THE ENGLISH POOR
IN THE EIGHTEENTH CENTURY

PLATE I

THE HUMOURS OF
ST. GILES'S.

[front.

The English Poor

in

The Eighteenth Century

A Study in Social and Administrative History

BY

DOROTHY MARSHALL

M.A., PH.D. (CANTAB).

LONDON

ROUTLEDGE & KEGAN PAUL LTD

BROADWAY HOUSE: 68-74 CARTER LANE, E.C.4

First Published 1926
by George Routledge & Sons Ltd
Reissued 1969
by Routledge and Kegan Paul Ltd
Broadway House, 68-74 Carter Lane
London, E.C.4
Printed in Great Britain by
Alden & Mowbray Ltd
at the Alden Press, Oxford

SBN 7100 6421 7

CONTENTS

The ceaseless activity shown by reformers in promulgating new schemes for the relief of the Poor is explained by the faults of the existing financial and administrative machinery of the parish. By the 43 Eliz. c. 2 the management of the Poor in each parish was entrusted to the overseers who were appointed annually and who were forced to serve or pay a fine. In practice the Justices exercised very little influence over them. Type of man chosen not suitable—untrained—unwilling—also economy not forced on them—therefore easy attitude towards expenditure and accounts—in many parishes not noticeably corrupt but careless and inefficient—and accounts neglected. But London parishes notoriously corrupt because the size of the out parishes offered more opportunities for peculation. Chief ways were by juggling with contracts—by falsifying disbursements to the casual Poor—by spending unnecessary amounts on parish feasts. Methods of collection were also open to suspicion—no method of receipt. Abuse of communion money highly probable. By end of seventeenth century Parliament tried to provide some check on the parish officers—the 3 W. & M. c. 11, followed by the 17 G. II. c. 3, which made the rate-books accessible to ratepayers. Sometimes individual vestries made efforts to control their officials—while another method of improving the administration was to engage a paid assistant overseer.

The money required by the overseers was raised by the Poor Rate. Difficult to estimate its amount at beginning of period because no statistics—forced to rely on contemporary statements until 1776. Between 1662 and 1782 rise noticeable both in country, as a whole, and in individual parishes. Increase fairly steady until the end of Charles II, then slow rise until the sixties, followed by sharp increase until end of the century. Amount paid by each parishioner fixed by overseers and churchwardens. Original intention seems to have been that each should pay in proportion to his ability—but rents soon came to be considered as an indication of this ability—and eventually through a confusion of thought only the occupier and not the owner was taxed. The

rule that the Poor's tax should be based on equal pound rate
not universal—traces of ability to pay—assessments on Land
Tax books—Stock-in-trade.

If money raised not sufficient other parishes could be rated in
aid, but this infrequent except between various hamlets in
northern parishes.

Overseers frequently accused of making unfair rates for their
own ends—appeal from such rates lay to Quarter Sessions but
they afforded little real protection.

Therefore the mechanism of the parish not well adapted to a
skilful administration of the problems of poverty.

Our-Door Poor Relief the least difficult and best executed branch
of the Poor Law, though it interested contemporary writers very
little.   As a result the overseers were left to raise the rates and
spend them as they would until in 1693 the 3 & 4 W. & M. c. 11
made an attempt to strengthen the authority of the Justices—
but new law not a success and had to be amended in 1722—even
then double authority of the overseer and the Justice open to
abuse.

Knowledge of the working of the law comes from—county records,
such as appeals to Quarter Sessions for relief or the payment of
pensions—parish papers.   Different forms of relief comprised :
The payment of a pension—amounts in South—in London—in
North—pensions to orphans, etc.—boarding out of children—
abuses of the system in London—terrible mortality among them.
Smallness of many of the pensions led to begging among the
parish Poor—to prevent this—expedient of badging the Poor
adopted first by individual parishes and then legalised by the
8 & 9 W. III, such a law was fiercely resented—but only repealed
at the end of eighteenth century.   Allowances sometimes given
to labourers in full work if they were overburdened with small
children—this practice dated from seventeenth century, and
was unpopular with social reformers—but was adopted on wide
scale after distress in the eighties.

Other reforms of relief were : Payment of rent or provision of
house room—either by allowing building on the waste or by
providing parish cottages rent free—sums paid in this way—
provision of clothes—sometimes parish bought the raw material,
sometimes complete garments—provision of fuel—relief and
medical attendance for sick paupers—sometimes called in local
bonesetter and sometimes regular doctor.   Very little indication
as to nature of these illnesses—small pox the most prevalent—
fits—accidents—treatment of lunacy.   As result of these medical
activities entered into contracts with local doctors.   Payments
for funerals—managed decently.   From these details clear that
parishes provided for their Poor in as adequate a manner as their
finances would allow.

Real aim of 43 Eliz. c. 2 had been to set the Poor on work but
the machinery of the parish was totally unfitted for this purpose
—and by 1660 only a few parishes made any effort to supply

their paupers with work. Contemporary opinion was unwilling to let the matter drop, and the employment of the Poor received fresh impetus with the incorporation of the Bristol Workhouse. Number of workhouses grew steadily in first part of the eighteenth century—in 1722 new Act passed to facilitate the unions of parishes for this purpose but few parishes availed themselves of it—government of workhouses usually rested with a committee of varying numbers—actual management entrusted to a master of low social status. Many parishes preferred to farm their workhouse to a contractor. Types of contracts : To supply the Poor with work—to receive all the Poor sent to the workhouse at a fixed price per head—to farm the entire Poor of a parish for a lump sum down—Contemporary opinion on these methods of contracting the Poor out—favourable opinions—unfavourable opinions predominate—dirt—disease—starvation prevalent in these workhouses.

Workhouses under parochial management not much better— parish too small to provide suitable buildings—inadequate food and clothes—workhouses overcrowded and tumbling down— terrible effect on children sent there.

Failure of workhouses due to impossibility of employing the Poor at a profit—proved impracticable from the start. Due also to the corruption and slackness of the parish officers owing to the non-attendance of the gentlemen of the Board of Governors. In towns overseers made money out of supplying the House with provisions at enhanced prices.

Therefore by middle of eighteenth century chief virtue of the workhouse was to prevent the Poor from asking for relief, and this seems at first to have reduced the number of those receiving relief. The workhouse was also used as a threat to force such poor as received out-door relief to be content with very small sums. But the importance of the workhouse as a deterrent was modified by the fact that in many places the workhouse was too small to receive all the chargeable Poor, and also by the favouritism of individual overseers towards particular paupers. The Report of 1776 shows that in most parishes large sums were still paid out for Out-Door Relief.

As a result of this failure criticism of the existing workhouses multiplied towards the middle of the eighteenth century, and new experiments were tried, notably the Hundred Houses in East Anglia. In these houses internal conditions appear to have been much better at first, though they afterwards deteriorated. Then, in 1782, Gilbert's Act emphasized the new tendency to take the management of the Poor out of the hands of the parish officers and to entrust it to a larger unit.

The failure of the parishes to employ the Poor led to the development of an instinct of self protection—in 1662 the Act of Settlements gave parishes the legal right to remove certain classes of persons who were likely to become chargeable—this led to much inter-parochial litigation before Quarter Sessions, and several loopholes in the Act had to be stopped by the 1 Jac. II, c. 17 as well as several less important acts.

Impossible to remove everyone who did not comply with these provisions, therefore overseers forced to make a selection—types usually moved—in country married labourer—in town single woman—persons who made no effort to gain a settlement often not molested unless fell on bad times. Procedure followed in cases of removal—examination before a Justice—order of removal—removal. Right of appeal lay to Quarter Sessions—frequently exercised because law was complex—parishes wanted to rid themselves of expensive paupers. Costs of these appeals—effect of these appeals and removals on the Poor involved—to return to a parish after removal an offence against the Vagrancy Laws.

Evidence to show that laws actively enforced—resulting inconvenience—attempt to meet it by a method of certificates—at first mere parish agreements—in 1697 made legal position of the certificate holder with regard to gaining a settlement—new laws with regard to certificates—estimate of the influence of this device. In this way parishes received complete legal protection against strangers, but in its fear other more questionable methods were adopted of keeping down the number of chargeable Poor. Women fraudulently married to alter their settlement—perversion of apprenticeship. Parish apprenticeship rested on the 43 Eliz. c. 2—its success in dealing with poverty depended on the place occupied by apprenticeship in the economic life of the country—apprenticeship after Restoration waning in influence—therefore value of pauper apprenticeship depended on thoroughness of the training received.

Two legal methods of pauper apprenticeship—compulsory—no chance of juggling with the Law of Settlement—reinforced by the 8 & 9 W. III, and fines imposed for refusal—which were regarded by overseers as a source of revenue—extent to which compulsory binding was prevalent. Voluntary apprenticeship popular with overseers because could be used to alter the settlement of the child involved since apprenticeship in a parish conferred a settlement there. Details of such apprenticeships can be gained from the indentures themselves—sums paid as premiums—in the towns—in the country—payments at stated intervals. Cost of the outfit of such apprentices.

Working of system in practice—type of trade to which children bound—in the country—in the towns—the pauper trades—silk trade—frame-work knitters—appeals of apprentices to Quarter Sessions reveal many cases of ill-treatment—masters often become insolvent and decamped. Our knowledge of pauper apprentices very scanty because too friendless to appeal in most cases—consequently many ran away and never served out their indentures—length of time for which they were bound also had this effect—if caught might be sent to the house of correction. Little public opinion on the question—workhouses were known to be bad places for children, therefore there seemed no alternative to apprenticeship though contemporaries realised its possible evils quite clearly—Acts of 1747 and 1767 attempted to ameliorate their lot—in 1778 length of apprenticeship shortened for the whole of England—by the end of the century serious attempts were being made to grapple with the evils caused by the parochial administration of the Poor in this field.

Another device of the overseers to prevent the growth of their chargeable Poor was to hinder the marriage of poor persons by encouraging the destruction of cottages—the result was to encourage the growth of bastardy—such children usually became a burden on the parish and a succession of laws were passed with a view to forcing the parents to provide for the support of their illegitimate children. Procedure after 1733—oath of woman before Justice as to the father of her child—arrest of man, who was forced to give security—opportunities for abuse. Treatment of pregnant women—removed to place of settlement if elsewhere at the time, as bastards took the settlement of the parish where they were born—if possible her own parish likewise turned her adrift—every other parish hounded her out. If parish failed to rid themselves of such women before their delivery, an affiliation order was served on the putative father—amount of these orders —appeals to Quarter Sessions against them—amounts actually recovered by the parishes from the parents—returns of 1773-74-75 imprisonment of reputed fathers—forced marriages between the parents—punishment of women. Whole attitude towards the question absolutely non-moral, yet despite such stringency, failed to suppress bastardy. Terrible effect of leaving administration of Poor Laws entirely to such small local units.

The failure of the parishes to provide for the Poor was largely responsible for the increase in vagrancy of which contemporaries complain. Vagrants dreaded because they spread small-pox— caused fires by carelessness. London particularly infested with vagrants of a rougher type—link boys—beggars—the blackguard—unlicensed hawkers—who found refuges in low lodging-houses—descriptions of such beggars.
Suppression of vagrancy had been entrusted to parish constable, though he was quite unfitted for this work—many complaints against the constables. Parliament tried to secure an improvement by passing new laws. The use of false passes. Definition of vagrancy, etc.—examination of such vagrants before the Justices—fresh definitions of vagrants—another large scale vagrant law. The financial machinery of the Vagrant Laws— the payment of the constable's expenses secured by a rate—reinforced by the 11 W. III, c. 18—the 1 An. st. 2, c. 13 ordered the rates for conveying vagrants to be fixed by Quarter Sessions —rates for conveying vagrants so fixed—after 1739 to be paid out of a general county rate—amounts spent in this way. The growth of the contractor system for passing vagrants—their methods—not, however, universal even late in the century. Improvements in methods dealing with vagrancy counterbalanced by the activities of the parish officers in turning their chargeable Poor adrift.

By 1660 it was clear that the Poor Law needed readjustment but the effects of the Act of Settlement were most unfortunate. It penalised not only individuals but also the development of the country by depriving the labourer of any incentive to look for work outside his parish, and by terrifying him with the harsh provisions of the Vagrancy Laws. This danger was intensified

CONTENTS

by the lack of educational and cultural facilities. Also the Act
of Settlement tended to brutalise the administration of the law,
though this brutality can be explained to a certain extent by the
character of the century.

The tragedy of the Poor Law was not one of low aims but of lack
of achievement caused by inadequate parochial machinery,
which was incapable of providing employment for the Poor, and
which, therefore, forced everything to be measured by financial
standards. Yet, despite its failure, the Old Poor Law has
valuable lessons for the reformer of to-day.

LIST OF ILLUSTRATIONS

PREFACE

In my original Preface to *The English Poor in the Eighteenth Century* I wrote "The purpose of this study is to give an account both of the way in which the Poor Laws affected the lives of the mass of the labouring Poor in the later part of the seventeenth–century and during the eighteenth–century, and of the contemporary attitude towards poverty. A good deal of light has been shed on the early period of English Poor Relief up to the outbreak of the Civil War, and again on the period that followed the outbreak of the Revolutionary War in 1793. But though much scattered information on the period in between is available in books dealing with other subjects there is, as far as I know, no one place to which a student desiring to obtain information on the various aspects of the working of the Poor Law in eighteenth-century England can go. Even Sir Frederick Eden's *The State of the Poor* is chiefly concerned with the latter period, while in his review of the history of the Poor Law he does little more than reproduce a series of opinions from various pamphleteers. It is hoped therefore that this study may do something to fill the gap."

Since then there have been two major developments. When I wrote these words the Poor Law with its unions and its workhouses, its relieving officers and its boards of guardians, was, apart from private charity, the main instrument for dealing with dire poverty and destitution, though even then it was losing some of its functions to other public bodies. To-day it is a thing of the past, as remote from most people's memories as the Old Poor Law which it replaced, and with which this volume deals. The result has been to make some of the comparisons contained in my Introduction, and some of the prophecies in my Conclusion, out of date. I have however allowed both to stand as I wrote them, though instead of the Poor Law we have a Welfare State with its retirement pensions, its National Health Service and its Ministry of Social Security. Yet however great the outward change, both in the climate of opinion, which now demands for even the most improvident or unfortunate of its citizens something above the stark level of mere subsistence, and in the apparatus of relief, the basic problem of relieving excessive poverty without encouraging the work-shy is still with us. While it remains unsolved the experience and the expedients of an earlier age can never be without interest both to the sociologist and to the historian. Indeed one might well repeat the old tag "The more things alter, the more they remain the same."

The second major development has been an increased interest in social history which, over the last forty years, has been considerable. When *The English Poor in the Eighteenth Century* was first published it was breaking new ground, though it was followed a year later by Stanley and Beatrice Webb's *English Poor Law History Part I, The Old Poor Law*, (1927). Since then much work, both published and unpublished, in the form of M.A. and Ph.D. theses, has been done on this subject. The greater part of this research has been concentrated on the period between 1793 and 1834, but enough has been devoted to that covered by this volume to confirm the general picture contained in these pages and also to make explicit some points which were only implied or undeveloped in them. Some of the most useful contributions in this field have been made by historians who have focused their researches on to particular counties or areas. The result has been to stress once again the dangers of generalization and the importance of geographical and economic factors in shaping the pattern of Poor Law administration. Because this was essentially local the problems that the parochial officials and the neighbouring magistrates had to face varied not only between town and country, which is obvious enough, but also between upland and lowland, between parishes dominated by one or two large land-owners and those parishes which were not, between parishes where some nearby industry offered steady employment and those where it was seasonal, depending perhaps on some watering place such as Brighton or Scarborough. These local differences can only be brought out by a painstaking examination of local records and the more those concerned with the activities of the magistrates sitting in petty and Quarter Sessions can be integrated with those of particular parishes, the more accurate the resultant picture is likely to be. My own impression, and until more work of this kind has been done it must remain an impression, is that in most rural parishes until the eighties the Old Poor Law worked reasonably well. Opportunities for maladministration and brutality there most certainly were, but though instances of both are not difficult to find, when Chadwick and his followers implied that these were the rule rather than exceptions, in rural parishes at least, they were overstating their case. Such incidents tended to be isolated ones, often with years separating them. But though regional studies have modified some older generalizations about the Poor Law they have confirmed the difficulties that all parishes, urban and rural alike, faced in trying to find remunerative employment for their paupers and also their determination to prevent settlements wherever they could.

Of the materials used the most important have been contemporary writers, Quarter Session Minute and Order Books, and parish accounts and papers. Throughout the period there was a great interest taken in the Poor and the supply of pamphlet literature is abundant and interesting. Many of the county records have been published, at least in part, and I have also examined the Cambridgeshire and Lancashire records in manuscript. In the study of parish accounts and papers, in addition to those read in manuscript, some excellent printed material has been available, while much interesting information has been gleaned from parochial histories.

The credit for anything that may be good in this book belongs chiefly to others, and to none more than to Professor Lilian Knowles, who not only read through each chapter as it was written, but gave me her suggestions and criti-cisms, both of which were invaluable. To work under her direction was to receive an education in research and without her help this book could never have been written. My thanks are also due to Miss M. G. Jones of Girton College and Mr Slater of Magdalene College, Cambridge, for the help and encouragement which they gave me in the early days of my research. I wish also to acknowledge my gratitude to Mr Vere Lawrence of Trinity College, Cambridge, for many valuable suggestions as to the arrangement of my material and above all to Professor Eileen Power who, since my first year at Cambridge, has been both an inspiration and a guide. To her I owe my interest in social history and I am proud to have been one of her students. I also owe a heavy debt of gratitude to Mr E. N. Parker who read through the whole of my manu-script and proofs with painstaking care. I should like to express my appreciation of the kindness of the Rector of Dunstable Priory and the officials of the County Halls of Cambridge and Preston in allowing me to use the documents under their care. Finally, I should like to take this opportunity of acknowledging my debt to Girton College for making it possible to undertake this research by holding first the Cairnes and then the Old Girtonian Studentship.

INTRODUCTION.

THE problem of poverty must, by its very nature, be one of vital importance to any civilized community, and so anything that tends to throw light on the methods by which past generations attempted to solve it, and on the results which they achieved, cannot be without real interest and value. A mere collection of facts, however, is apt to be both uninspiring and bewildering unless the principle lying behind and co-ordinating them into a unified whole, can be discovered. In the record of the English Poor Laws this co-ordinating principle is seen to be that of public responsibility for the Poor, and the entire history of these laws is comprised in the acceptance and application of this assumption. Consequently it is only by seeing for whom this responsibility was incurred, by whom it was incurred, of what it actually consisted, the methods by which it was discharged, and the results that followed, that the tangled skein of the history of English Poor Relief can be unravelled.

In any country, and at any time, the treatment which is meted out to poverty must exert vast influence on the moulding of a people, and this is particularly true of the England of the seventeenth and eighteenth centuries. The scope and activities of the Poor Laws were much wider, and far more generally diffused, than they are to-day. In the first place they affected a much larger proportion of the population than is now the case. After 1662 the overseers of the poor had certain rights over all persons who did not inhabit a tenement worth £10 a year or more. They could remove anyone who came under this category, who might be suspected, however vaguely, of being "likely to become charge-able" back to "his or her legal place of settlement." This clause in theory affected not only the old, the infirm, the helpless, and the infants, but also all those agricultural labourers who worked for, and were depend-ent on, their wages ; it affected the great class of manual workers of every kind ; it affected most of the smaller manufacturers, such as the spinners, the weavers, the dyers, and the shearers ; it affected, too, the large class of small craftsmen, the blacksmiths, the carpenters or the tailors.   In short, as the Poor Laws had power not only over those who were actually chargeable, but over those likely to become so, their operation included the greater part of the lower working class under the desig-nation of "The Poor".

Secondly, not only had the Poor Law officials authority over a larger section of the nation than they have to-day, but also they were expected to do more for them, since only a very considerable measure of poverty, and not utter destitution, was required of applicants for relief. In other words the parish was not only a relieving, but, in some cases, a preventative agent.   The original intention of the 43 Eliz. c. 2 had been threefold.   The parish was to provide work for the unemployed ; it was to furnish a free technical education to its poor children, and to the children of persons who were too poor to maintain them, by binding them out as apprentices. Thirdly, it was to relieve the "lame, impotent, old, blind, and such other among them being poor and not able to work".   As time went on, however, its scope became wider and wider, until by the eighteenth century its responsibilities were multifarious.   It was expected to maintain the poor when they were ill, as well as to provide free medical attendance, physic, and nursing. In time the Overseers entered into definite contracts with local doctors for this purpose, though there is not one word in the statute book beyond those quoted above to suggest that they were empowered to take such a course. If a pauper died the parish paid the funeral expenses, which frequently included the tolling of the bell, and bread and beer for the bearers. Its other activities comprised the provision of clothes, fuel, food, and similar necessaries for parishioners who were in want ; paying rents or finding houses for poor persons ; helping women whose husbands were in prison ; paying allowances to labourers over-burdened with children ; and assisting poor men with small sums of money to enable them to buy stock to follow their trade. All this was in addition to the statutory duties of collecting the poor rates, paying weekly or monthly allowances to the above enumerated classes of the poor, and binding out children.

The fact that the influence of the Poor Laws was so wide-spread assumed particular importance after the Restoration, because from that date England embarked with increasing rapidity upon that career of industrial and social change, which was to transform her into the England we know to-day. The conditions with which Charles II had to cope were very different from those which prevailed at the passing of the 43 Eliz. c. 2. This Act, in which Elizabeth co-ordinated her former measures for the better relief of the poor, was part of that re-organization which she carried through in almost every branch of the economic life of the country. England had broken away from the framework of the Middle Ages ; the day of the serf, the manor, and the knight was over ; these were giving place to the artisan, the paid labourer, the parish, the trader and the merchant. Such sweeping changes had tended to disorganize society ; and new regulations were needed on all sides. One result of the disappearance of the old order had been the increase in poverty and vagrancy. It was to cope with these problems that the Act, which was to provide the basis for English Poor Relief for so long, was passed. At first it was admirably suited to the conditions under

which it had to function. For the England for which
Elizabeth had enacted this law was very different from
the England of the Restoration. The majority of the
population were still engaged in agriculture, and the
parish was the most important unit in a life that was
constructed to meet the needs of a rural community,
rather than those of the town dweller. The vital factor
in the economy of the day was the self-sufficiency of each
district. Trade was still largely local, and industry, in
most places under the control of the guilds, fluctuated
little either in quantity or in place. Moreover, com-
munications were very bad, and there was no great
fluidity either of work or of provisions. Consequently
it was a real necessity to stop vagrancy, and to provide
work for people in their own parishes. For in many
parishes there was neither more work than the parishioners could perform, nor a larger food supply on which
they could draw than would keep them during the
winter months. While this was the case, the parish was
the only effective unit which could be used for the relief
of the Poor.

By the time of the Restoration this was no longer
wholly true. A new England was coming into being in
which social conditions were changing to such an extent
that the poor laws were no longer in harmony with the
life of the people. The 43 Eliz. c. 2 directed that poor
persons were to be maintained and provided with work
by their own parish if the need arose, but it did not say
definitely who were to be considered the poor of a parish,
or how such work was to be organized. While the
population of a parish was more or less stable it had not
mattered greatly ; now it mattered to a more serious
extent. From the Restoration onward, trade, both
foreign and internal, had increased tremendously ;
and industry had grown in proportion. But the very
increase in trade had brought increased instability with
it. Where before it had depended on the known requirements of a steady home market, now it depended on a

market that varied with the diplomacy of Europe, with foreign fashions and vagaries, and even with the ability of the merchants who served such a trade. Increased trade in time came to mean increased specialization, and, more than ever before, certain districts began to produce certain goods and to depend on other districts for the goods which they did not produce themselves. Defoe, writing in 1704, could say that it was the " excellence of our English manufactures that it is so planted as to go through as many hands as it is possible ". And this tendency of districts to specialize was beginning to be a real thing even in 1660. Combined with the fluctuations of trade, it meant that a depression in any one branch of industry might hit a particular district so hard as to curtail considerably the demand for labour in that part. Therefore, though the trade of the country might be flourishing, the centres of labour would not always be the same. The new lines on which industry seemed to be re-organizing itself indicated that labour would have to develop a mobility it had not known before, and flow to or desert certain areas as the law of supply and demand required.

The increase of trade meant also an acceleration in the growth of town life. People automatically began to collect round centres where work was better organized. Where labourers collected, there retailers gathered, and dependent trades sprang up. As a result, the country was no longer a collection of rural parishes, which, with the exception of the old trading towns, is what it had mainly been, although numerically the rural parishes predominated until the end of the eighteenth century. The growth of the towns in turn affected the old parish organization ; for where formerly this had been applied to wide spaces and a community where each man knew his neighbour, now it became increasingly only a division of a prosperous, rather huddled, and very busy town. Therefore, in the towns at least, the parish was no longer the logical unit of local government.

The increase in the numbers of the urban population led to an increased demand for foods of every kind, and to satisfy this men began to turn, tentatively and distrustfully at first, to the new methods of agriculture introduced from Holland.   Moreover, towns which depended on the sale of their manufactures for the money with which to buy their food, required good roads to get in touch with their markets.   This meant an increase in road building, which later developed into the turnpike system.   Between Elizabethan England and 1660 many of these changes had taken place, though they were still tentative, experimental and accidental, but the crop of the eighteenth century was already showing a faint green above the subsoil of the past.   In short, it was an era in which many of those industrial and social problems which now agitate our economic life, were engendered. Anything, therefore, that helps to illuminate the life of the worker during this period is of considerable interest, for much of the psychology of the working man of to-day can only be explained by reference to the generations which lie behind him.   Accordingly the question upon whom this tremendous responsibility devolved becomes one of paramount importance, and it is something of a surprise to find that so large a branch of the administration was relegated to purely local authorities, without the provision of due oversight by any central supervisory authority.

Indeed, the outstanding feature which marks off the years from 1662 to 1782 as a definite period in the history of English Poor Relief is its intense parochialism. It was the hey-day of the parish officer, whose activities were checked or stimulated only by the Justices in Quarter Sessions, acting as a court of appeal.   This was in direct contrast to the earlier history of the administration of relief in this country.   From Elizabeth to the outbreak of the Civil War the central government had exercised a strict control over the parochial officers— a control which had manifested itself in two ways.   One was the active supervision of the Privy Council over the details of relief. Time and again parishes were forced to return an account of their exertions in this direction. Officers were required to report as to whether their parish was providing work for the unemployed, and relief for the aged and impotent ; they were asked whether poor children were being placed out as apprentices, and whether vagrants were being duly punished. In this way did the Crown endeavour to ensure that the law should be obeyed.

The other device employed for the benefit of the Poor was the regulation of the corn market in times of scarcity. Between 1581 and 1630 an intricate mass of detailed provisions had been framed for that purpose. This was the system embodied in the famous Book of Orders, the object of which was artificially to lower the price of corn in times of scarcity, in order that unnecessary hardships should not be inflicted on the labouring part of the community. It included, also, special provisions which aimed at allowing the Poor to buy corn before the dealers took possession of the market. To the same end, that of securing the food supply of the Poor, the municipalities, and particularly London, were encouraged or coerced into storing corn, to be sold to the Poor at a reduced rate in time of dearth.

Scarcely a trace of either of these expedients is to be discovered in the administration of the Poor Law, after its reconstruction at the time of the Restoration. The Courts through which the Privy Council had exercised its power had been abolished, and had the Crown even wished to exercise its old influence, it lacked machinery to give expression to its will. Accordingly the parishes were no longer called upon to give an account of themselves, while the regulation of the corn market likewise ceased. This was not because the old periods of scarcity had become a thing of the past ; the year 1661 was almost one of famine, while often in the next two reigns prices were very high, and the century ended with a five years' dearth. The change in policy was further marked by the fact that after 1670 the import of corn was restricted until prices rose to nearly 80s. per quarter, and that in 1673 an experimental bounty, made permanent in 1689, was given on the export of corn. Doubtless this new attitude arose in part from the fact that the English corn market was more highly organized than it had been in the days of Elizabeth. By the end of the seventeenth century London had become the great corn market for England ; to it was brought the corn from the counties, and from it, the grain was re-exported. Consequently, there was not the same danger to London of starvation in a dearth, and simultaneously improved means of transport rendered the prospect of local famines less serious. In part, too, the abandonment of the system framed in the Book of Orders was probably due to the royal consciousness, that the Poor were no longer so menacing an element in the country, as they had been in the past. In the days of the Tudors, when the sovereign had no standing army and there were many claimants to the throne, it was felt as vital to the royal interests that the Poor should not be allowed to wander up and down the country-side, sowing the seeds of discontent. Accordingly, as a precaution against their rallying round a rebel leader, they were to be given work in their own parishes, and in time of dearth were not to lack for food. But now the establishment of a standing army had dispelled this earlier fear.

Moreover, the result of the Civil War had been to change the relationship between the King and his poorer subjects. Much of the power which the King had exercised on their behalf had passed to Parliament. But Parliament, at this time, was keenly interested in many things besides the Poor, for the state of trade, the question of the relationship between the two Houses, and the pressure of foreign affairs, all demanded its attention. Thus, though it might and did pass acts dealing with the Poor, it could not always supervise their

execution, wherefore responsibility for their fair administration was delegated to the parishes. Accordingly this
period became one of parochial *laissez faire*. Each
parish was free to go its own way, checked only when it
came into conflict with some individual or body which
had legal rights of its own, for the enforcement of which
appeal might be made to Quarter Sessions. This was
the procedure followed by parishes which had been
injured by other parishes, by people who had been
unfairly assessed to the Poor's rate, and by paupers
who could not obtain their allowances. But, except for
the restrictions of this nature, the parish officer was
supreme.

The parishes were not only responsible for the details
of the administration in this period ; they also influenced
the broad principles of the law. Except for some
isolated acts for the safeguarding of the ratepayers, all
the bills which became law were based on parochial
practice. Those clauses, for instance, which permitted
the badging of the poor, or which authorized the use of
certificates, or which permitted parishes to join together
to build workhouses, were all based on actual previous
parochial experiments. This was true even of the Act
of Settlements itself. Indeed, it would be roughly
accurate to say that Parliament sanctioned no law which
had not previously received the approval of a number
of parishes.

Yet in spite of the very considerable powers vested
in the parish officers, the men who were chosen to serve
in these capacities were untrained in the business of
public administration. They were legally compelled
to serve such an office if appointed, but they held office
for only a year, and were unpaid. To undertake the
responsibility for the management of the Poor was
considered an obligation inherent in the possession of
lands or houses within the parish. In theory, the idea
that a man owed a public duty to the place in which he
lived, if he had means to discharge such a trust, was

excellent, but in practice it worked abominably. Since the office was unpaid, despite the loss of time which it involved, men either tried to avoid it, or else used it for their personal advantage. Even if a man eager to do his best for the parish were appointed, the fact that the office was annual meant that as soon as he got at all familiar with the business he was superseded by the next Overseer. Frequently, too, the men who were appointed to such parish offices, were themselves of no high social standing. The law had directed that the Overseers of the Poor were to be chosen from among the substantial householders, but in practice gentlemen and persons of substance preferred to pay a fine rather than undertake so troublesome a task. As a result the responsibility for the management of the Poor fell on the farmers or on the small tradesmen—in each case men who had their time fully occupied with their own business. Moreover, they were quite unused to the niceties of public administration ; and it is not unusual to find Overseers who could only make their mark. Consequently their aim was to get through the parish business with as little trouble to themselves as possible. A careless, lazy administration was the utmost that could be expected from such men, whose highest ambition was to get through their year of office as best they might. The worst that could be anticipated was a state of intolerable corruption, such as, particularly in the large city parishes, appears often to have been the case.

The results of casting the responsibility for the relief and maintenance of the Poor upon officers so appointed were not happy. In the first place, the country was deprived of any uniform poor law, since there was no machinery to subordinate the interests of the part to the welfare of the whole. And so each parish fought for its own interest, not caring upon whose shoulders might fall the burden, which it had itself evaded. The benefit of the community and of the pauper was continually sacrificed to the interests of the parish. For example,

when a wanderer suspected of small-pox came into a
parish no steps were taken to place him in quarantine,
and instead of receiving relief he was bribed or driven
from the village to spread the infection further, rather
than that the parish should be at a charge for him, until
at last he sank down in some parish too weak to go
further, where perforce he had to be relieved. Such was
the common practice of the day, and it was one which
took no regard for the welfare either of the community
or of the individual. In the same way, persons endeav-
ouring to gain a settlement were sent back to their own
parish, unless they could give security or get a certificate.
Parishes wrangled and contested cases at Quarter
Sessions, so that sometimes the unfortunate object of
contention was removed two or three times in the same
year, thus having his chances of gaining a fair living
utterly destroyed. Where children had gained a separate
settlement from their parents families were ruthlessly
broken up. A common instance of this is to be found
in the case of a widow with children who has married
again, her second husband belonging to a parish other
than that of her first. In a case of this kind she acquired
her new husband's settlement, while her children by her
first marriage retained their father's settlement. When
this happened all the children above the age of seven
were given over to the Overseers of that parish in which
they were settled. In all these ways the parishes acted
with a lack of humanity and a blindness to all interests
but their own, which is almost incredible.

   The reason for much of their callous behaviour is to
be found in the question of the Poor Rates. Since each
parish was financially responsible for its own poor, its
first and most vital interest was felt to be the keeping
down of the rates. Hence its willingness to do anything
to " save the parish harmless ". The whole history
of the administration of parish relief during this period
of parish domination is the history of a long struggle
between their moral and financial responsibility for the

Poor—a struggle in which the desire to keep the rates low was the victor. For though in the sphere of actual poor relief itself, such as the provision of money, clothes, and houses, the parishes were not ungenerous, in every other branch of the administration the true intent of the law was perverted for financial reasons. The records of the workhouses, of parish apprentices, of the laws regulating bastardy, and of the failure of the vagrancy laws, all afford illustrations of this fact.

Another result of leaving so much responsibility to the parish officers is to be found in the petty corruption that disfigured the whole administration of the law. Since there was not a proper system of oversight, and since many vestries were self-electing and select, the opportunities for jobbery with the parish poor money were numerous, and since the Overseers were unpaid, it was but natural, considering the public morality of the day, that many of them should take advantage of it. A further manifestation of the slackness which disfigured the whole management of the Poor, was the rise of the contractor system. Because many parish officers had neither the skill nor the desire to perform the business themselves, they were only too glad to shuffle the responsibility on to someone else, who was willing to undertake it on pecuniary grounds. The method employed was for the parish officers to contract with some man who should be responsible for the entire administration of one particular aspect of their business. For instance, contracts were entered into with doctors for medical attendance, or with joiners to supply coffins at a fixed rate. The most popular form of contract was that which arranged for some outsider to take over the conveyance of vagrants or the management of the parish workhouse. In the former case the vagrant contractor would undertake to convey all vagrants, who might be sent along a particular route, for a lump sum down per year, whilst in the latter the workhouse contractor either received so much per head for all the poor sent into the workhouse, or else contracted to maintain all the poor of the parish for a lump sum per year. In the latter instance he practically relieved the Overseers of all their duties. As the parishes invariably drove as close a bargain as they could, and as the contractor had his own profit to make, the results for the poor were not fortunate. In consequence of these and of other abuses, the administration of relief was subjected to an increasing wave of criticism as the eighteenth century wore on.

This discontent found its first practical expression in a bill for the better relief of the Poor, which Thomas Gilbert succeeded in piloting through the Commons in 1782, and which in due course became law. Gilbert's Act, as it is commonly called, was a gesture of revolt against the domination of the parish officer. Other writers had pointed out the deficiencies of the system, and had advocated a more drastic supervision of the Overseers' activities than Quarter Sessions had afforded, but Gilbert was the first man to have sufficient public opinion behind him to get his proposals carried into law. By this Act such parishes as wished to avail themselves of it were granted the right of forming unions for the better management of the Poor. There was to be a common workhouse for the aged, the infirm, and the infants, while the able-bodied were to be provided with work outside. The responsibility for the undertaking was to be vested in certain elected gentlemen, who were to supervise the Overseers, practically reducing them to mere rate collectors. In this way the isolation of the single parish and the domination of the parish officer were to be annihilated.

Not only did the Act of 1782 end the purely parochial administration of the Poor, it also marked the beginning of a new mental attitude towards them. With the fall of the paternal government of the early Stuarts public opinion had gradually grown harder and still harder on the Poor. Until nearly the close of the seventeenth century there still had been some writers who regarded poverty as a misfortune which disturbed conditions, bad trade, and low wages had brought down upon the poorer classes. But before 1700 it became increasingly fashionable to regard poverty as a crime, caused by the excesses and follies of the Poor themselves.

It was claimed that the Poor were poor because they would neither work nor save, and because they were at once lazy and extravagant. Consequently, the first part of the eighteenth century was a time when severe discipline was advocated. Both in theory and in practice workhouses and contractors were the expedients advocated and employed. Then with the rise of prices after the '70's there came a gradual change of opinion, as conditions began to throw some doubt on this hypothesis, and the general attitude became softened by a more sympathetic outlook. The Act of 1782, which aimed at making the workhouses decent places of retirement for the old and the unfortunate, illustrates this new line of thought no less than it exemplifies the distrust felt towards the parish officer. In the fields both of administration and of opinion the Act of 1782 marked the end of a period in the history of English Poor Relief, though, unfortunately, the era which followed it, and which ended with the Act of 1834, was fully as disastrous in its results. It must, however, be admitted that the seed which bore such evil fruit had been sown during the time of untrammelled parochial responsibility.

THE
ENGLISH POOR IN THE
EIGHTEENTH CENTURY

CHAPTER I

THE CONTEMPORARY ATTITUDE TOWARDS
THE PROBLEM OF POVERTY—OPINION

Just as it is impossible to understand the significance of a man's action until we know the environment and influences which have moulded him, so it is impossible to understand any branch of legislation until we know something of the forces which inspired it, both in conception and in administration.   In other words, some understanding of contemporary opinion is a vital prologue to the study of any phase of a past age.   Such opinion may have accorded ill with the practice of the time—it may have had little direct influence on legislation—but, inevitably, since laws are administered by men, it pervades their details and becomes the force by which the bones of legislation are moved.   This is especially the case when legislation deals with such a subject as the regulation of the Poor, which affects the lives and pockets of ordinary men.   The Poor Laws, moreover, were administered, not by paid officials, but by ordinary citizens as a civic duty.   That meant that contemporary opinion on the subject of the Poor was, in many cases, the opinion of the men who actually worked the machine.   Therefore, in order to know the spirit in which the statutes dealing with the Poor were administered, it is necessary for us to study, as a preliminary, the social and economic atmosphere of the time to which they belong.

During the Middle Ages religion permeated every

sphere of life. Hence it is not surprising to find that the earliest motives for relieving the Poor in England were predominantly religious. At an early date, we are told, the third part of the income of every church was to be devoted to this work. In the same way hospitality and charity to the Poor were stressed as being good works worthy of all Christian people. To give alms was a means of grace to the giver, even if the gift were ill-advised, and more likely to create than to remedy poverty. The doles from the monastery gates, the open table kept by wealthy nobles, the gifts of food and money at weddings and at funerals, were all indiscriminate charity, inspired partly, no doubt, by a love of display, but also by the religious idea that to give alms to the Poor was a means of grace for more fortunate persons. To be poor was not regarded as a fault of man, but as an inscrutable act of Providence : both rich and poor alike were members of one Church ; both were brothers in Christ. While these beliefs obtained common accept-ance, the main object of charity was the giving of alms to relieve, and not to prevent, poverty. Speaking generally, one might almost say that throughout the early Middle Ages there was no public consciousness that poverty ought to be prevented. The Bible had stated that, " ye have the Poor with you always ", and at a time when theology and sociology were inextricably mixed, this seemed reason enough for leaving things as they appeared to have been ordered by Providence.

It was therefore natural that the parish, which was the unit of ecclesiastical administration, should play a large part in the organization of charity. When England moved out of the Middle Ages the Tudors found the parish a convenient division for local government, such as the repair of the roads, and other functions of a non-religious kind. So when it became necessary to provide systematic relief for the Poor, the parochial machinery was adapted to meet the situation, leaving an indelible mark on the history of poor relief in England.

The Reformation destroyed the old idea of the fellowship of Christ, and in Protestant countries faith, not
works, became the slogan for Heaven ; and, once Charity
had been robbed of a vague mysticism, men attempted
to tackle its problems in a practical manner. Mean-
while, with changing social conditions, the problem itself
had changed, and the extremities to which the poorer
sort were reduced threatened to become an intolerable
nuisance to the State. The reasons for this have been
enumerated often ; the decay of serfdom, which meant
that men were free, but also free to starve ; the breakdown of the self-sufficiency of the manor ; the increase
of sheep farming ; the end of civil war and the abandonment of large bodies of retainers ; the dissolution of
the monasteries—all have been held responsible for the
flood of vagrancy and pauperism which distinguished
the social history of the Tudor sovereigns. Accordingly,
what people, and especially the governing classes,
chiefly desired, was not an opportunity for indiscriminate
alms-giving, but a method for the prevention of poverty.
For poverty was regarded as a potential danger to the
State, and was, therefore, a peril to the King. At a time
when no monarch was so firmly seated on the throne
that he, or she, did not fear rebellion, persons who went
up and down the country-side, starving and discon-
tented, and linking up the country with a web of dissatisfaction, were regarded as a menace. For these
Poor were capable of forming the nucleus around which
any one of the Pretenders, who from time to time aspired
to the English throne, might form an army. In short,
the Poor must be relieved, if not on religious grounds,
then for the sake of ensuring political security, and so
Prevention and Punishment became the watchwords of
the government when dealing with poverty. Elizabeth
endeavoured, by apprenticeship and by yearly hirings,
to prevent persons from falling into poverty ; she tried
to put down vagrancy by whipping, and she aimed at a
decent relief for the impotent poor, chiefly to prevent

them from begging.   Above all she tried to find employment for all who wanted it by ordering the parish Overseers to set the Poor of their parish on work.   In this way she hoped to prevent the Poor from wandering. The sixteenth century was an age of State regulation, and such provisions were in accordance with the public opinion of the time.   In a paternal state, it was an impossible idea that men might be allowed to starve for want of due regulation.   The fellowship of the Church had given way to the autocratic authority of the sovereign, but rich and poor were still members of the same family.

One effect of the Civil Wars was to sweep away this paternal conception of the peculiar relationship between the Crown and the Poor.   Henceforth the stress was laid, not on the group, nor on the King, but on the individual. The cult of Independency emphasized this tendency by its appeal to the separate conscience of each man.   More than ever were men encouraged to think and act for themselves.   By the time Charles II had come to the throne, the leaven of individualism had gone too far to be counteracted by any power of his, even had he wished to stop it.   In the age that followed, the Poor were like the proverbial bundle of sticks, which could be separated and broken one by one.   Deserted by Church and King, when the prevailing creed was " the devil take the hindermost," the rôle of " hindermost " nearly always fell to them.

The last half of the seventeenth century was a period of transition.   Neither the old paternal supervision of the early Stuarts, nor the harsh materialism of the eighteenth century, was yet in complete possession of the field.   Old motives for relieving the Poor persisted, though often in a changed form ; but, at the same time, new ideas on the subject were clamouring to be heard. As a consequence these years are full of apparent contradictions, and on all sides there is a seeming confusion of thought.   Some writers are found who still hold the views of the older school, while others advocate the use of stern measures towards the Poor. Though the result of this conflict was to determine men's attitude towards the problem of poverty for nearly threequarters of a century, it is difficult to say which view was predominant before 1700.

Religion still continued to exercise some faint influence over the administration of relief, but to say how much was lip-service only would not be easy. Even this influence was inherently changed from that which had held sway throughout the Middle Ages. To give alms was no longer a mystic act of grace, but a practical duty towards God. " Suppose, Sirs," wrote Hains, " there were no Profit to be reaped. That what we contribute is only a mere Act of Charity, accomplishing the happy Reformation, Comfortable Imployment and Maintenance of the Poor. Consider, I say, if this were all, whether it would be safe to keep that interest or money, which we ought to part with, and improve for God's glory and the good of many of our poor Neighbours ; since by so doing we may incur his displeasure and our own ruine for ever." [1] The Poor, even to such persons as were still influenced by a religious motive, were no longer an opportunity, but merely a responsibility, and in time even this aspect of the religious duty of relieving the Poor became entangled with other motives not even remotely religious. By the middle of the succeeding century Bailey found nothing incongruous in writing in the same paragraph that it was both our duty to God, and very good for our trade, to provide for the Poor. Thus he wrote, " To provide a comfortable Subsistence for the Poor, is Most certainly a Duty highly obligatory upon every Person in whom the traces of moral virtue are not quite obliterated ; the performance of which is equally required by Policy and Religion. This is a Charity of the utmost extent ; which, if conducted according to the following plan, by employing the Poor in Parish Workhouses, will very much promote the

Commerce, Wealth and Peace of this Kingdom.   These
Houses will also become proper Schools to train up the
Children of the Poor to Religious Sobriety and Industry,
who would otherwise be brought up in Sloath, Ignorance
and Vice.   They will likewise be nurseries for Spinners,
Weavers and other Artificers, in the Woollen, Linen and
Cloth Manufacture, and give Occasion to the Exercise
of many other Trades and useful Employments."[2]
Such an extract illustrates the great gulf which divided
the religious motive for relief in the Middle Ages from
that which influenced men in the early eighteenth
century.   The latter was not strong enough, and lacked
the driving force to make it a real and effective incite-
ment to the relief of the Poor.

The paternal idea of the Tudors and early Stuarts
persisted longer.   The material conditions, which prevailed for the first few years after the Restoration, were
favourable to its continuance.   After the late political
disturbances, the country was in a very disorganized
state ; much land had changed hands, and no one was
sure of his title to it ; a sense of unrest, fatal to industry,
was abroad.   Moreover, from 1660–63, 1678–9, and
1693–1700, corn was scarce, and prices were high.
Writers speak as if trade were in a desperate condition.
Davenant said that the Balance of Trade was £1,993,207
against us in 1662.[3]   From all accounts they were
difficult years for the labouring part of the community.
Hains, writing in 1674, says, " So general and loud for
diverse years past, have been the complaints, for want
of trade and money throughout this nation ; and so
pressing are the necessities of most men, that there is
scarce any person that can be insensible to it. . . .
Poverty seems to have invaded the whole nation.   Leases
being thrown up constantly in the country, and tradesmen breaking daily in the City . . . and Labourers
generally, if they have families, are ready to run abegging,
the Poverty of most Parishes being such that they can
hardly supply or relieve them."[4]   Even allowing for

some exaggeration, conditions were so bad that men must have been well aware of the hardships which they imposed on the poorer sort. In this connection it is interesting to note that during the seventeenth century the majority of tracts dealing with the questions of poverty were written when corn was dear. For instance, out of twenty-two pamphlets dealing with the Poor, eighteen were written in years when the price of corn was high, and only four when it was low. This looks as if, during the seventeenth century, poverty was still believed to be the result of circumstances rather than of depravity, and as though it were felt that in time of need it was still the duty of the more prosperous classes to discover some means by which the Poor could earn a fair living. Thus, during these years, writer after writer propounds views in accordance with these sentiments. Hale, speaking of the employment of the Poor, says, " It would be an abundant recompense, by accustoming the poor sort to a civil and industrious course of life," [5] even if such employment involved the authority which organized it in some financial loss. Sir Joshua Child held similar views as to the responsibility of the government, regarding it as " our Duty to God and Nature so to provide for and employ the Poor," whether such employment should " turn to present profit or not." [6] Such employment, he thought, would be amply worth while if it kept the Poor from begging and stealing. Other writers thought, " that it would be safer, more profitable, and less chargeable to these kingdoms to imploy the poor that want other employment, in making Inclosures and Fortifications or in Planting trees or in making Store Houses or Work Houses, or in other public structures, than to suffer them to be idle and take ill courses." [7] However little these views were translated into action, there is abundant evidence to show that men still thought that no man who was willing to work should be allowed to lack employment, and that it was the function of authority to provide such employment. With these writers there is no hint of *laissez faire*, no suggestion that the balance of unemployment should be redressed by the laws of supply and demand.

By the end of the seventeenth century the economic outlook had changed. In spite of unemployment and temporary distress the trade of the country had been growing steadily. Davenant said that in 1686 we had "near double the tonnage of trading ships to what we had in 1666,"[8] and that rents in some parts of the country had risen from twenty to twenty-six years' purchase, and in others from fourteen to seventeen or eighteen. In 1698 the Balance of Trade was reported to be £43,320 8s. 1d. in our favour, and every year trade was increasing. Our exports, which were valued at £3,525,906 18s. 6d. in 1696, had risen to £16,365,953 0s. 7d. in 1760.[9] Moreover, owing to the increased use of enclosures and the new methods of agriculture, both of which were growing in importance throughout this period, the food supply of the country was not so precarious as in former years. This change in the material condition of the country produced a natural reaction in men's attitude towards the Poor. For in spite of this increase in the national wealth and prosperity the Poor Rates continued to rise. This was more than contemporaries could understand, and a new bitterness superseded the old sense of responsibility towards the Poor. After the eighties this new spirit became very noticeable in the writings of Dunning and Locke. They protested that the rates would never be lowered by providing the Poor with work, but only by driving them to obtain work for themselves, and to this end they advocated considerable sternness. In the next century this school of thought received a powerful adherent in Defoe. By 1720 the idea of providing work as a method of relief had practically died out, and the men who advocated workhouses were animated by a determination that the Poor should not have something for nothing. It was with this object that Overseers were empowered to confine all their poor in workhouses, and to refuse them relief if they objected to this treatment. Until the close of the sixties in the eighteenth century, opinion with regard to the relief of the Poor favoured the strict execution of such provisions, and writers aimed, not at softening, but rather at tightening, the administration of the Poor Laws. By the seventies, however, there were increasing signs that writers had progressed as far along these lines as they intended to go, and that a reaction in favour of more lenient treatment towards the Poor was setting in.

Such was the general trend of opinion with regard to the Poor during this period. The whole question was one which aroused much interest, and there is no lack of writers to illustrate each phase and point of view. But whether they treated poverty as a misfortune or as a crime, and whether they wished to reform circumstances or individuals, in one thing they were unanimous, namely in their desire to devise some plan or regulation by which to check the Poor Rates in their upward flight.

In dealing with the question of the Poor most writers followed the three great lines of classification adopted by 43 Eliz. c. 2. This act divided the Poor into the aged and impotent, children, and such persons as were able but unemployed. Not very much controversy raged about the best methods of dealing with the two former classes. Neither in the seventeenth nor in the eighteenth century did writers waste their time on the case of such persons as by illness or age were unable to maintain themselves. It was popularly supposed that the number of these persons would not be large, once the able-bodied Poor had been absorbed into industry, and it was considered that they might be safely left to the parish officer to relieve as aforetimes. When an author was engaged in advocating the establishment of workhouses, he usually suggested that certain quarters might be assigned therein to such poor as were incapable of doing anything in their own support, on the ground that they could be more cheaply maintained in that way than by the payment of separate allowances. Other writers advocated out-door relief for these types of paupers, but it was not a point on which discussion waxed hot.

The second class were the infant poor. These were made up of orphans, deserted children, and children whose parents were unable to maintain them without help from the parish. In these circumstances the Overseers and Churchwardens were empowered by 43 Eliz. c. 2 to bind out the children belonging to their own parish as apprentices when they reached the age of seven or more. Public opinion strongly approved of the employment of children, and the ideas of a later age on the subject of education and the need to foster a child's self-development, would have been met with a blank uncomprehension, had they been expounded to the average social reformer of the eighteenth century. Mandeville, writing in 1723, said, " Few children make any progress at school, but at the same time are capable of being employed in some business or other, so that every Hour of those of poor People spent at their Books is so much time lost to Society. Going to school in comparison to Working is Idleness, and the longer Boys continue in this easy sort of Life, the more unfit they'll be, when grown up for downright Labour, both as to Strength and Inclination. Men who are to remain and end their days in a Laborious, Tiresome and Painful Station of Life, the sooner they are put upon it at first, the more patiently they'll submit to it for ever after."[10] Despite the growth of the Charity School movement, charity to children in the seventeenth and eighteenth centuries meant enabling them to earn their own living at the earliest possible moment, no matter how laborious their life might be. That at one Charity School the girls had been induced to work some twelve hours a day is stated as a fact calling for approbation.[11]   In this case, part of the money gained went to the parents, and it is hinted that great success has been achieved in

A VIEW OF THE CHARITY CHILDREN IN THE STRAND

winning over the parents by this bribe. During the seventeenth century many writers advocated the setting up of spinning schools to teach poor children how to spin. Among their number was Dunning in 1686, Yarranton in 1677, and Locke in 1697, while Hains wrote various pamphlets on the subject. Besides spinning woollen and linen yarn, it was suggested that schools for lace-making and kindred employments might be set up.

A majority of writers blame the evil education, or lack of education, which the children of the Poor received, for the increase of poverty and vagrancy. Sir Joshua Child held that " the children of the Poor are bred up in Beggary and Laziness, do by that means become not only of unhealthy bodies and more than ordinarily subject to many loathsome diseases, whereof many of them die in their Tender Age, and if any of them do arrive to years and strength, they are, by their idle habits contracted in their Youth, rendered for ever after indisposed to Labour, and serve only to stock the Kingdom with thieves and beggars."[12] Another writer said that such ill-training had " Ruined many a hopeful Plant " while a third compared Idleness in Youth to the Seed-plot of the hangman's harvest. [13]

This feeling that the problem of training the young in habits of industry must be solved, if the Poor Rates were to be reduced, was shared by all writers. Whatever men had to say in theory about the value of pauper apprenticeship, in practice they could see that its results in many cases were far from happy, and that there was real need of further action in this direction. The establishment of working schools was the favourite expedient suggested by seventeenth century writers ; Hains, Yarranton, and Locke were all advocates of this scheme. In the eighteenth century the workhouse ousted the working school from its popularity among the writers of the day. In theory such places were to be well equipped to train children up in habits of industry and to teach them a trade. In practice, however, the matter proved otherwise. Throughout the period, writers, though differing as to their remedies, stressed the point that if the younger generation could be trained up to habits of industry and frugality, a great advance would have been made in dealing with the whole question of poverty.

To both 17th and 18th century writers the crux of the problem was the position of the able Poor. The other aspects of poor relief are passed over in a little space so that they can concentrate all their time, ingenuity, and pen-craft on the problem of finding some method of coping with the able Poor which shall at once reduce their numbers and their expenses per head. According to Sir Matthew Hale, "Although the relief of the Impotent Poor seems to be a Charity of more immediate Exigence, yet the Imployment of the Poor is a Charity of greater Extent and of very great and important consequences to the public Wealth and Peace of the kingdom as also to the Benefit and Advantage of mankind."[14] The question was, in fact, one of unemployment rather than of poor relief. It was thought on all sides that, " could all the able hands in England be brought to work, the greatest part of the burden that now lies upon the industrious for maintaining the Poor, would immediately cease, for, upon a very moderate computation, it may be concluded, that above one-half of those who receive relief from the parish, are able to get their living."[15] How great the numbers of the unemployed really were it is impossible to tell, as different writers give such widely divergent answers, which even the lapse of years between them makes it impossible to reconcile. Haines says that there must be at least 200,000 maintained by the Poor Rates and by begging,[16] while Locke in 1697 estimates their number at 100,000.[17] Lawrence Braddon supposed that " all the Poor in Great Britain, which in time may come under the Authority of this Corporation, are 1,500,000 souls, and of these there will continually be 300,000 Persons who, through

Infancy, Age or Infirmities, will be incapable of Labour."[18] This extract is more valuable as forming some guide to the popular estimate of the proportions between the able and the impotent Poor, than as containing a statement of actual fact.

It was universally felt that if any good was to be done with the question of unemployment it was vitally necessary to find out what was its fundamental cause, and, by remedying this, to stop the rot from spreading any further. Accordingly the first part of every treatise deals with what the writer supposed to be the root of the trouble ; and whatever plan he proposed in the second part was based, as was natural, on his findings in the first. To understand any of these plans it is therefore necessary to know to what causes contemporaries ascribed the growth of poverty. Though the number of men who wrote on the subject was large, the causes to which they assigned the growth of the Poor Rates were not numerous, and can be roughly divided under five heads, which are : Trade depression and consequent lack of work, the prevailing lowness of wages, the laziness of the Poor, the luxury of the Poor, and lastly the Poor Laws themselves. Of these five explanations the first two were characteristic of the seventeenth century, the next two of the eighteenth, whilst the last was put forward by various writers in both periods.

Writers of the first years after the accession of Charles II held the belief that the main cause of the prevailing poverty was the decrease of trade and industry. It is difficult to say whether the state of trade was quite so desperate as contemporary descriptions imply, but, even allowing for some pardonable exaggeration, it appears to have been sufficiently unsettled to justify the belief of those writers who blamed the circumstances of the times for the amount of poverty which existed.

A second cause to which seventeenth century writers attributed much of the distress of the time was the lowness of wages. It was claimed by many men that this, rather than any actual lack of work, was the real root of the trouble. In 1699 it was said that, "Many cannot now earn above sixpence or eightpence a day with the greatest toil."[19]   It is interesting to see that Cary and Firman, both men who had had practical experience in organizing work for the Poor, blamed the lowness of wages for the amount of poverty which existed. Thomas Firman was a seventeenth century merchant of Aldersgate who had started the practice of giving out flax-spinning to the poor of the Parish to spin in their own homes. "There are," he wrote, "many thousands whose necessities are very great and yet they do what they can to live by their own honest Labour to keep themselves and many times would do more than they do, but for want of employment, several that I now have working to me, do spin some fourteen, some sixteen hours in twenty-four, and had much rather do so than be idle."[20]   But in spite of great personal keenness he was not able to make his scheme pay, and he reckoned that he lost £200 out of £4,000 per year. He explained that unless the Poor would spin 800 yards for a penny there was little profit in it, and to do that meant so great a toil that "till the Magistrates will do their duty and see the Laws put in execution against Beggars, and the People grow so wise, as not to encourage this wicked course of Life, I have little hope to see this matter much amended."[20]   Cary was a chief mover in the Poor Reforms at Bristol, and the setting up of the Workhouse there, and he bears testimony to the same thing. "But we soon found that the greatest cause of Begging did proceed from the low wages of Labour ; for after about eight months our children could not get half so much as we expended."[21]   It is also worth noting that in "An Account of several Workhouses," published in 1725, it is frequently reiterated that the labour of the Poor will not pay for the money expended on them, and that the chief use of the workhouse in the matter of reducing the rates is that it acts as a deterrent. Sir

Matthew Hale, whose "Provision for the Poor" Eden thinks was written about 1659, though it was not published until 1683, says, " There are many poor that are able to work if they had it and had it at reasonable wages."[22] Davenant thought that part of the trouble, at least, was caused by lack of work, for he says that, though part of our Poor by reason of our slack administration are suffered to remain in sloth, yet " the other, through a defect in our Constitution, continue in wretched poverty for want of employment, though willing enough to undertake it."[23] The trouble appears to have been the difficulty of getting work at a living wage. J. Hayes, writing of the clothing trade, said that the poor wanted work at such wages as would give them a reasonable support, his estimate of a living wage for a family consisting of a husband, wife, and four children, being not less than ten shillings a week between them,[24] and Hale also gives this sum as the decent minimum. Dunning was less sympathetic, and complained that in times of bad trade, when " Renters of Farms and others cannot give so large wages as such expect," good workmen prefer to live on the parish, rather than work for less than their usual wages.[25] But, as Hale shows, there were two sides to this question. " It is not unknown," he said, " how some covetous masters in hard times, if they are well-stocked and of abilities, will set to work many Poor, but they must take such wages as they are not able to live upon."[26] What a sudden depression in any trade might mean to the Poor employed in it is illustrated by the following Petition of the Middling and Poorer Sort of Master Shoe Makers against the order that the Curriers should sell only whole hides. They protest that if they cannot get leather in small quantities as they require it, thousands of the trade " will, in all likelihood, be under a necessity of leaving their Families to their respective Parishes, to travel Foreign Countries for Bread, to the great Detriment of the British Nation."[27] This threat of emigration, coupled with the risk of being thrown on the Parishes, was the chief weapon employed in any dispute with the Government. The chief reason for it lay in the fact that France was trying to improve her manufactures at the expense of England, and to do this English workmen were tempted over to start the new trades. This was particularly true of the woollen manufactury. Thus, the woollen manufacturers declare that without due encouragement the persons it employs " must inevitably perish, or be an immediate heavy Charge (which is already in many places almost insupportable) to the respective Parishes to which they belong, or (which would be of very fatal consequences), they will be obliged to remove into foreign countries, where they will exercise their trades, and consequently will teach those Nations to perfect their Woollen Manufactures, to the great Prejudice, if not to the entire Destruction, of our own."[28]

By the commencement of the eighteenth century the view that poverty was caused primarily by low wages had fallen into disrepute. Theorists held that the responsibility for what distress existed must be laid on the shoulders of the working class themselves, and one of the first indications of this new attitude is to be found in a tract, " The Trade of England revived," which was published anonymously in 1681. In it the author stated that " We cannot make our English cloth so cheap as they do in other countries, because of the strange idleness and stubbornness of our Poor, especially in all places within fifty miles of London, where the Poor are most numerous, where wool is cheaper than in most places and so it would be a very good place for trade. But these Poor are so surly that most of them will not work at all, unless they might earn as much in two days as will keep them a week. And when they do work they will often mar what they do."[29] Dunning, writing five years later, on the increase of the Poor Rates, affirmed positively that it was " Not occasioned by any Dearth or Scarcity of Necessitie there being never a greater plenty ; nor for want of employment, there being never more, nor through smallness of wages, that being never so great. But by Idleness, profuse Expenses, the ill-bringing up of children and the younger sort."[30] This extract furnishes an explicit contradiction of the view of poverty which was still held by writers influenced by the Elizabethan ideal. When Dunning wrote his " Plain and Easie Method " corn was cheap, there having been no sign of a scarcity since 1679, and as a consequence he was less tolerant than writers who wrote when provisions were dear. Even so, Locke, though he wrote during a period of high prices, took much the same view of the causes of poverty, for he said, " If the causes of the evil be looked into, we humbly conceive it will be found to have proceeded neither from a scarcity of provision, nor from a want of employment for the Poor, since the goodness of God has blessed these times with plenty, no less than the former, and a long peace during two reigns gave as Plentiful Trade as ever. The growth of the Poor must, therefore, have some other cause, and it can be nothing else but a relaxation of discipline and a corruption of manners."[31]

In the eighteenth century writer after writer declared his adherence to this view. On all sides rose the cry that wages were not too low, but too high. It was felt that, while mechanics and servants demanded wages which, to quote contemporaries, " were excessively high," England would never be able to compete with France in foreign markets. As Braddon wrote, " It must be confessed in the now course of trade that the bringing down of our wool and other materials to a low rate, and reducing the wages of our manufacturer to a level, at least, to what the French and Dutch give upon like occasions, is absolutely necessary to support our foreign trade."[32] On all sides there came a demand for labour. " The Farmers' Wives can get no Dairy Maids," wrote Defoe, " their Husbands no Plowmen, and what's the matter ? Truly the Wenches answer they won't

go into Service at 12*d*. or 18*d*. a Week, while they can
get 7*s*. to 8*s*. a Week at Spinning ; the men answer they
won't drudge at the Plow and Cart, hedging and ditching
and threshing and stubbing, and perhaps get £6 a Year,
and coarse Diet, when they can sit still and dry within
Doors and get 9*s*. or 10*s*. a Week at Wool Combing, or
at Carding and such Work about the Woollen Manufactury."[33]   In the March number of the Gentleman's
Magazine for 1734, Vanderlint called for an increase in
husbandry, so that a fall in the cost of food might produce
a corresponding fall in wages.[34]   In common practice,
however, it was often found that cheap food meant not
cheap but dear labour, since, as their wants were easily
supplied, it was increasingly difficult to induce the Poor
to work.   In support of this view Joshua Gee stated
that it was a known fact that " It has been remarked by
our Clothiers and other manufacturers, that when Corn
has been cheap they have had great difficulty to get their
Spinning and other Work done.   For the Poor could
buy Provisions enough with two or three Days' Wages
to serve them a Week, and would spend the rest in
Idleness, Drinking, etc.   But when Corn has been dear,
they have been forced to stick all the Week at it ; and
the Clothiers have had more Work done with all the
ease that could be desired, and the constant application
to Business has fixed their minds so on it, that they have
not only had money enough to purchase Food, but also
to provide themselves with Cloath and other necessaries,
whereby they live comfortably."[35]   In this connection
it is interesting to note that in several years during
which corn was particularly cheap there was a slight
retrogression in the volume of our export trade.   Such
was the case in 1700, 1718, 1719, 1723, 1738, 1739, and
1744,[36] and this fact lends some colour to the view that
cheap bread did mean a difficulty in getting labour.
Throughout the eighteenth century the greater number
of the pamphlets written about the Poor were published
in years when Corn was cheap, as if that, rather than the

scarcity of provisions, was apt to cause a crisis in the affairs of the working class. The majority of the population were still engaged in agriculture, but even so the trade, and therefore the industry, of the country was increasing enormously. To a large extent the spinning and weaving, though particularly the former, were carried on as a bye-trade by the families engaged in agriculture, and the increased work involved by a good harvest might account to some extent for a falling-off in the amount of manufacture produced. Moreover, trade was increasing out of all proportion to the increase in population—which meant that, in years of good trade, manufacturers would be hampered by a lack of labour from producing the goods for which the merchants could find a vent. Nothing would be more exasperating to a man who needed hands than the sight of vagrants begging in every street, while he had to pay money, which he wanted as capital for the expansion of his own business, towards the relief of persons whose labour he could well employ. As Massie put it, " The greatest part of the Poor Rates of England and Wales are paid by Freeholders, Farmers, Merchants and Tradesmen ; which several classes of men go through great Labour, or Fatigue of Body or Mind, according to their stations, so that being obliged to maintain the Poor People in Idleness must be disgusting."[37] The sense of irritation which such a situation was calculated to produce explains much of the harshness with which even good and philanthropic men regarded the Poor.

These tracts may be regarded as protests against the raised standard of living which was beginning to come into operation among the Poor about this date. Such an outcry is perfectly comprehensible among people who thought it was essential that the drudgery of society should be done by those members of it who " in the first place are sturdy and robust and never used to Ease or Idleness, and in the second soon contented as to the necessities of Life. Such as are glad to take up with the coarsest manufacture in everything they wear, and in their Diet have no other aim than to feed their Bodies when their Stomachs prompt them to Eat, and with little regard to Taste or Relish, refuse no Wholesome Nourishment that can be swallowed when Men are Hungry, or ask anything for their Thirst but to quench it."[38]   When this was the standard of life, and the function of the social organism assigned to the poorer sort by the consensus of opinion of the time, it was no wonder that each instance of laziness, drunkenness, or extravagance was regarded as menacing the whole fabric of society, and as imperilling national Wealth. " The Labour of the Poor is the Treasure of the Rich," was a proverb freely quoted, but it was feared that the Poor might cease to labour, and so destroy the trade upon which English prosperity was built.

Idleness was not the only charge laid to the door of the Poor.   They are also accused of spending their time, of which they had defrauded the State, in profligate living, in luxury, and particularly in brandy drinking. Locke was very emphatic on the subject.   So, too, was Dunning, who said, " It's generally observ'd, That not only more Ale and Brandy is sold in single Ale houses than formerly ; but the number of such Houses and Shops are also increased, that the money spent in Ale and Brandy in small country shops and Ale houses amounts to a vast, and almost incredible sum, did not their payment for excise manifest it."[39]   The complaints about the increase of dram drinking are very numerous, and, in some cases, worthy of the most violent prohibitionist.   Part of the charge of Sir John Gonson to the Grand Jury of the Royalty of the Tower of London in 1728 ran as follows, " Nothing is more Destructive to the Health or Industry of the poore Sort of People, on whose Labour and Strength the Support of the Commonalty so much depends, than the immoderate Drinking of Genevea.   It is common for a starving sot, intoxicated with this or other like Liquors, to behold his rags and nakedness with a stupid Indolence, and either in sence-less Laughter, or in low and insipid Jests, to banter all Prudence and Frugality, drowning his pinching cares, and losing with his Reason all anxious reflections on a Wife, Children perhaps crying for bread in a horrid empty Home. In hot tempers it lets loose the Tongue to all the Indeciencies and Rudness of the most Pro-voking Language, as well as the most hellish Oaths and Curses, and which is frequently followed by Quarrels and Fightings, and sometimes hath been the cause of Murder. Besides all this, these houses are the Receptacles of Thieves and Robbers, and often the Original of them too ; for when a Wretch has spent or wasted that which should support himself, and his Family, it is here (in the brandy shops) that they Associate and turn House-breakers, and street robbers, and so by quiet Progression at last make an exit at the Gallows."[40] Such was the contemporary official attitude towards dram drinking.

More harmless luxuries also came in for their share of condemnation. The chewing and smoking of tobacco, the taking of snuff, the wearing of gay clothing—all were adjudged to be inexcusable extravagances. After the rise in the rates, which began to be marked about 1770, there was also a tremendous outcry against the use of tea, sugar, and white bread in poor men's families. To the use of these articles, indeed, contemporaries did not scruple to attribute the difficulties in which the poor found themselves, and they affirmed that with better domestic economy the present rise in the rates would have been unnecessary.

There was still a minority who looked elsewhere for the causes of the increasing poverty, and who considered the Poor to be more the victims of circumstance than the original cause of their poverty, extravagant and improvident though they might be. Massie was, per-haps, the most interesting writer in the eighteenth century who held these views. He found two causes which he held to be responsible for the increase of poverty. The first of these was the enclosing of the common fields, which even before 1760 was considerable, though it was carried on with nothing like the same rapidity as in the last part of the century. He contended that people were being turned off the land more quickly than they could be absorbed into trade, and that the effect of enclosures was to remove " Multitudes of People from our Natural and Fixed Basis of Land to the Artificial and Fluctuating Basis, Trade."[41] This, he said, accounted for the immediate surface poverty of the moment. But the permanent evil he traced to " that very first law that was made to provide for the poor."[41] Other scattered writers agreed with this dictum. Child, soon after the Act of Settlements was passed, said that one must not blame the execution of the law, but the law itself ; and that it was useless to declare that we had very good laws which were very badly executed, for " There never was a good law made that was not well executed, the fault in the law causing the fault in the execution."[42] Davenant bears out this statement by saying that " The corruption of mankind is grown so great that now-a-days Laws are not much observed which do not in a manner execute themselves."[43] In 1735 a Committee of the House of Commons passed a series of resolutions to the effect that the laws regulating the Poor were defective, that they were difficult to execute and of little use. But, in spite of this condemnation, nothing was done, and Mr. Hays, who had been the leading spirit in the movement for reform in the Commons was unable to get his bill accepted. Yet notwithstanding the lethargy of Parliament on the subject, when, as one writer stated, " Many thousands of the incapable Poor are almost starved for want ; thousands of them not having above ninepence per head per week, for Lodging, Diet and all other Necessaries,"[44] many thinking people must have condemned the existing system as a failure.

Thus a feeling grew up on the part of some that the Poor Laws were responsible for creating much of the poverty which they were supposed to relieve, and on the part of all that they had failed either to lessen the number of the Poor, or to relieve them adequately. This general consensus of opinion was the opportunity for all who were interested to bring forward their own suggestions for a better management of the Poor. The central idea of the majority of these tracts was to set the able Poor on work, the difference between the various writers lying only in the means which they suggested to attain this end. These, like the causes of poverty, can be grouped under certain heads, such as a revival of trade and the protection of the home market and of home industries, the provision of work by local authorities, either by working schools or other methods, such as the formation of joint-stock companies for the purpose, the enacting of such regulations as would compel the Poor in self-defence to find work for themselves, and lastly, compulsory work enforced by a strict workhouse system. Most of the proposals put forward for lessening the burden on the Poor Rates can be placed under one of these headings. The first and second remedies proposed are characteristically seventeenth century ; the third expedient was most prominent for the last twenty years of the seventeenth and the first twenty of the eighteenth, while the workhouse is mainly the favourite panacea of the eighteenth century writers.

If a writer thought that a large quantity of men would work provided they could obtain work on reasonable terms, then he saw in a revival and expansion of trade the best way of lessening unemployment. This was the point of view of many of the seventeenth century writers before 1695. Their aim was to stimulate trade in the belief that to do so was automatically to decrease poverty. In detail the movement was by no means disinterested, and its principal leaders were men who were concerned in the great woollen and silk industries. During the second half of the seventeenth century the groans of the woollen weavers were especially loud over the decay of their trade, which, they prophesied, would lead to general poverty and a fall in the price of wool, a result which in its turn would hit the landed interest. Their chief grievance was the export of wool to France, where it was being worked up with such good effect that manufacturers complained that there was no longer any outlet there for English cloth, and that they were losing their markets in consequence. Also, besides the regular export of wool abroad, a very large quantity was smuggled out of the country, the running of wool, especially to France, being a very lucrative employment. Accordingly, the first cry of the woollen manufacturers was that, if poverty were to be prevented, the export of wool must be stopped, for " the Export of unwrought wool hath destroyed our Foreign Markets for the Sale of our Cloth."[45] Another storm of protests was raised against the French luxury trade, as it was called. English fashions demanded French goods, e.g., silks, velvets, and wines, but the French did not encourage the importation of English products. It was a trade much condemned by contemporaries, who argued that, as the French would not take our cloth in exchange, we had to pay in specie for trumpery fripperies, which brought no increase of wealth to the nation. Hains, in his " Prevention of Poverty," gives as the general causes of poverty, " First the daily decrease of Goods and Commodities of our own growth and exportation. Secondly the double increase of foreign Goods and Commodities, brought over more and more from beyond the seas."[46] " But doubtless," he says, " it is the many £100,000's which our bad Husbandry and ill conduct sends every year beyond the seas, which we see again no more, this is the Grand Cause of our Miseries." It was prophesied that if we continued this trade we should be ruined, since it tilted the Balance of Trade against us, and destroyed even our home markets by permitting the sale of French goods. On the other hand it was argued, " If money were not transported, then our own manufactures, which are much diminished and become less than they were forty or fifty years ago, would now find quick markets and yield good prices, to the great encouragement of manufactures; but the contrary is notorious."[46] This clamour certainly stopped the trade for a time, and when William III. came to the throne it was formally ended, though throughout the eighteenth century a great trade was done in smuggling French brandy and silks into England.

No sooner had their grievance concerning the French trade been redressed than the woollen weavers and the silk manufacturers found another enemy attacking their prosperity, and threatening to overwhelm the land with poverty, or so, at least, they said. This was the increased popularity of printed linens and calicoes, which were driving some kinds of woollen and silk goods from the market. So the woollen and silk manufacturers waged a determined war against their use under the pretext of preventing poverty.[47] As a result of their propaganda an Act was passed in 1720, prohibiting the use of printed linens and calicoes.

Not all the attempts to cope with unemployment by stimulating trade were made in the interests of industries already well-established. There was an important group of writers who thought that the popularization and spreading of the linen manufactury, which was little practised in England, would do much to solve the problem of poverty, besides having the additional advantage of shifting the Balance of Trade in our favour, since in the present course of trade much money was exported yearly to Russia and the North German states for linen yarn. It was hoped that by growing the flax in England, and doing our own spinning and weaving, England would at once become more self-supporting and, at the same time, find employment for her Poor. "Then," wrote Yarranton, "will they need no relief from the Parish, nor will there be any complaining in the streets."[48] He thought that Warwickshire, Leicester, Northampton, and Oxfordshire would be the best counties in which to start the industry in England, because in those counties the land was suitable for growing flax, and there was no other staple industry, while food was cheap, and the district was served by the Thames, Avon, and Trent.   Moreover, as this region occupied a central position with regard to the rest of industrial England, he hoped that the Linen manufactury would be gradually diffused thence through the rest of the country.   The author of the " Trade of England Revived " favoured the northern counties as a place suitable for the planting of the linen trade,[49] his contention being that in those parts there was plenty of good cattle land which could be used for growing the flax, while there were good ports from which to export the finished products.   The cost of living, too, was less in the north than in the south, and, therefore, he thought, the poor might be induced to work for cheaper rates than they could be made to accept elsewhere.

Moreover, the linen manufactury was recommended as being particularly suitable for employing the poor because so much of its cost price went in labour.   It was estimated by a man with practical experience in the trade that " three parts of four, even of that cloth which comes not to above two shillings an ell, will be paid to work to the spinners and weavers."[50]   It was, however, essentially a pauper industry, in which wages were very low.   But as it demanded neither great skill nor strength, whilst the outlay on tools and raw material was small, it was an easy trade by which to employ the poor. " This manufactury," wrote Hains, " was an employment for the weakest people ; not capable of stronger work, being widows and children and decrepit and aged people, now the most chargeable, as likewise for Beggars and Vagrants, who live idly and by the sweat of other Men's labours."[51]   Thus the linen manufactury was advocated as a means of absorbing those people who were too old, feeble, or unskilled to find employment in other trades. While this remained the case, linen spinning must inevitably continue a pauper industry, and, in point of fact, the great majority of the yarn produced in Great Britain was spun in Ireland.

Many suggestions were put forward, not only with regard to the type of work on which it was considered advisable to employ the Poor, but also as concerned the methods by which this work should be organized and distributed. The simplest of these proposals was that the parish officials should make arrangements with some local clothier to give out work to all parishioners who might apply for it, and to pay them at fixed prices for the work which they did. This was the normal method of the seventeenth century, not only with regard to paupers, but also for ordinary labouring people, who in general received their work from the local clothier and worked it up in their own homes. Where it was applied it relieved the Overseers of all trouble beyond that of making the necessary arrangements with the clothier. This was the method advocated in "An Appeal to Parliament that there may not be one beggar in England" in 1659; and at the end of the century Dunning was proposing to deal with poverty by means of a destitution test of such a nature.[52] The difficulty was that the Poor of a parish consisted, at least in normal times, of those people whom the manufacturers had no wish to employ while they could get other labour, and so it was often difficult to find a contractor who would employ the parish poor; or, if he did, he would contract for such low rates of wages that the industrious workman would be penalized. Such a plan was only possible if it were certain that the Poor really desired work and would do it when they were given opportunity. With this method, also, there was no supervision, and the work turned out might be faulty or the material spoilt, while, if the people employed were paupers, it was difficult to have any hold on them by way of penalties. There was further the danger that the paupers so employed might embezzle the raw material with which they were entrusted. For all these reasons it was felt that some better method of organizing pauper labour was needed, and accordingly the other method advocated in the seventeenth century was the setting up of working schools. Robert Hains was a great exponent of this idea and wrote many tracts on the subject. In 1677 he published his " Proposals for building in every country a Working Alms House as the best expedient to perfect the trade and manufacture of linen Cloth." Hains himself had invented a machine which, he claimed, would enable spinners to earn ninepence instead of sixpence a day. He was very anxious to encourage the spinning of flax in England, together with the setting up of working schools, so that a market might be provided for his invention. Yarranton, also, advocated that spinning schools should be set up to teach the spinning of linen thread to both children and adults who wanted employment. His proposals were based on the schools which he had seen in Saxony while he was studying the iron industry there.

The period from 1660 was an era of industrial experiment at home, of expansion abroad, and, to a large extent during the first two decades of the eighteenth century, of speculation. Accordingly, it was quite in keeping with the spirit of the age that some writers should propose to treat the poor as a business proposition. The old maxim (as already quoted) said, " The Labours of the Poor are the Treasures of the Rich," and speculators of the time evidently thought that they might extract ore from such a mine. Several writers put forward the idea of running the poor on the lines of a joint-stock company. Sir J. Child, one of the first men to take this view, thought that it might be done without trying to make a profit by giving a social value to the position of a " Father of the Poor."

Most writers were not so optimistic, and their plans were drawn up with the idea of running the Poor at a profit, which was to be distributed in the usual way.

The general underlying idea behind most of the schemes was that the promoters should be incorporated as a company having the use of the Poor Rates for a given number of years, managing, in return, all the Poor—impotent, aged, children, and able. It was hoped that by skilful management much profit might be reaped from the labour of the latter class, while the others might be provided for in the most economical manner by reason of their numbers. Lawrence Braddon's scheme actually appears among those other schemes by which speculators tried to raise money in the year of the Bubble. One of the earliest prominent writers to put forward such a scheme was, as has been said, Sir Josiah Child, the eminent East India merchant, who wanted to incorporate a company under the title of The Fathers of the Poor, with extensive powers to receive money, to build work-houses, and to set the Poor to work. He wished also to have the right of transporting vagrants and other incorrigibles to the colonies for seven years.[53] Eden considered his plan unduly inquisitorial, even for the reign of Charles II, and thought that Child was "like Necker, more qualified to manage the details of a country house than to correct errors of legislation."[54] His plan was, in spite of Eden's criticism, less hare-brained than those of some of his successors, and even as late as 1739 Sir Matthew Decker advised its adoption with certain modifications. There is an ingenious proposal in Davenant's "The probable methods of making a people gainers in the Balance of Trade." A company, known as "The Governors and Corporation for maintaining and employing the Poor of the Kingdom," was to subscribe £300,000 and to receive a charter for a period of twenty-one years, during which time it was to receive a definite proportion of the Poor Rates. This corporation was to "Provide for the real and Impotent Poor good and sufficient Maintenance and Reception, as good or Better than hath at any time within the space of —— years."[55] The company is likewise to have the

right of employing all the Poor who cared to come to it
at threequarters of the market rate of wages on a six
months' contract, in return for which concession it is to
maintain all the able poor who apply to it on these
terms, whether they can be employed or not. Davenant
seems to have thought the scheme quite practical, and
as good a plan as any for setting the Poor to work.
Perhaps the most ambitious of the writers who tried to
promote the interests of society by establishing a company of exploit pauper labour, were John Bellars and
Lawrence Braddon. The former was a Quaker who
published his first treatise in 1695, under the title of,
" Proposals for raising a College of Industry." He wrote
various other books between this date and 1723, all of
which outline or elaborate the same plan. His aims
were threefold : profit for the rich, a plentiful living for
the Poor, and a good education for youth ; his first book
is prefaced by the tag, " The Sluggard shall be cloathed
in Raggs, He that will not work shall not eat."[56] His
plan was to establish colleges of Industry, a certain
proportion of whose inmates would, by their labour,
maintain the whole college, while the profit from the
labour of the remainder would go as interest on the
money lent by the Founders. These colleges were to be
built on enough land, and to contain representatives of
enough different trades to be self-supporting, so that
once they were in working order they would be able to
maintain themselves and have a surplus of profit to be
given to the Founders. They were not to be workhouses so much as co-operative societies, and there was
to be adequate accommodation for such married couples
as wished to join the society. Bellars promised under
his plan that the Poor would " be made rich, by enjoying
all things needful in Health or Sickness, Single or
Married, Wife and Children ; and if Parents die, their
Children well educated and preserved from Misery and
their Marriage incouraged, which now is greatly dis-
couraged."[56] These colleges were only designed to

meet the case of the able-bodied, but unemployed, Poor,
and were for those who " are thrown out of any Trade,
as being more than Sufficient to supply the general Want
of the nation."[56]   In his " Essays on the Poor,"
published in 1699, and again in 1723, he insisted that
one of the great benefits his colleges would confer, if
widely adopted, would be an increase in the food supply
of the country.   He says that " with many commodities
the Market is overstocked . . . which is a great un-
happiness of many of our merchants, that they make
commodities when nobody wants them . . . whereas
the same Labour in Husbandry they used in making
their Manufactures would have raised much more Food
than the money they got for their manufactures will
buy them."[57]   He evidently feared that a great increase
in industry would be followed by a scarcity of food,
owing to the trend of labour to pass from the land to
trade.

Lawrence Braddon, too, had a most elaborate scheme
for setting up collegiate cities.   He wished to start by
building three great hospitals for all the Poor within the
Bills of Mortality, one for the sick and lame, one for
" those whose years have rendered them incapable of
labour," and one for children aged less than three.[58]
All the able Poor were to be accommodated in collegiate
cities, each of which was to contain 20,000 inhabitants.
The corporation was to have the use of the Poor Rates,
but only after the cities had been built and were ready
to receive the Poor.   He hoped that eventually the
corporation would extend all over Great Britain, and
by so doing would have 600,000 people's Labour for
nothing, besides the Poor Rates, occasional Charities,
and forfeitures to the Poor.   In some ways Braddon
was a man of ideas.   He was interested in agriculture,
and proposed that attached to the cities should be
experimental colleges for " studying the Improvements
in Husbandry, Gardening and Forestry," where gentlemen's sons might be taught agriculture for £30 a year.

He also suggested that two million acres of wheat culti-
vated under the new method would yield enough grain
to be kept in public granaries against a time of scarcity.
Moreover, in manufacture, Braddon held remarkably
modern opinions on the value of specialization. " Let
each manufacture," he said, " be divided and sub-divided
into as many Branches as possibly it can and let each
Person be obliged to keep to *one part* only and not use
himself to work upon Things which require Performances
of every different kind."[58]   Of all the many proposals
made for the employment of the Poor, the idea of
running them for a profit is one of the most interesting.
It marks most definitely the fact that the Poor from
being fellow-countrymen had become a distinctive
species, a sect apart.   That the Poor, because they were
poor, should be collected in colleges or cities, the sole
qualification for which was unemployment and poverty,
casts an illuminating light on the mentality of the early
eighteenth century.   It was an interesting proposal,
but was allowed to lapse into oblivion after the specu-
lations aroused by the South Sea Bubble had died away.
Even in the experimental years of the early eighteenth
century such plans can hardly have been considered as
practical economics by thinking men who knew the facts
of the case, and the utter failure of the Charitable
Corporation in 1733 is a significant commentary on what
would most probably have happened had any such
plans been seriously put into execution.

Such schemes as those outlined above illustrate the
fruits of paternalism carried to excess.   But even while
they were being put forward, with more or less serious-
ness, certain vigorous writers, such as Dunning and
Locke, were advocating plans which contained the germs
of the policy of *laissez faire*.   These men argued that
what was wanted was not regulations for the provision
of work, but regulations which would force the Poor to
find work for themselves.   Thus Dunning suggested that
the parish obligation to employ its Poor might be

manipulated in such a manner as to make the Poor eager to find work for themselves.[59]   To achieve this end, he suggested that the able Poor should be sent round to the able parishioners in turn, each of which should be obliged to employ them for a certain number of days, but that "their wages be less so that the masters be willinger to employ them and that they may rather get work for themselves."[59]   Such paupers as refused to be employed in this manner were to be put to hard and meaningless tasks under penalty of starvation if they refused, until they were reduced to obedience.   In the early eighteenth century this school gained a powerful advocate in Defoe, who summed up these new tenets briefly when he wrote, "It seems strange to me from what just grounds we now proceed, upon other methods and fancy that it is our Business to find them work and to employ them, rather than to oblige them to find themselves work and go about it."[60]

This attitude towards the able but unemployed Poor was not of very long duration.   By 1722 it had been practically superseded by a general belief in the efficacy of workhouses to deal with poverty.   It was chiefly interesting as marking a transition between the solicitude which required that work should be found for the Poor, and the harsh determination of the eighteenth century to compel the Poor to work.   The workhouse was the favourite panacea for all the social ills of the eighteenth century, but it was itself the invention of an earlier date. Bridewell had been in some sense a workhouse.   The working alms-houses and hospitals which Hains advocated so eagerly, were drawn up on workhouse lines. Child, when he outlined his scheme for the incorporation of the Fathers of the Poor, included in it power for the corporation to erect workhouses.   It was not, however, until 1699, when Cary published his account of the workhouse set up at Bristol,[61] and when other big towns followed Bristol's example, that the idea seized the imagination of the day.   It was generally felt that workhouses were the only sure method by which, at once, the rates might be reduced, and the production of the country increased.   The wave of enthusiasm bore fruit in the act of 1722, which gave parishes a permissive right to join together to erect workhouses and to refuse relief to persons who declined to enter them.   It was hoped that many benefits would accrue from this act. At a former date Davenant had written, " If the legislature would make some good provision, that workhouses might in every parish be erected, and the Poor such as are capable compelled to work, so many new hands might be brought in as would indeed make English manufacture flourish."[62]   It was also hoped that the establishment of workhouses would do something to deal with the question of vagrancy, by way both of prevention and of cure.   By training children in habits of industry, and by providing them with a trade, it was thought that the future generation would have less temptation to turn vagrant.   As for the present generation, workhouses would provide a place where vagrants might be set to work, for they were the type of person who could "in no other way be so effectively brought to industry and order as when reduced to so narrow a compass or confinement under fitly qualified rulers, officers and Regular Government."[63]

Thus, for one reason or another, workhouses were advocated by most of the eighteenth century writers. Hale's scheme had dealt largely with the employment of the young, but that was only on paper ; the workhouse set up by the Bristol Corporation did in fact attempt to deal with the question by establishing a kind of training school for the youth of the city.   Cary was sanguine of the success of his method, and, writing on the question in 1722, suggested that the Poor Law should be reduced to one statute, and that facilities should be provided for encouraging corporations to set up workhouses.   Such corporations, if formed in the country, were to approximate to the size of the average hundred, and were to consist of a workhouse and a house of correction. In 1735 a Mr. Hays, M.P., actually carried a bill for the reform of the Poor Laws as far as the committee stage in the House, in which he advocated that every county should be divided into districts, each with its own workhouse and house of correction ; the aged, the impotent, and the children were to be provided for in hospitals. Alcock, in 1752, advised that three different kinds of houses be established to deal with the poor, one for the industrious and impotent, one for the sick, and the third, a house of correction, for vagrants. Perhaps the most elaborate plan for a workhouse system is to be found in H. Fielding's " A proposal for making an effectual provision for the Poor." He drew up his plan for Middlesex, that being the county with which he was most conversant, but he hoped that it might afterwards be extended to other counties. In it he suggested that there should be two great divisions, a County House for the industrious, which would also contain wards for the sick and aged, and a House of Correction for vagrants, which, beside work-rooms and lodgings, should be equipped with dungeons and fasting rooms. Labourers out of work were to come to the County House, where work would be found for them, but the regulations, even for these voluntary inmates, were so strict that few would care to avail themselves of the privilege. The usual routine was to be organized very much on the lines or an ordinary prison to-day. The fact, that, as a concession, labourers who came voluntarily to the County House were to be allowed to exercise themselves for two hours on Sundays and Thursdays in the closed garden, under the supervision of two warders, is sufficient commentary on the manner in which the unwilling would be treated.[64] Yet Fielding was a magistrate, had had some practice in the regulation of the Poor, and was a humane man. Bailey was dissatisfied with the standard and quantity of the work done in the average workhouse, and thought that it

E

might be improved by the registration of such workhouses under the Society for the encouragement of
Arts, Manufactures and Science. This he intended to
effect by a system of rewards and premiums. But of
all the writers who uphold the workhouse solution for
the regulation of the Poor, Massie has the most modern
flavour. He wished to have a national establishment
with nine Commissioners, fifty-two Commissioners-
General, and a properly paid staff of secretaries and
clerks. The law of settlements was to be abolished, and
workhouses and houses of correction were to be set up
where they were most required. In many ways Massie
is the most interesting of all the writers of the first half
of the eighteenth century, who devoted themselves to
the question of poverty.

There were, however, some dissentient voices raised
against workhouses. Defoe in particular was their
determined enemy, both on economic and on social
grounds. He considered that to set up workhouses was,
economically, to rob Peter to pay Paul. There is a
pamphlet, published under the name of Philanglus,
which is probably by him, and in which the writer
controverts the popular view, holding " that the Poor of
the wool manufactures does want work, is in Truth too
apparent to be denied, and therefore the trade cannot
employ more Poor than it now does, but to the prejudice
of the Clothing Trade." If, as people seemed to think,
there was a demand for hands in the woollen industry,
" the Poor themselves would soon find their way to the
wool manufacture without the expense of building
workhouses or raising money and Joint Stock or an Act
of Parliament to inforce them to it."[65] Defoe's
" Giving Alms no Charity." was written on the same
theme to defeat a bill of Sir Humphrey Mackworth's,
for setting up workhouses in every parish. Writing
again in 1723 under the name of Andrew Moreton, he
said, speaking of workhouses, " They have an evil
tendency for they mix the Good and the Bad ; and too

often also make reprobates of them all. . . . If we are to have workhouses, let there at least be separate Wards and Tables ; let some difference be made between once substantial and contributing householders and vagabond wretches, let all communication between the parties be cut off, that the innocent children of unfortunate men may not be corrupted."[66] These remarks on the internal condition of workhouses were, in many instances, only too true ; and conditions became worse rather than better as the century advanced. But to most people the workhouse remained the only method by which the Poor could be driven to work. Indeed, it may be said to epitomise the attitude towards the Poor which prevailed during the first half of the eighteenth century.

By the middle of the century, however, there were signs that a change was coming over men's attitude towards the employment of the Poor in workhouses. They believed in the theory as much as ever, but they were far from satisfied with the way in which it was carried out. Accordingly, after the fifties there was a gradually swelling number of publications, almost all of which suggested modifications in the workhouse system. These tracts are interesting not only because of the dissatisfaction which they expressed with the contemporary organization of these places, but also because in them are to be seen the first faint signs of a more lenient attitude towards the Poor. Fielding voiced this discontent when he wrote, " That the Poor are a very great burden and even a nuisance to this kingdom ; That the laws for relieving their distresses and restraining their vices, have not answered those purposes ; and that they are at present very ill provided for and worse governed, are Truths which every man will, I believe, acknowledge."[67] A few years later Massie also bore witness to the ineffectiveness if the Poor Laws. Accordingly both men brought forward schemes for new and improved workhouses. A suggested alteration, which was very often made, was that the parish was too small a unit for the employment of the Poor, and that workhouses, under paid officers, ought to be established either in every Hundred or in every County. This was Fielding's solution.   Massie would have abolished the Act of Settlement, and built workhouses where they were most required.   A number of writers inclined to the establishments of districts, which should be larger than the parish, yet smaller than the county. Joshua Tucker suggested that " The New Plan, whatever it is to be, should not be too large, any more than too confined.   A Parish District for instance and a Parish Work House have been proved to be generally too confined.   But, on the other hand, is not a County District by much too large and unwieldy ? [68]   At least one writer, however, protested that the trouble was not that the parishes were too small, but that they were too large.[69]   Others advocated the abandonment of the workhouses, and wished the Overseers to give out work to the Poor, to be done in their own homes, as had once been the custom.

In these enquiries into the actual running of the workhouses, instances of the hardships which were inflicted on the Poor within their walls came to light. In 1758 Massie blamed the strictness with which the Poor Laws were executed for much of the poverty of the country.   In 1773 John Scott wrote a pamphlet to expose the wretched situation of the Poor, and to incite people to make better provision for their necessities. Three years later Dr. Trotter advocated the establishment of Hundred Houses, on the ground that the present workhouses were unduly hard on the deserving poor. Gradually this discontent with the old system became more wide-spread and more pronounced, till finally it even began to show some signs of translating itself into action.   After the seventies the number of petitions for the repairing or enlarging of workhouses, or for the building of new Hundred Houses in East Anglia, became noticeably larger than it had been in the first part of the century. Evidently some little attempt was being made to improve the lot of the Poor in this respect.

It was not only the Poor who were regarded with more leniency as the eighteenth century grew towards its close. A new attitude towards the under-dog was coming into being. This showed itself in many ways. In 1760 Hanway contrived to obtain a bill to better the condition of the parish babies who were born in work-houses within the Bills of Mortality, where they died of bad air and neglect, and sometimes of deliberate intent. He worked unceasingly for the betterment of the children of the Poor, and in this he was at least partially success-ful. It was through his activities that something was done to lighten the lot of the poor chimney sweepers. At the same time John Howard was engaged in his struggle against the prison organization of the day. Before he started his reform movement, the condition of the English prisons was simply indescribable for filth, lack of decency, starvation, and cruelty. In 1788 Wilberforce entered on his campaign against the slave trade, and even at an earlier date he had been interested in the subject. On all sides a new interest was being taken in the rights and conditions of men.

It is interesting to speculate as to how far this new spirit was inspired by French influence. The latter half of the eighteenth century was, on the other side of the Channel, a period of intense speculative philosophy. Savants ruminated over the nature of man, over the nature of governments, and over the " Rights of Man." In 1762 Rousseau published his *Contrat Social*. Man became to men a matter of supreme importance, and the rights a man possessed, by the very virtue of his being, were held to be sacred and indestructible, even by the State itself. It was natural that English writers should be influenced to some extent by the ideas which were exciting the whole learned world of France ; it was in accordance with their national character that they should transform this speculative interest into practical activity.

On top of this new humanitarian sentiment several factors arose, which forced thinking men to turn their attention to the state of the Poor. The general dissatisfaction with the interior economy of the parish workhouses has already been noticed, as having had a tendency in this direction. After the end of the sixties the price of corn rose and remained high, and this in its turn adversely affected the general cost of living. At the same time the Poor Rates rose rapidly all over the country. The combination of these two factors forced men to study the relation which wages bore to prices, and to make some note of the conditions under which the Poor lived. An examination of the facts made it evident that in many cases the high price of food offered the Poor the alternative of starving on a parish allowance or of being subjected to the dirt and discomfort of a workhouse. This condition of things was not new; but now men, beginning to look upon it with new eyes, were filled with horror and disgust. At an earlier date no man would have written, " Our feelings for the sufferings of the Poor are daily wounded. At the same time that millions of money are apportioned for their use, we know that thousands are labouring under the severest trials which poverty and disease can inflict ; and we reflect with indignation on the other hand that thousands, who ought to earn their daily bread, by the sweat of their brow, are maintained out of the Poor Rates without employment, a reproach to the community and to themselves.[70] Such sentiments are more in accordance with those which prevailed in the first years of Charles II. than with any which were common in the earlier part of the eighteenth century.

As a result of these feelings men began to compare the state of our Poor at home with the other objects of the new humanitarianism. Of what use was it, they asked, to free slaves abroad when English men and women suffered from such evils ? Thus Scott wrote, " In a country wherein it has been declared in the first Court of Justice that slavery is unknown, and that the owner of a negro has no power to compel his slave to return to America, without the latter's consent, we meet with the following punishment inflicted on a poor fellow for leaving his wife and children chargeable on the parish (or rather to speak more properly in these hard times, for not staying to starve with them or rot in gaol)." [71] The punishment to which he alluded was the brutal one of ordering three whippings, with a week's interval between each. Fifty years before, such a punishment for the like offence would have called for commendation, not condemnation. Still later Applegarth wrote, " But though the Price of Provisions has been enhanced for many Years last past, beyond what it was formerly ; yet alas ! the Wages of the Poor Peasants have not been raised more than about one Sixth ; that is to say from one Shilling per day to fourteen Pence ; so that the case of this Sort of People, as well as of the Soldiery, is extremely piteous and deplorable." He then goes on to say, " Now as much hath been said lately (with great Propriety), in Favour of the African Slaves in the West India Islands ; suppose, Reader, we were to say something in Behalf of John Bull's children (who are worthy of at least some notice)." [72]

Thus by the end of the century a complete revolution had taken place in men's thoughts with regard to the Poor. The danger was no longer that those in authority might be too severe, but that they might be too lenient. It is difficult to fix a date, even approximately, when this new attitude first gained a hold over men's thoughts. The middle of the century saw much dissatisfaction with the way in which the Poor Laws were administered, but the dissatisfaction was levelled not at their leniency, but at their lack of effect. By 1775, however, a new sympathy towards the Poor was appearing in writer after writer, though it was not until Gilbert's Act was passed in 1783 that this new policy received anything like official recognition. Even then the Act was only permissive ; but it was nevertheless significant. Just as to a watcher on the banks of some tidal river the moment when the boats at anchor swing their sterns down stream, is a sign that the tide has turned and is flowing out, so Gilbert's Act was a sign that the tide of public opinion had turned, and that the current was flowing once more towards leniency and indulgence.

CHAPTER II

THE ADMINISTRATIVE AND FINANCIAL
EQUIPMENT OF THE PARISH

THE ceaseless activity shewn by reformers in promulgating these new schemes, few of which depended on the overseers and churchwardens for their effectiveness, is explained by the faulty financial and administrative machinery of the parish. The responsibility for the Poor rested on the churchwardens and the overseers of the Poor, who by the 43 Eliz. c. 2. were to be nominated from among the substantial householders by two or more neighbouring justices. But whatever may have been the early practice, in the period under review the usual procedure was for the vestry to decide the overseers for the following year, and send a list to the justices with the request that they would nominate the first two names. Thus in reality the choice of officers to deal with the Poor rested with the parish itself, and they were usually appointed on some fixed system of rotation. Once appointed the justices exercised very little control over them, for though the Act provided that within four days after the end of their term of office they should submit their account to the justices, this examination was apt to be perfunctory.[1] Also, by a ruling of a later date, it was decided that if the overseer were prepared to swear to his accounts, it was not necessary for him to produce details. In the same way, the provision that the rates made by the overseers should be signed by the justices before they could be collected, was rendered nugatory by a legal decision declaring that though their signature was indeed necessary before the rate could become legal, yet the justices had no power, either to refuse to sign or to alter the assessment, however unjust it might seem to them to be.   In short, their action was purely administrative.[2]   Hence there was very little effective control over the way in which the parishes assessed, levied, and spent their poor rates ; and by their liberty in this important matter of finance the way was prepared for them to take what freedom they would in other branches of the poor relief.

Throughout the period, but particularly in the latter half of the century, contemporaries were united in complaining that the parish officers were neither efficient nor honest.   The truth of this statement it is difficult to prove, except in particular instances, but the law offered a considerable number of loopholes, of which men wishing to indulge in corrupt practices might avail themselves, while the very fact that the overseers were unwilling, unpaid, annual officials, must have made for bad administration.   The average overseer was either a farmer in rural parishes or a shop-keeper in urban ones ; he was engaged in earning his own living, and was generally unwilling to waste more time and thought over his troublesome duties than was absolutely necessary. It was to his interest to keep the machine running until his year was over, but not to start new experiments, which he would never have the opportunity to carry through, and which the next overseer would probably discard.   Moreover, he was usually quite unqualified for his task, and in some instances could not even write, but was reduced to making his mark.   One cannot write down all overseers and churchwardens as embezzlers and defrauders ; the most to be said is that their circumstances did afford opportunities for fraud, of which, in many cases, they availed themselves.   But more definite than this it is impossible to be.

Moreover, economy was not forced on them ; the income within which they must keep was limited only by public opinion, and by the ability of the ratepayers to pay. If the money in hand proved insufficient, the justices at Quarter Sessions appear always to have been amenable to the levying of another rate, when the overseers could prove that it was necessary. Thus there was little incentive to economy, and the lack of control must have led to an easy attitude towards the question of expenditure and accounts. If an overseer entered up honestly the money he expended and received, and took nothing material in the way of perquisites of his office, he had done all that could possibly be expected of him. Probably many parishes attained something of this standard. The administration was neither economical nor efficient, but, at the same time, it was not noticeably corrupt. Perhaps the parish officers " did themselves well " when they met over the parish business, and made a little out of the goods which they supplied to the Poor ; but in many cases the amounts of money that passed through their hands were not large enough to allow of much dishonesty. The impression left by ordinary parish accounts drawn from country districts or quite small towns, is one of honesty. Sometimes, however, the justices who signed the accounts at Easter as by law directed, do not seem to have been altogether convinced, The Westbury accounts for 1700 were evidently signed in a spirit of suspicion, " allowed of this Account if true "—and the names of the justices follow. In many cases it must have been difficult to know whether the accounts were true or false, since they consisted merely of stray entries on loose scraps of paper, more for the benefit of the overseer himself than for the information of anybody else. The following entry sheds rather a lurid light on the state of many parish accounts :

" Paid John Richardson for Collecting all theese Accounts the Best he could and Putting them in this Book for 20 years past they haveing been neglected all that time.. £1 0s. 0d."[5]

Eden also noticed that in many parishes, into whose affairs he had enquired, the accounts for all but the last few years had been lost or destroyed, as being things of no importance.[4]   Thus at Cumwhitton (Cumberland), he says : " The overseers' accounts of Disbursements for the Poor are lost, except for a few years back ; and, even then, only the sum total expended each year, is entered on the parish books."[5]   In other cases the parish officers would give no information as to the expenditure on the Poor, and what accounts he could get were very muddled and confused ; yet this was as late as 1797.   Thus law, custom, and training alike conspired to make the administration of the poor law, at best careless and extravagant, and at worst full of loopholes for personal profit.

The poor law administration of the London parishes was noticeably corrupt, even to contemporaries.   They afforded more chance of personal wealth to the parish officers than did the poorer rural parishes, or those of the small country towns.   Large masses of people were crowded into them, and it became a question of relieving, not merely half-a-dozen widows, a few labourers with large families, and a few bastards, but, in many parishes, several hundred poor persons a week.   The mass of money dealt with afforded an opportunity for peculation. In towns, also, where the officers were drawn from the shop-keeping class, much money might be gained by juggling with contracts or diverting the money laid out for the Poor through certain channels.   A large number of the City parishes were managed by select vestries, which meant that, though the overseers of the Poor might be, in theory, chiefly responsible for the Poor, in practice all the important pecuniary decisions were taken by the vestry.   Contracts were disposed of, or the Poor's money allotted, within the vestry and among the members of it, or among their friends, without any outside interference.   Thus it was not difficult for the parish vestrymen to use the Poor Rates in such a way as to benefit their own pockets.

There were three chief ways of making parish offices

a profitable concern.   One way was by placing contracts
in such a manner as to get a commission on them, or by
supplying the Poor with their own goods at an enhanced
price.   In 1714 an enquiry was held into the management of the Poor Rates in the Parish of St. Martin's-
in-the-Fields.   This parish was chosen for the enquiry
because it had been represented as the most free from
abuse.   If this were so, the condition of the other
parishes is best left to the imagination.   The placing out
of contracts appears to have been a common device, for
the Committee reported :

> " That whatever is wanting for the Use of the Church,
> supposing the Accounts of Qualities and Quantities to be
> fairly given in, is bought at the worst Hand, and paid for at
> extravagant Rates ; because the Persons who furnish their
> Goods, or their Work, are, for the most part, such as have
> been churchwardens and vestrymen."[6]

Another department of expenditure very difficult to
check arose from the weekly disbursements to the casual
poor.   The position of these casual poor was outside
the settlements act ; not being the settled poor of the
parish, according to the act of 1662, they had no right
to receive relief there.   In London parishes particularly
there were always certain destitute persons who drifted
into a parish in search of work, or who, after working
in a parish for a time without acquiring a settlement
there, fell sick or into some other misfortune.   In
addition, there were the Scotch and Irish emigrants,
who legally had no right to relief in an English parish,
and who, therefore, could not be moved until they were
actually chargeable, when the proper procedure was to
remove them to their own country.   Technically these
people had no right to parochial relief, but practically
it was simpler and cheaper to give them relief than to
discover their real settlement, to remove them, and,
perhaps, as a sequel, become involved in a law dispute.
So it became the custom to relieve all persons who were
in need for the time being, whether they had a settlement

in the parish or not. These were termed the casual poor. The same Committee before referred to reported :

> " That, the Books being filled with great Multitudes of Names, and of Sums distributed at several times to Persons carrying those Names it was impossible to distinguish which were fictitious, and which were real ; but the most part must be taken upon Trust."[6]

It also added that, as to the cost arising from the casual poor, which in 1713 amounted to £1,794 12s. 7d., and in the next year to £1,876 16s. 4d.,

> " it amounts yearly to near One third above what is distributed to the known or standing Poor : and it is in this Article, principally, that the Committee is of Opinion the Publick may be more than ordinarily imposed on ; several small articles being blended into this, under the name of Extraordinaries, to make it appear the greater."[6]

The suspicions of the Committee were further roused when its members came to examine the vestry clerk, through whose hands passed the payments to the casual poor, and found that though

> " the said Erridge, over and above his standing salary, raised in the Three Years, great Sums out of the said Poor's and Parish Money, amounting to above £832."[6]

yet with regard to these same casual poor they

> " could get no good Account from him of them : Sometimes he said, They were like as Settled Poor, though not entered upon the Pensions ; sometimes, that they were such as had received some Misfortune accidentally in the Parish : And being further demanded Whether he had the Warrants from the Justices of the Peace for relieving the sick Poor, according to Statute ; he said, He had : But when his books were produced to that Intent, he could not shew so much as one single Instance satisfactorily to the Committee."[6]

Their final judgment on Erridge, and on the general methods of account-keeping adopted by the vestry, was that these accounts made it

> " appear how necessary a Person this said Erridge is to the governing Part of the said Parish when such Accounts shall be suffered to pass."

They also stated that throughout the enquiry they had taken the accounts " De bene esse," but that " by several Instances already discovered, the Committee finds Reason to doubt the Truth of many of them."

This allowance of the casual poor was very difficult to check, and in cases where it was distributed by one or two men it was impossible to say whether all the money entered under that head had actually been paid out. The only record of the transaction was that set down in the account books, and entries like the following could not possibly be checked :

> " 1709 May 5 To a lame Woman going to Worcester..o–2–o, 19 To one in Want..o–1–6, 22nd To ditto..o–2–o, Aug. 19th To a poor Person..o–o–6, To another..o–1–o, January 27 To a poor Family..o–4–o, March 4 To a servant in Mitre Court..o–2–o, April 17 To one very ill..o–5–o."[7]

Instances of this kind of entry could be multiplied indefinitely. It was the normal way of entering up the amount of casual relief. In one case, it was ordered by the Middlesex Justices, sitting at the Court House in Bloomsbury, that " Whereas divers great Sums of Money have been of late Years unnecessarily expended in this Parish," for the future " the Pay Master for the Time being, when he pays any money on Account of the casual Poor, or Pensioners, or Parish Nurses, to any other Persons than the poor persons or Nurses themselves do take Care to set down the names of the Persons to whom such Money is paid, for his Security and our Satisfaction, in Case of Disputes concerning such Payments."[8] It was not the corruption of the parish officers alone which went to swell the amount of the payments to the casual poor. The Poor themselves took advantage of the inadequate arrangements for the checking of such sums by coming for their allowance twice, under one pretext or another. In 1816 it was declared a common practice of the poor to go from parish to parish getting casual relief from one, on one day, and from another on the next. Where the Poor could blame the officers, and the officers the Poor, it is not surprising that both parties prospered at the expense of the ratepayer.

Another cause of expense was the unnecessary feasting indulged in by the parish officers at the parish charge, whenever they had cause to transact any parish business. In the large urban or city parishes the abuse was more pronounced, as the feasts held there were of a more luxurious type. The accounts of the senior churchwarden, who also paid the casual poor and superintended the poor rate of St. Dunstan's-in-the-West, are honeycombed with tavern reckonings. Thus in the autumn of 1709–10 it took three separate meetings, each of them occasioning refreshment, to settle the Poor's Book. " August 25 At the Golden Lyon and Horn with the Deputy and others about settling the Poor's Book.. 0–9–8, Sept. 6 At the Horn after settling the Poor's Books..£2–4–0," and lastly, " Sept. 27 At the Horn upon signing the Poor's Book..0–16–6."[9]   Sometimes, not content with this total of expenditure, he entered the same items twice, upon different pages, such as (page 21), " June 10 With the Deputy and others at the Horn..£0–6–6," and on page 28, June 10, " Spent at the Horn with the Deputy and others..£0–6–6."[9] Evidence of the same extravagance comes also from the report on St. Martin's-in-the-Fields, where the following entries are made in the accounts of a certain Mr. Jeremiah Rose, " Spent by ditto on several vestrymen and overseers at several Taverns, and Crowded into several Articles..72–0–0."[10]   With the price of food what it was at the time, this sum was enormous, and would have maintained a dozen paupers for a year. A vivid commentary, in a case showing even greater extravagance than the last, is furnished when we read, " Spent by ditto at One Dinner at the Mulberry Garden..£49–13–9."[10] These more extreme instances are taken from the wealthy London parishes, compared with which, some of the small rural parishes were very moderate in their

PLATE III

The Rev'rend Rosy Priest with mirthful glee,
Tosses the Glass to Church Prosperity,
His Jolly Clerk no less elated view,
Better to an'm here then in a Pew.

A Parish Feast humbly Inscrib'd to His
Guards, Mennbers, Vestrymen, Questmen, and
Vizard-masters &c. by Gazzan.

The Meager Reader graips a Fowl his prey,
Another the Sir Warden does convey,
Whilst the Arch Beadle unto Spoil inclines,
Wraps the third Bottl unto Scrawn in his Cloak.

A PARISH FEAST

[face p. 64

requirements. At Batley they only " pd at a meeting at Ben. Beaumonds..1–0," and even at the " Accts taking at Ben. Beaumonds..5–0 " cleared their expenses.[11] But something was always expended on refreshment on these occasions, and, since there was no effective check on such indulgence in this direction, it was a practice capable of great extension. Sometimes the parishioners, when the vestry was an open one, and allowed them to express their opinion, tried to put a stop to this feasting at the parish expense. Pannal, for instance, determined " that there shall be noe money spent or allowed upon any accounts or lays-taking about the parish concerns but shall be all dispatched in the vestry without any charge to the parish."[12] Such regulations, though often made, were rarely kept ; Leyton parishioners reiterated again and again that the parish officers were not to spend more than a certain sum on dinners after beating the bounds and on similar occasions, but, from the accounts, and from the way in which the decree is repeated every few years, it does not appear to have been very effective.[13] Since the parochial officers received no actual pay for their work, they intended at least to compensate themselves by a little jollity.

Not only were the assessments and disbursements made by the churchwardens and overseers exposed to the charge of jobbery, but the methods of collection employed by many of them were also open to suspicion. For one thing, there was no satisfactory method of receipt, and this alone allowed the accounts to be considerably " cooked ". The Committee which considered the state of St. Martin's-in-the-Fields was very suspicious over the way in which the vestry treated the question of arrears ; for it found,

" That the Arrears of the Poor's Rates, amounting yearly to a great Sum, and, in these forementioned Three Years, to £1,187–14–6, are given in as desperate and wholly lost to the Parish ; Whereas upon Perusal of the Books of Arrears

F

by the Committee, it appeared, that many Persons therein
named are very sufficient, and of Quality and Reputation ;
and that from some of them the arrears had been demanded ;
so that the Committee has grounds to believe that several
of them may have been collected, though never brought to
account afterwards."[14]

Defoe found the fact that the parish authorities gave no
receipts a great grievance, as undoubtedly it was.   He
wrote :

" If the Government receives but a Shilling of a Subject
there is a Receipt given for a Voucher, but Parish Officers
give no other Satisfaction for your Payment, than crossing
the Book with a Pencil, which may be rubb'd out with a
Piece of Bread at pleasure, and you are obliged to pay over
again.   Nay, while they have all the Cards in their own
Hands, if they are not honest, they may make duplicates of
their books and collect the same rate over and over again ;
as has been the Case in several Parishes."[15]

Defoe, however, once on a tide of eloquence, was a little
apt to be carried away by the possibilities of the case.

One highly probable source of corruption, though not
actually a poor rate, was to be found in the administration of the money taken at the Communion collection,
which was supposed to be expended for the relief of the
Poor.   Certainly the Committee before mentioned found
cause to suspect that this was the case at St. Martin's,
concerning which it reported :

" As to the Altar or Offertory Money, the Committee
cannot but observe, that the Method used in St. Martin's
Parish for collecting Sacrament Money, is such as is liable
to great Frauds ;   being without Check or control, and,
according to the Confessions of the Churchwardens themselves, wholly left to the Discretion of such as collect it,
and those they pretend sometimes to account to ;   Whereby
there is reason to believe, this great and signal Piece of
Christian Charity offered to God for the sole use of the Poor,
at the times of most solemn Devotion, is, notwithstanding
the Directions given by the Rubrick (which orders, That
the Money given at the Offertory shall be disposed of to such
Pious and Charitable Uses as the Minister or Churchwardens
shall think fit ;   wherein if they disagree, it shall be disposed

of as the Ordinary shall appoint) diverted from its primitive Use and Designation, and turned to the private Profit of those who ought to be most exemplary to others for Piety and Charity."[16]

St. Martin's was not the only parish which indulged in fraud of this kind. The vestry of Leyton appears to have had doubts as to the probity of its churchwardens on this point also, for, among other regulations restraining their expenses in other ways, comes the notice,

"It is ordered y^t ye Money collected at Communions, ye sum shal be entered down in ye Parish Book, and how and to w^h it shal be from time to time disposed."[17]

That such money, even more than the poor rates, could be calmly diverted to doubtful uses, regardless of the source from whence it came, is a striking commentary on the public morality, and on the religious feeling of the time.

By the end of the seventeenth century Parliament had realized that to leave the sole power of making rates to the churchwardens and overseers, without any check whatsoever, other than the nominal one imposed by the Justices of the Peace, made an abuse of that power singularly easy. Accordingly, in the 3 W. & M. c. 11, some slight check was provided by the enactment,

"That there shall be provided and kept in every parish (at the charge of the same parish) a book or books wherein the names of all such persons who do or may receive collection shall be registered, with the day and year when they were first admitted to have relief, and the occasion which brought them under that necessity."

But more interesting than the actual expedient employed to restrain the arbitrary power of the overseers, is the reason given in the preamble to that Act, which shows a decided distrust of the parochial officers. It is because

"many inconveniences do daily arise in cities, towns corporate and parishes, where the inhabitants are numerous, by reason of the unlimited powers of the overseers, church-wardens and overseers of the poor, who do frequently, upon

frivolous pretences (but chiefly for their own private ends)
give relief to what persons and number they think fit,"

that new provisions had to be made.   In all probability
the members knew the truth of the statement which
they made, for most of them were country gentlemen
and either had been or were justices of the peace.   Hence
they did not legislate from hearsay alone, but from
practical experience of the methods of the parish officers,
knowing that these were given to making rates " upon
frivolous pretences."   After this nothing more was done
to restrain the power of the overseers and churchwardens
to assess and levy rates until the 17 G.II. c. 3, in the
preamble of which very much the same phraseology is
used as that employed in the earlier Act.   To regulate
this power, it was felt, publicity was the best weapon
to employ ; if the officers could no longer strike in the
dark, parishioners would then be able to protect themselves against unequal and unfair rates.   Accordingly,
it was enacted

" That the churchwardens and overseers, or other persons
authorised to take care of the poor, in every parish, township
or place, shall give, or cause to be given, public notice in the
church of every rate for the relief of the poor, allowed by
the justices of the peace, the next Sunday after the same
shall have been so allowed ; and that no rate shall be deemed
or reputed valid and sufficient, so as to collect and raise the
same, unless such notice shall have been given."

By this means, each parishioner would know what he
was paying, as compared with his neighbours, and would
be able to detect any glaring inequality.   In the rate
book belonging to the parish of Monkwearmouth the
following entry shows the Act in practice :

" I hereby certify, to whom it may concern, that the rates
in the preceding pages were read by me in the parish church
of Monkwearmouth, in the time of divine service, the 6th
day of April, 1777, by me, Sach. Crawford, parish clerk."[18]

Up to the passing of this Act the rates were inaccessible
to any but the officers of the parish, unless they were

produced before Quarter Sessions by order of the Court. This power gave officers unlimited facilities for making unequal rates, and for favouring some persons at the expense of others, since no one could know with certainty what his neighbour paid. This was another of the points on which Defoe felt strongly.

"Why," he wrote, "are not their Books open to general Inspection, that we may see by whom the Money is paid, to whom it is paid, and whether any is left to be carried on to another Quarter, and lessen the succeeding Charge : This would be but fair Dealing, and I think, reasonable satisfaction to be given us for our Money. But there are too many Parish Feasts, to admit of such honest administrations, the Spit is too often saddled, and the Bottle goes too merrily round, for the Ease of the Parishioners."[19]

To this length, however, the Act did not go, and the overseers' account books remained inaccessible to all but the vestry, though it was provided

"that the churchwardens and overseers of the poor, or other persons authorised as aforesaid, in every parish, township or place, shall permit all and every inhabitants of the said parish, township or place to inspect every such rate at all seasonable times, paying one shilling for the same ; and shall upon demand forthwith give copies of the same, or any part thereof, to any inhabitant of the said parish, township or place, paying at the rate of sixpence for every twenty four names."

This did at least mean that it was possible to find out how the rate was assessed, and how much was collected. It did not, however, give any check on the amount of the rate which the officers decided to raise, or on the purposes for which it was employed. If the officers refused to obey the provisions of the Act they were forfeit £20 for every such refusal, to be recovered by suit. Another Act passed the same year, dealing with the same subject, ordered that all the rates made for the relief of the Poor should be entered into a book specially kept for the purpose, and that fourteen days after all appeals from such rates were determined they should be entered up in the said book. The book in question was to be kept in a public place, where all persons so assessed " may freely resort," it was to be handed on to the succeeding overseers, and was to be produced at Quarter Sessions when any appeal concerning rates was heard and determined. (Further than this, however, the law did not go.) Parliament obviously did not trust the parish officers to act honestly, and therefore enacted that the actual assessments should be entered into a book to which the ratepayers should have free access. In other words, it provided some control over the assessment and the collection of the poor rate, but practically none, apart from the provisions that the names of all receiving relief should be entered in a book and called over once a year before the vestry, and that the order of a justice should be necessary for the granting of relief, over the disbursements.

Apart from such action as Parliament took on the question, attempts were made at different times and by various vestries to control this irresponsible expenditure of parish money. Such attempts were, on the whole, most likely to be made by open vestries in places where the number of ratepayers was not too large for effective action, or where the vestry, though a closed one, yet comprised most of the important ratepayers. For in these cases it was possible, as well as, from their own personal point of view, desirable, that the expenditure of the officers should be controlled, not only with respect to their outlay on feasts, but also as regarded their actual administration of the poor relief itself. Where the vestry was a select one in a large parish, the whole question of control was different. The overseers in this case acted as the servants of the vestry, rendering account to them, and obeying their decisions. In this type of vestry the extravagance would seem to be, not the personal work of the overseers, but the fault of the vestry as a whole, and particularly of the chief churchwarden, who appears to have meddled freely, as indeed by law he was entitled to do, with the affairs of the Poor. In the open vestry the chief parishioners might exercise a little restraint, but in the select vestry, the vestry itself was the only check on the overseers, and it depended on the members themselves, and on the type of parish which they administered, whether such a check were exercised or not. To take the instance of an open vestry, at Cowden, in 1695,

> " it was agreed at a full meeting of the Parish that if any officer, Churchwarden or Overseer, do buy, or allow of the buying of any clothes, or give any relief to any poore Inhabitant of the Parish or otherwise charge the Parish without he or they call a vestry then such Officer or Officers shall bear the loss of such monies as he or they shall lay out, or give away without the consent of such vestry."[20]

No officer was expected to relieve a poor person upon his own responsibility, except in those parishes where the payment of casual relief played a large part, and where the officer was definitely responsible for its management. Otherwise the question of those who should receive relief was supposed to be submitted to the vestry.

Sometimes it was difficult to prevent the officers from acting as if they were free agents ; hence the action of Cowden in disowning any debts which the parish officers might incur through acting without the sanction of the vestry. At Hawkshead the difficulty evidently was to make the parish officers do their duty, and keep and present their accounts ; for on 31 May, 1725, the following entry appears among the minutes :

> " We whose names are hereunto Subscribed do hereby agree that if any Parish officer or officers within our Parish of Hawkshead in the County Palatine of Lancashire do neglect his or their duty in his or their office to the detriment of any of the severale divisions within the said Parish of Hawkshead that such officer or officers so neglecting his or their duty or refuse *or* neglect to give his or their Accounts when lawfully Summoned or if any person or persons misapply any of the Parish money he or they are to be

prosecuted at the expense of the several divisions of the said parish of Hawkshead."[21]

Besides endeavours to make the control of the vestry over the parish officers a real thing, another method of securing an economical and effective administration of the poor law was to appoint an assistant overseer with a small salary, who was to help the annually-elected overseers, so introducing some continuity of policy and knowledge into the parish. The parishes which adopted this method were always in a minority, and the practice itself was extra-legal, though it was a device which found favour in the eyes of the poor law reformers towards the end of the eighteenth century. But instances of the appointment of such overseers are to be found at a considerably earlier date. At King's Lynn, as early as 1656, the Mayor and Justices of the town agreed to appoint one Robert Green to act as a kind of paid over-seer with a salary paid out of the hall. He received strict injunctions, however, that he " doe not alone judge what is fitting to give this or that p'ty that is in want, but to certifie and be as assistant to the Mayor and Justices as other oversears in that *p* icular."[22] More-over, it was ordered, " That the other overseers doe not neglect their office in meeting at the Church notwith-standing such an assistant to bring in their money and assist in making assessments if need be."[22] Manchester had a paid overseer from an early date ; for when the question of a workhouse came before Parliament in 1730, a certain Mr. Bowker, who was " Overseer of the Parish and hath been so for Ten Years past, for which he receives a Salary of Thirty Pounds per Annum," was called upon to give evidence.[23] Another growing northern town, Liverpool, adopted the practice early. At the beginning of the eighteenth century, Liverpool was still a small town, but throughout the century it was growing rapidly, and the number of its poor, together with the problems connected with their management, grew in proportion. As a result of this rapid growth, the need was felt for a better system of organization than that afforded by statute. To meet this need, as early as 1724, it was decided

> "That Mr Ed Crane be allowed for his trouble in assisting the overseers and paying the roll weekly, which he undertakes to doe for the year ensueing, haveing one of the Overseers to go allong with him weekly, the summe of £15 out of the next years Ley."[24]

In 1743 the vestry appointed Thomas Wharton to be overseer, along with those duly elected, at a salary of £20 per year, and he appears to have done most of the administrative work in connection with the poor.

In the same manner Thomas Ford was appointed assistant overseer by the vestry of Burton-on-Trent in 1730 at a salary of £4, paid quarterly.[25] In all these ways the vestries made an effort to check the opportunities for corruption, offered by the machinery of the Poor Laws, and to secure a more efficient administration.

The 43 Eliz. c. 2, had authorized the churchwardens and overseers of the poor of each parish "to raise weekly or otherwise, by taxation of every inhabitant, parson, vicar or other, and of every other occupier of lands, houses, tithes, impropriate, propriations of tithes, coal mines or saleable underwoods in the said parish, in such competant sums of money as they shall think fit," for the purposes enjoined on them elsewhere in the Act. Throughout the period this rate had been rising steadily until it threatened to become a heavier burden than the majority of parishes could support. As a result, overseers found that, whatever their personal inclinations or theories might be, everything had to be sacrificed to the main objective of keeping the poor rate within manageable proportions, and this fact, combined with bad administration, reacted most unfavourably on many branches of their activities.

It is difficult to estimate, even roughly, the amount of money paid in poor rates every year for the last half of the seventeenth century. Each parish levied and collected its own rate; there was no centralizing authority which made any record of the yearly amount of this rate, and the only evidence procurable at all is to be found in the parish account books. Thus there was no one source to which contemporaries could go if they wanted information on the subject, while so many of the old account books for that period have been lost, that to-day, even if the tremendous labour of searching the records of all the parish account books were undertaken, there would still be many gaps. Thus the only information which can be got on the subject comes from estimates, formed and recorded by contemporaries, of the total amount of the poor rates of the country.[26] These estimates, moreover, vary, no two being identical.[27] But on one thing the writers are agreed, namely, that the Poor's Rate was everywhere increasing.[28] Hains in 1677 writes of "the heavy Burdens most Parishes lie under to maintain their Poor, which daily increase."[29] Dunning in 1686 said that the Poor's Rate "is near double what it was thirteen years since, and like to double again in a shorter time."[30] In 1760 the Justices and Grand Jury of the General Quarter Sessions for the county of Norfolk petitioned the House of Commons as follows :

"That the charge of maintaining the Parochial Poor of this Kingdom is become so extremely burdensome, that the Occupiers of Land and Houses are scarce able to bear it : That an Evil of this Nature should be so long and so sensibly felt in a Trading Nation, which wants Hands in Husbandry, and in every branch of business, the Petitioners apprehend must be owing to some defect in the Laws and to the Want of a more effectual Method of providing for the Poor, by which the Aged and Impotent may be better sustained and the Idle and Profligate, in some measure, made serviceable to the Community ; and it was with the utmost Satisfaction the Petitioners observed the serious Attention paid in the last Session to this Matter : And therefore praying the House to take the Premises into further Consideration and grant such Relief as shall seem meet."[31]

The latter half of the eighteenth century also saw many applications to Parliament for private bills to regulate the Poor of particular places, all of which pleaded the necessity imposed by rising rates. In 1776 this growing complaint received official corroboration, when the Committee of the House of Commons, which had been considering the laws concerned with the Relief and Settlement of the Poor, reported :

> " That it is the opinion of this Committee that the money raised for the relief of the Poor is a grievous, and if no new regulations are made, will be an increasing burden to the Public."[32]

Various figures are fixed by contemporaries as representing the amount of the Poor's Rate at the end of the seventeenth century, though these estimates can be taken as nothing more than rough conjecture. Perhaps the most complete is that given in Dr. Davenant's " Essay upon Ways and Means of Supplying the War," in which is given " An estimate of ye Poor Rate for one Year made in ye latter end of King Charles ye 2nd's Reign," and which, the author said,

> " was Collected with great Labour and Expence by Mr. Ar. Mo. a very knowing Person. He hath not the Account of Wales, but according to the proportion Wales bears to the rest of this country in other Taxes, the Poor Rate there must have been about £3,375. So that the Poor Rate, at that time, through the whole Nation was about £665,362."[33]

He then proceeded to give a list of what he considered to be the Poor Rates of each county, which may be of some interest :

> " Bedfordshire..£6,911, Berkshire..£9,800, Buckinghamshire..£14,800, Cambridge and Ely..£9,128, Cheshire and Chester..£5,796, Cornwall..£9,257, Cumberland..£4,988, Derbyshire..£7,953, Devonshire and Exon..£34,764, Dorsetshire and Pool..£13,884, Durham, Northum'land and Berwick..£13,620, Essex..£37,348, Gloucestershire and Gloucester .. £19,600, Herefordshire .. £8,687, Hertfordshire..£10,760, Huntingdonshire..£5,850, Kent...

£29,875, Lancashire..£7,200, Leicestershire..£11,600, Lincolnshire and Lincoln..£31,500, Northamptonshire..£21,516 Nottinghamshire..£11,760, Norfolk and Norwich..£46,200, Oxfordshire..£7,950, Rutland..£3,730, Salop..£13,375, Staffordsh^r and Litchfield..£7,150, Somersetshire and Bristol..£30,263, Southamptonshire..£13,173, Southfolk..£25,750, Surrey and Southwark .. £15,600, Sussex..£18,720, Warwickshire and Coventry..£9,800, Worcestersh^r and Worcester..£10,640, Wiltshire..£18,240, Westmorland..£1,890, Yorksh^rn^th York and Hull..£26,150, London, Mid. & Westminster..£56,380."[33]

In his total of £665,362, Gregory King more or less concurred, for he estimated that there were " 849,000 Families decreasing the Wealth of the Kingdom to the extent of £622,000 per annum "[34] in 1688. Dunning took a peculiarly gloomy view of the whole situation, while still another writer estimated the Poor's Rates at £840,000.[35]

Probably by the end of the century the poor rate for the whole country was between £650,000 and £700,000 per year. As has been seen, its increase was bitterly resented by contemporaries. In considering the significance of their groans as to the intolerable increase, we must remember that the amount of ready money circulating in the country was very limited, and that it was quite possible even for persons comfortably circumstanced to be straitened for actual coin. The permanent income of the Crown for carrying on the government of the country amounted in 1663 to no more than £1,081,710 6s. For, though the Commons had voted Charles II. a revenue of £1,200,000 a year, in actual fact he was never able to obtain it, a large number of his difficulties throughout the reign being occasioned by this same lack of ready money. So, if Davenant's estimate of £622,000 a year for the poor rate is not a gross exaggeration, it will be seen that this did in fact amount to half the sum of money necessary for carrying on the work of government. It is only by comparisons of this character that it is possible to estimate the weight of the burden which the poor rates imposed on contemporaries. It must, however, be admitted that at the time of the Restoration an average poor rate fluctuated between 3*d*. and 4*d*. in the pound, and this was very often estimated on half the real rental. In industrial parishes the rates always tended to be heavier owing to the hardships caused by a trade depression.

The first trustworthy figures for the rates of the whole country are those given in the schedules returned to Parliament in consequence of the Committees of 1775 and 1786. The parishes were regularly circularized, and definite returns made as to the amount of money raised for the Poor. The total poor rate for 1776 was £1,523,163 12s. 7*d*., so that Fielding's round number of a million in 1754 was, in all likelihood, roughly accurate. The rates in this schedule are returned both for each separate parish and for the whole country. Thus, to take a few examples, the net expenditure for the Poor in Bedford, according to Davenant, was £6,911, while by the reports of 1776 it was £16,662 17s. 1*d*., and by those of 1787, £20,977 0s. 11*d*.; in Cornwall in the first instance it was suggested as £9,257; in 1776 it was reported to be £22,004 11s. 10*d*.; while in 1787 it was £28,531 19s. 9*d*.; in Essex the first figure was £37,348, the second £74,067 3s. 5*d*., and the third £94,569 14s. 6*d*. Therefore, supposing the first set of figures to be approximately true, the comparison by counties shows the tremendous increase that had taken place in the poor rate within a hundred years. By 1787 the total amount paid by the parishes of England and Wales in Poor Rate was £1,943,649 15s. 10*d*. as opposed to the £665,362 suggested by the " very knowing Person " who collected the figures for Davenant.

The same rise can be seen in individual parish accounts. This tendency appears in parish after parish, but the rate at which the rise took place, and the particular years which were milestones in the leap forward, differ from parish to parish in accordance with local circumstances. One trait which most parishes have in common is, however, the fact that the increase in question was anything but a steady one. That is to say, though 1750 might show an enormous increase on, say, 1700, yet 1725 might be much higher than 1727. The rates did not go up in steady progression, but fluctuated wildly. At Westbury the poor rate in 1668,[35] and for many years before that date, had been 2d. in the pound ; in 1671 it was increased by a halfpenny,[35] and after this it never fell below 3d. In 1681 the rate increased suddenly to 9d.,[35] but from then on to the end of the century 6d. or 8d. rates prevailed. In 1699, again, the officers were forced to levy two rates for that year, one for 6d., the other for 3d.[35] The same variability is to be seen at Lapworth, where in 1690 the rate still stood at $1\frac{1}{2}d$. in the pound. By 1697 it had reached $4\frac{1}{2}d$., and in 1700 it suddenly jumped to 10d. Then as suddenly for the next two years it fell to $4\frac{1}{2}d$. again, and by 1703 it was once more at 9d.[36] The poor rate at Kettering behaved in precisely the same fashion.[37] It would be interesting to know how much influence the administration of the various overseers had on these fluctuations of the rates.

But though individual rates might go up or down, it is impossible to deny the existence of a general rise, or even to say that contemporaries were exaggerating unpardonably. Between the end of the seventeenth century and 1782, rates doubled and quadrupled themselves in parish after parish all over the country. At St. Leonard, Wallingford, in 1699, the amount raised in rates was £5, and by 1714 it had risen only to £10 16s. 11d. ; but by 1774 it had soared to £80 16s., and by 1782 to £154 13s. At Tiverton in 1680 it was £499 18s. 9d., and in 1782 £2,183 11s. 11d. At Rodmarton in Gloucester in 1680 the poor rate was £12 9s. 10d., and in 1782 it was £71 12s. 3d.[38] In Birmingham the rates rose from £325 17s. 7d. in 1676 to £10,943 10s. 3d. in 1782,[38]

and in Liverpool from £160 in 1702 to £1,000 twenty
years later.[39]   Both these centres were, however, towns
with rapidly growing populations, where the rates
might be expected to increase as the places grew in
numbers and in importance. But a reason such as
this cannot be advanced with the same strength everywhere.

In the majority of places, despite yearly fluctuations,
the increase in the rates may be regarded as being
fairly steady from the end of Charles II.'s reign till
the sixties of the next century.   Probably a sharp rise
had taken place shortly after the Restoration owing
to the general distress of the country, of which the
Settlements Act itself was a manifestation.   This rise
resulted in the outcry of contemporaries against the
rates.   The next sharp rise appears to have come
between 1760-82, though in most parishes it occurred
during the seventies rather than the sixties, owing to
the gradual and increasing growth of distress, and thanks
to bad harvests.   For instance, the poor rates in
Houghton Regis rose from £188 14s. at 1s. 6d. in the
pound in 1771, to £323 11s. 11d. at 2/6 in 1782;[40] at High
Walton in 1772 they were still only £8 3s. 10½d., while
ten years later they amounted to £65 3s., at 4s. in the
pound.[40]   At Hawkley they rose from £33 12s. 11d.
in 1760 to £133 6s. 10d. in 1782,[40] while at Leicester
a rate worth £735 19s. 4d. in 1776, yielded £926 14s. 3d.
in 1782.[40]   In many places this rise at the beginning
of the latter half of the eighteenth century is noticeable,
and it was from this period until the reforms of 1834
that the rates for the relief of the Poor became increasingly a burden.

The amount payable by each parishioner towards the
support of the Poor was fixed by the churchwardens
and overseers of the Poor, and this function placed
considerable power in their hands.   The original intention of the law appears to have been that each parishioner
should pay in proportion to his ability to do so.   When

the population of a parish was small and stable, and
when everyone knew everyone else's business, this was
not so difficult to arrange with some show of fairness.
In many cases, however, rent became, at an early date,
a rough calculation on which it was possible to base a
tax that in theory depended on ability to pay. In other
words, a man's rent came to be regarded as an indication of his general financial position ; and on this,
as a result, was levied an equal pound rate for the
relief of the Poor. This method of taking rent as a
basis of calculation for the levying of the poor rate had
several results. In the first case salaries, fees, and wages
were left out of any estimate as to ability to pay, chiefly
because salaries and fees would be the property of persons
from whom it might be difficult to collect, while weekly
or yearly wages were so small that it was useless to
attempt to tax them towards the support of the Poor.
Secondly, rents were only rated to the occupier, and
not to the owner as well. This was because a certain
confusion had grown up in the public mind, and it was
considered unfair to tax the same thing twice over,
once from the tenant and once from the landlord.
The reason for such obscurity arose from the fact that
it was not seen that the rent paid by the tenant was the
measure of his ability to pay towards the support of
the Poor, so that the rent received by the landlord might
in the same way provide some basis of calculation.[41]
In the same manner it was decided that an owner could
not be rated for rents he received, or for land that he
held, outside the parish. Such questions as these were
finally settled by legal decision made in the High Courts,
on cases taken to them by way of appeal.

The rule that the Poor's Tax should be calculated
on an equal pound rate based on rent was not, however,
universal. Traces of the older system based on ability
to pay are found in parish after parish. In 1733, for
instance, when an act to regulate the vestry of St.
Mary, Whitechapel, was before the House, the following

evidence was given, " That the Rate assessed amounts
to £2,262–13–0 and is made discretional, by the vestry,
on the real and personal Estates, that if it were a Pound
rate the Poor would be greatly oppressed."[42]   Mr.
Philip, giving evidence before the same committee,
further said, " That, if the Poor were maintained by a
Pound rate, it would fall heavy on the Inn-keepers,
whereof there are numbers, who pay £100 per Annum
for their House, when Gentlemen, worth £3,000 or
£4,000 live in Houses of £50 per Annum : That it has
been the constant Method in the Parish, to make the
several rates discretional."   That there was a good deal
of bitter feeling is evident, for one witness described
how, after leaving a vestry, an open one in this case,
" he was hissed, and spit upon, because he was for a
Pound rate."   In another case, a number of persons
who lived in Kingston-upon-Hull, but were not freemen
of the town, complained that they were charged " with
an arbitrary personal Payment of a certain Weekly Sum,
without any regard to the Yearly Rent or Value of
their respective Houses, greatly exceeding in general,
the assessments laid on the other inhabitants."[43]   St.
Mary Magdalen, Bermondsey, petitioned in 1758 " That
it would be a great convenience to the said Parish, if
an equal Pound Rate could be laid on all the Occupiers
of Houses, Buildings and Lands, but that such a rate
is not now established by law."[44]   In the parish of
Kensington all the rates, both for the relief of the poor
and for other parochial matters, were assessed according
to the Land Tax books of the parish for the time being ;
accordingly the parish petitioned that the Act (29 Geo.
II.), by which this provision had been enacted, might
be repealed upon the ground that

> " for many Reasons no fair and equal Pound Rates can be
> made in the said Parish, according to the Poor Laws, so
> long as the Parochial Rates continue to be governed by
> the Land Tax books, and rather, for that the Land Tax
> Books being made out but Once a Year, and at a different

Time from the Parochial Rates, which are made at least Twice a Year, many losses of Poor Rates happen to the Parish thereby, besides the Difficulties accruing to the Officers in collecting the same."[45]

Perhaps the most vexed question of all was whether a tradesman was liable to be taxed on his stock-in-trade. The action of the Courts was very uncertain and contradictory in this respect, and throughout the eighteenth century, in spite of the fact that legal opinion was undecided, some parishes continued to assess their poor rate on stock-in-trade, while in others the practice was utterly foreign and obsolete. Thus at Monkwearmouth in 1778 the poor rate was made on a basis of

" Rentals 6d. per pound per month and $\frac{3}{4}d$. and $\frac{1}{2}$ of a farthing per keel per month for every keel the ship carries, and a penny three farthings per month for every fittage and ballast keels."[46]

In a fishing centre of this type, the ships of the fishermen were equivalent to the stock of the trader, and appear to have been rated as a matter of course.[47]   Hale was clearly of the opinion that stock-in-trade ought to have been rated to the relief of the Poor, but he bears witness to the difficulty of putting it into practice, and writes of the difficulty in raising money for the Poor.

"Because those places, where there are most Poor, consist for the most part of Tradesmen, whose Estates lie principally in their Stocks, which they will not endure to be searched into to make them contributory to raise any considerable stock for the Poor, nor indeed so much as to the ordinary Contributions : But they lay all the rates to the Poor upon the Rents of Lands and Houses, which alone without the help of the stocks are not able to raise a stock for the Poor, although it is very plain that Stocks are as well by Law rateable as Lands, both to the relief and raising a stock for the Poor."[48]

This expedient of taxing stock-in-trade was adopted in several private Acts for the building of workhouses, when it was necessary to raise a large sum for the poor, as, for instance, at Bristol and Norwich.   But whenever a parish attempted to force its tradesmen to contribute on this basis considerable friction ensued.   In 1777 a test case was brought before the High Court by Bradford,[49] Wilts, but the decision, being based on local custom, was not conclusive, and the question continued to be one of much difficulty well into the next century, when it was finally settled by Parliamentary action.

If the money raised by these means was not, owing to the poverty of the parish, sufficient to relieve the chargeable poor, then it was provided by 43 Elizabeth c. 2 that

> " Two Justices shall and may tax, rate, and assess, as aforesaid, any other parishes, or out of any Parish within the Hundred where the said Parish is, to pay such Sum and Sums of Money to the Churchwardens and Overseers of the said poor Parish for the said Purposes as the said Justices shall think fit according to the Intent of this Law : And if the said Hundred shall not be thought by the said Justices able and fit to relieve the said several Parishes not able to provide for themselves as aforesaid ; then the Justices of Peace at their General Quarter Sessions, or the greater Number of them, shall rate and assess, as aforesaid, any other of other Parishes, or out of any Parish within the said County for the Purposes aforesaid, as in their Discretion shall seem fit."

It is difficult to say how far this provision of the law for the relief of poor parishes was carried.   The clause referring to rating parishes in aid outside the Hundred may be regarded as practically a dead letter.   Apparently justices did sometimes, however, rate parishes within the Hundred for the relief of another parish over-burdened with Poor.   Thus at Lewes in 1690 the Justices in Quarter Sessions ordered that Patcham should pay £17 16s. 6d., Hangleton £4 16s. 9d., East Aldrington £6 1s. 1½d., Blackington £4 2s. 10½d., and Ovingdean £6 0s. 10½d. yearly towards the relief of the poor of Brighthelmstone.[50]   But to rate in aid does not seem to have been a device frequently employed, in spite of

legal permission to do so.   There is, however, one great
exception to be made to this statement, and that
concerns the parishes in some of the northern counties.
By the Act of 1662 provision had been made that
where, on account of the size of the parishes, which
in Lancashire, Yorkshire, and Westmorland sometimes
straggled over ten miles of difficult country, it was not
convenient for two overseers to manage the whole
parish, then each hamlet or chapelry should appoint
its own overseers and manage the Poor exactly as if it
were a separate parish.   To all intent, these hamlets
remained independent of each other, though sometimes
the justices would force the wealthier division to come
to the help of its poorer neighbour.   Even this limited
rating in aid does not seem to have been widely
practised.[51]

It will be seen, therefore, that the whole question of
rating was one of considerable complexity owing to the
original vagueness of the law.   Parish officers were not
quite certain in the first case on what basis to calculate
their assessments, and consequently local variations
came into being and prevented the law from attaining
any real degree of uniformity.   Thus real property,
estimated by its annual rent, and calculations based
on land tax, on stock-in-trade, and on personal property,
were in all places, either singly or in combination, the
basis on which the poor rates were assessed.   This made
it impossible to lay down a general rule with regard to
the assessments for the Poor.

But, quite apart from the legal difficulties of assessing
the poor rate, the parochial officers were accused of
making unfair rates for their own ends.   In either case,
when a parishioner thought that the rate levied on him
was illegal or unfair, the appeal lay in the first instance
to Quarter Sessions, which had the right, either to
quash the whole rate as unfair and order the churchwardens to make another one, or to amend the rate
so far as it concerned the one particular person who had

appealed. Quarter Sessions could not, however, make a whole rate itself ; it could only amend, or return the whole rate to the parochial officers to be re-made. In many cases the Justices in Session would refer the question, as was their constant practice on other points, to one or two justices who lived in the neighbourhood and who, therefore, might be expected to know something of the rights of the case   The number of instances in which the Sessions decided against the rate made by the parish officers, gives some colour to the complaint of the time that the poor rates were not always fairly assessed, and that the vestry taxed lightly, or not at all, its own friends, making up the deficiency by extra taxation on other parishioners. Sometimes, as at Shenley, the churchwardens and overseers were actually presented to Quarter Sessions for making unlawful rates.[52]

In many ways Quarter Sessions afforded but little protection against corrupt practices in the assessment of the rates. Frequently, through bad management, or other causes not specified—Defoe would say inordinate feasting—the money first raised proved insufficient, and the justices were asked for permission to levy another rate. The reasons alleged were many and various ; that the needs of the poor had been so great, owing to the war, that the overseer had to spend his own money on their relief, or that there were so many empty houses in the parish that the rate had not realized the amount which had been expected. Generally the necessary permission was given without question. But from some admissions in the report of the Committee on the Poor Rates, appointed by the House of Commons in 1714, it seems likely that a number of these extra rates were, in reality, unjustifiable.[53]

From these details it will be seen that the mechanism of the parish was not such as to facilitate any solution of the problem of poverty. The officials were untrained and annual, there was no real check on the malversation of funds, and the interest of each parish was in favour of a rigid economy, which often expressed itself in methods detrimental both to the neighbouring parishes and to the state of the Poor at large. Nevertheless, it was through these unconnected and unrelated units, that such national poor relief as there was, must be administered. To realize the means which they had at their disposal is to understand the failure of the parish. When a body is diseased no group of doctors, however eminent, could work a cure by each prescribing for one part alone, irrespective of the treatment followed by each of his colleagues.

CHAPTER III

THE PARTIAL SUCCESS OF THE PARISH IN THE SPHERE OF POOR RELIEF

THE part of the 43 Eliz. c. 2 which the imperfect parochial machinery found least difficulty in carrying out was the " necessary Relief of the lame, impotent, old, blind and such other among them, being poor and not able to work." The history of outdoor relief is important for two reasons. It was probably the most continuously, as well as the best, executed branch of the poor law ; and had, also, an important influence in shaping its after history. It owed its continuity to the fact that it was the easiest part of the law to set in motion and keep in working order. There was no complicated machinery to be dealt with, and, unlike the provision of work, it did not make too great demands on the overseers' capacity. To collect the rate and share out the proceeds among the parish poor presented no great difficulties, whilst the needs of the old and infirm, of children, and of the sick, made a more obvious appeal to human sympathy. Thus, when other branches, notably the provision of work, broke down during the lack of oversight in the Civil Wars, it is probable that a meagre amount of poor relief went on in most parishes. In this way it had a continuous history. It was probably also the most widely executed part of the law. For every person removed there were probably half-a-dozen relieved ; for every child apprenticed there were probably several boarded out. Even in parishes which possessed a workhouse, outdoor relief was not entirely abolished, while in many parishes, where there was no workhouse, the chief duty of the overseers comprised the relieving of the poor by the grant of monthly pensions, by the gift of clothes, and by the provision of house room and fuel. What loomed most largely in theory—the provision of work—did not to the average overseer appear half so important as the work connected with outdoor relief, since this was the aspect of the law with which he was most conversant.

Secondly, the history of outdoor relief was also important owing to the way in which it moulded the fate of the " Old Poor Law," and reacted on the legislators of 1834. It would not, indeed, be great exaggeration to ascribe to the administration of outdoor relief at the end of the eighteenth, and during the first three decades of the nineteenth century, the absolute breakdown of the law. The primary cause of this collapse was the crushing pressure of the rates, a burden largely due to the increasing profusion with which outdoor relief was given at the close of the century. It is, therefore, a matter of interest to see how such relief was managed at an earlier date, and to enquire whether the seeds of such collapse were inherent in the system.

Yet, in spite of its importance, contemporary theorists spent but little time on the subject, all their attention being given to schemes for making the Poor work. Writers contented themselves with protesting that the parish poor received excessive pay, without attempting to suggest what they would deem an adequate amount Guides were written for the use of officers in settlement cases, but the amount of relief necessary to support life, the question as to who should be given relief, and any indication as to how much ought to be given to various classes of paupers, received barely a comment. In this sphere of their responsibility the parish officers were left without even advice.

The business of poor relief was carried out by the same set of officials who assessed and collected the rates, and this double function of raising the money, which they alone were authorized to spend, put an undue amount of power into their hands. Yet for almost a century after the passing of the 43 Eliz. c. 2, the overseers were allowed to disburse the money as they pleased, without any legal check. But as the old self-sufficiency of the parish began to break down, under the weight of the economic and social changes which were taking place after the Restoration, opinion became troubled as to the advisability of leaving everything to the discretion of the overseers. Accordingly the 3 & 4 W. & M. c. 11, passed in 1693, decreed that no relief should be given, except in time of emergency, without the authority of a justice of the peace, and that all persons receiving relief should have their names and " the Occasions which brought them under that Necessity " entered in a book kept for the purpose. Every Easter the names in the book were to be scrutinized afresh. But the Act did not prove as successful in preventing the granting of " unreasonable relief " as had been hoped, for many of the Poor, having been refused by the overseer, went behind his back and complained to the justices, who often, ignorant of the real circumstances, granted the relief asked for. By a new Act, passed in 1722, no pauper was to go to the justice until he had first been refused by the overseer. The justice was then empowered to call both the parties before him and examine the case. Even when the justice was near at hand, as in a town, or where he dwelt in the great house in a village, such procedure would occupy at least a morning, waiting on the justice. But in many a rural parish, five to twenty miles of bad road might separate it from the nearest justice, and the business could not take less than a day, which the overseer, with his own affairs to conduct, could ill afford. The result was that the clamorous pauper, who threatened to appeal to the justice, tended to get more than his fair share of relief, at the expense of more modest claimants. Such was the effects of leaving the administration of poor relief to men who had only the odds and ends of their time to devote to it. For as soon as a parish grew at all populous it was clearly impossible for an overseer to make those inquiries into the real conditions of the recipients of relief which are so necessary, and which even to-day the paid poor law officer finds it difficult to carry out except in a perfunctory manner.

Our knowledge of the actual working of the law comes from two main sources—the county records and the parish papers, especially the overseers' accounts, the latter being the more important as Quarter Sessions did not interfere greatly in questions of relief. Before the passing of the 3 W. & M. c. 11, poor persons were in the habit of bringing their petitions for relief before the Court. After hearing such a complaint the Court would make an order and the matter would be finished. Sometimes the overseers were merely ordered, e.g. to " take into their Care and Consideration the poore Condition of Nicholas Stamford his wife and five smale children who are very poore and allow unto them such weekly relieffe as there wants and necessities shall require."[1] But in other cases they were ordered to pay a definite weekly sum, as when the overseers of Swaffham Prior were ordered to pay to John Cracknall and Joseph Almi " two infirm persons and incapable to work to provide for themselves—twelve pence per week a piece."[2] But once individual justices were empowered to deal with cases of this character, petitions to Sessions for poor relief grew less, and Quarter Sessions became largely a Court of Appeal.

The questions relating to the administration of poor relief, which were brought before Quarter Sessions by way of appeal, can be grouped under three main heads. These are, firstly, appeals by overseers against orders for relief granted by single justices ; secondly, appeals made by paupers asking that the arrears of their pension might be paid to them ; and thirdly, appeals from overseers to enforce the law obliging persons of " sufficient ability " to be responsible for the maintenance of certain of their poor relations. Normally an overseer appealing against an order for relief was successful, either in getting it totally abolished or in obtaining a substantial reduction. The reasons pleaded were usually that the circumstances had altered since the granting of the order, or that the justice had been misinformed. Sometimes the overseer made an application that the pension might be voided altogether, as when the officers of Ellerton appealed against an order " to pay a man 6*d*. weekly, he being sickly and infirm, since which he hath recovered his health and is now able to labour for his living, yet though work hath several times been tendered to him, doth wilfully refuse the same and wanders idle about the country."[3] The Court discharged the order.

The second class of appeals, those from paupers asking that the arrears of their pensions might be paid, show that it was one thing to obtain an order from the justice, but quite another to get the actual pension from the parish. For instance, a complaint was made by George Day, an inhabitant of Caldecot, "he being a lame person and very aged and having but one hand to help himself," that the overseers had disobeyed the order of Sir Henry Pickering granting him relief. Accordingly the Court, having verified his statement, ordered him a pension of two shillings a week and fourteen shillings a year for house rent if the parish did not find him a house ; while all his arrears of pension were also to be paid. This type of case is decidedly common, and emphasizes the lack of any machinery, other than the cumbersome method of appealing to Sessions, for enforcing the parish officers to carry out the law.[5]

The third class of case which it was customary to bring before Quarter Sessions, acting as a court of appeal, related to the maintenance of pauper relatives These appeals might be brought forward by the pauper himself, but were usually the work of the parish officers,

who based their action on the provisions of the 43 Eliz.
c. 2, by which " the father and grandfather, and the
mother and grandmother, and the children of every
poor, old, blind, lame, and impotent person, or any
other poor person not able to work, being of sufficient
ability shall at their own charges relieve and maintain
every such person " as the justices shall direct. In
accordance with this statute, the Justice, on appeal
by the overseers, would consider whether the person in
question were of sufficient ability, and if so, would
make an order compelling him to pay so much weekly
to the overseer of the parish where the poor person
resided for his or her relief and maintenance. This
provision was rigidly enforced, as being of practical
value in relieving the poor's rate.

The most important form of relief given by the overseers was a small weekly or monthly pension, known
as the collection or the parish pay, and in theory given
to the aged, impotent and sick, and to children. The
Poor Book of Westbury-on-Trym, which is extant from
1654-1700, gives a very detailed picture of the kind of
relief given and the usual amounts of the weekly pay.
To establish a standard is difficult, but the whole tone
of the book, as far as its own parishioners are concerned,
is generous and sympathetic ; it represents, possibly,
the best that a parish could do. The paupers who were
in receipt of the regular parish allowance were probably
for the most part old, for after their names have appeared
for a few years there generally follows the account of
the money expended at their funeral. The rest appear
to be mostly children. Many of the allowances so
granted must have been supplemented by some work
or other means, for many of them were not sufficient to
ensure even bare sustenance. In many cases they were
eked out by the overseer himself, who, besides paying
a regular weekly sum, gave intermittent gifts of clothes
and fuel, and occasional money doles. In many cases,
too, house room was provided. Thus, in 1664, William

Coats received twelve months' pay at three shillings a month, and Agnes Smith the same at a shilling a month.[6] In addition, the following items occur in the accounts for that year, " payd for a payer of shoes for William Coats .. 4.2, geaven to William Coats at sev times .. 05.00 and geaven to Agnes Smith at sev times 02.06."[6] Next year both allowances were raised a shilling a month, but that did not prevent William Coats from receiving another 1s. 6d. " at 2 severall times." In 1668 there comes an entry: " payd for a shroud for Agnes Smith and burying .. 06.06."[6] During this early period regular pensioners were receiving six shillings a month, and none less than two and sixpence.[6] At the end of the century six shillings formed the usual payment, rising in some cases to eight. Thus from 1662-1700 there is a slow but steady rise in the amount of regular relief given. Much larger sums, too, were expended at the close of the century in extra payments and in the provision of clothes and other necessaries. But even so, the allowances can hardly have been considered excessive. Other parishes paid roughly similar amounts.[7] Lapworth in 1704 " paid for 3 weeks table for Eliz. Hall .. 4.6."[8] At Poole equivalent sums were being paid ; in 1697, according to the list, the overseers allowed " Widow Parker 00–04–00, Ursuall drake .. 00–08–03, Widdow stockley and children .. 00–10–00, Widow Linsfield .. 00–04–00, Mary Wedden .. 00–04–00."[9] At Leeke the overseers paid as much as £8 18s. per year to " James Davenport, blind," in addition to his house rent, which cost fourteen shillings.[10] The Quarter Sessions books also give a certain amount of information as to the sums given in weekly relief, which coincides with the picture presented by the parish accounts and vestry minutes. In Cambridgeshire and Middlesex, according to their evidence, the average sums ranged from a shilling to one and sixpence per week, though specially hard cases sometimes received two shillings.

Conditions in London are always supposed to be slightly different from those ruling in other parts of England. Consequently, when the average pension in the southern counties ranged from a shilling to one and sixpence, that of London was from fourpence to sixpence per week higher. The following extracts will illustrate this difference. Thus at St. Margaret's, Lothbury, " At a meeting of some of the Auditors for the poore of the parish of St. Margaret, Lothbury, London, it is ordered that Mr. Richard Stonhill Churchwarden of the same parish doe henceforth pay to widow Gilbert & to Widow Edmett two poore ancient Pensioners of the same parish who are very necessitous twelve pence a peece weekly till further order to the contrary."[10]   This was in April, 1669; by December of the same year it was evidently found to be insufficient, for the following entry appears : " At a meeting of some of the Auditors for the poore of the parish of St. Margaret Lothbury, London. It is ordered that Mr. Richard Stonhill Churchwarden of the same parish be desired to pay henceforth two shillings a piece weekly to widow Gilbert & widow Edmett two poore ancient Pensioners of this parish."[11], [12].

In the northern counties the sums paid away in weekly allowances were consistently less than they were in London and the south. This fact is confirmed both by the account books of various parishes and by the general trend of the entries in Quarter Sessions. The following examples are taken from " A true copy or List of the Poore of Ribchester and their necessity. And their monthly allowance sine ye 29th April, 1693.

Paid to Margarett Sharples, being old and not
able to worke p. one month   02–00
paid to Elizabeth Tindell, being lame and not
able to worke for a month.   01–00
Paid to James Sharples, being sick and not able
to worke for a month.   04–00
paid to Richard Newsham being lame and not

able to keep himselffe p. month besides his
apparell 06–00
paid to Ann Hacking being troubled with the
falling sickness monthly besides her apparell 05–00"[13]

In this parish one shilling and sixpence was the highest
amount paid per week, while the lowest came to no
more than fourpence. From the Lancashire Quarter
Session papers it would appear that pensions varied
from 6*d.* to 2*s.* a week, but instances of the latter were
very rare, and were confined to widows burdened with
several children. Single old men and women were given
a shilling at the very most and more usually ninepence.
Much the same standard seems to have prevailed in
Yorkshire at the close of the seventeenth century.[14]

Besides the adult Poor there were always a certain
number of children for whom the overseers had to make
provision. Some of these were the sons or daughters of
poor parishioners, who had died leaving them penniless,
others were bastards, whose parentage might be in
doubt, or whose mother had been forced to come to
the parish for relief. A third class of children were
those who had been deserted with the intent that they
should be brought up by the parish. Desertion was
frequent, particularly in London and the larger towns,
and entries such as " 19th Aug : 1674 paid for Blanketts
and other necessaries for Moses Throckmorton, left in
New Court .. 00–09–08,"[15] recur repeatedly. Children
of this class would be dependent on the parish for every
detail of existence almost from birth.[16] The treatment
which these children received differed very much with
the type of parish to which they were consigned. Infant
mortality was terribly high throughout the period, but
in the rural parishes the children do not appear to have
suffered from deliberate ill-treatment and neglect ; in
more crowded areas, however, and particularly in
London, few of the children who were left to the parish
under the age of three ever reached adolescence.

The usual method of providing for such children was

to board them out with other poor families, who were glad to take them for the sake of the money. Accordingly, entries dealing with parish children are common in the overseers' books, and it is from them that we get the clearest details as to what this practice involved. In many cases the children were boarded out with women who were themselves receiving relief, either in money or in kind, from the parish. This was the regular practice at Westbury. Some women regularly had a child to look after. Thus in 1690 the overseers " payd to Charity Jones for keeping Ann Williams 51 weeks at 1/8 ye week .. £3-16-06," and seven years later they " Paide Charity Jones 13 months pay at 6s. a month for Whit Churches boy .. £03-18-00."[17] This seems to have been the usual amount paid for boarding out these children. In 1690 they " payd for keeping Harvey's Boy from ye 18th of Aprill to the 14th ffeauary being forty weeks at 1/6 ye week.. £03-04-06."[17] Sometimes the allowance was more generous. Thus in 1697 the parish " Paid for keeping a Bastard to Sarah Scudamore 2 months pay at 10/- p. month comes to .. £01-00-00," but the same year this was reduced and they " Payd to Sarah Scudmore 4 months pay for keeping ye same child at 8s. a month."[17] In the same year the payments made at Poole in Dorset were on much the same scale, but not quite so liberal. Among the names of the " poore people to be pd by ye weeke " is " Honor Rider for one Child..1–3, goode Ash ffor Keeping of on Child..1–6, goode Bushell for keeping of two Children..3—, Susan phileps for on of Materes Children..1—," while " Adam Stroode for himselfe and dum Child " only got half-a-crown.[18] In addition to the weekly pension, the children boarded out by the parish were provided with all that they needed in the way of clothes, the weekly sum merely relating to the provision of food and lodging. In the course of several years a child might cost a parish a considerable sum before it was finally apprenticed.

The following entries taken from the Westbury books from 1682 to 1686 all relate to the same boy. " 1682, paid for harfees boy 13 moneths at 8s...£05–04–00, paid for a suit of Cloath for harfees boy..£00–09–04, paid for 2 pair of stockins..£00–02–06, paid for 2 paier of shoes..£00–04–00, paid for a new hatt and mending of cloaths and shoes..£00–02–10, paid for putting in harfees boy in the free school..£00–03–00." The next year, 1683, they expended " for 2 payer of shoes and mending for harfee..£00–05–04, paid for 2 payer of stockings and making 2 shirts..£00–02–06, paid for making a suit and drawers for him..£00–02–06 and paid for stuff for the drawers pocketts and buttons ..£00–02–04." In 1684 the following items were entered up on his behalf : " paid for harfee 13 m at 8s. £05–04–00, paid to Mr. Knight money that he laid out uppon harfees boy..£00–10–04." The following year they again " paid for Harvies Boy 14m at 8s. p.m. ..£05–12–04, payd for stockings and shoos and a payre of drawes for Haries boy..£00–06–06." In 1686 the entries respecting him come to an end with the following payments : " By 9 moneths pay to Widow Hopkins for Harvies boy at 8s. p. moneth..£03–16–00, By moe payd ye widow Hopkins for shirts, shooes and mending of Harvies Boyes clothes..£00–07–06."[19] This example —and similar instances are common—gives a clear picture of the way in which a small parish in a more or less rural district solved the problem of what to do with the children who were left chargeable to it, and who were not old enough to be put out as apprentices.[20] The practice appears to have worked satisfactorily. The money paid for board and lodging, though not extravagant, was slightly more than was paid to any parish pensioner, and probably fairly adequate, when supplemented by clothes and any other incidental charges. In any case, the parish children so boarded out were probably as well lodged and fed as children of the same social class who lived at home on the family earnings. In the Westbury accounts there is nothing to indicate that the rate of mortality was higher among the parish children than might ordinarily have been expected. In this respect parishes would be bound to differ, but speaking generally, and having regard to the standards of the time, we may say that this system of boarding out, when followed in a parish where everyone knew everybody else's business, was as good as any that could in that age have been devised.

In London, however, conditions were different, and the lot of a child who was left to the care of a parish by the death or desertion of its parents, or from any other cause, was a sorry one. Such children were either nursed carelessly in the parish workhouse by a woman often totally unfit to have the charge of children, and under conditions which would have taxed the skill of any nurse to rear the child, or they were boarded out by the parish officers to be reared outside the workhouse. This, however, was no alleviation of their fate, for the women who undertook the charge were ignorant and for the most part greedy—actuated solely by the desire for the two shillings or two-and-six paid weekly in recognition of their services. The result was that hardly any of the children so boarded out with parish nurses survived more than a few months. Nor was their death caused by mere neglect and ignorance of nursing ; frequently it was due to starvation, since the nurses converted the pittance received with the children to their own use. The extraordinary thing is that this state of affairs was known to exist and even to be common, and yet for a long period nothing effective was done to prevent it. As early as 1676 Jasper Gaunt, writing on " The Natural and Political Observations upon the Bills of Mortality," states as quite a natural state of affairs that " of the 229,250 which have died, we find not above 51 to have been starved to death, except helpless children at nurse."[21] Nor does he add one word of indignation that such an exception should have to be made. In 1684 it came to the notice of the Quarter Sessions that one Mary Compton had starved and murdered several infants committed to her care as children's nurse by the overseers.[22] In 1715 a committee of the House of Commons was appointed to consider the question of the poor rates in the metropolis, and for this purpose investigated the records of the parish of St. Martin's-in-the-Fields, which was supposed to be more free from abuses than some. In the course of the inquiry certain facts with regard to the nursing of parish infants transpired. " Mr. Grisdale, clerk of St. Martin's Church being sent for, and his Book of Burials being perused for the Three last Years, the committee observed, That the Proportion of Children far exceeds that of men and women, and, being examined touching the same, said, That one year with another, there was about 1,200 christenings and that above $\frac{3}{4}$ of those die every year."[23] Accordingly, the Committee reported to the House " That a great many parish Infants, and exposed Bastard Children, are inhumanly suffered to die by the Barbarity of Nurses, especially Parish Nurses, who are a sort of People void of Commiseration, or Religion hired by the Churchwardens to take off a Burden from the Parish at the cheapest and easiest Rates they can ; and these know the manner of doing it effectively as by the Burial Books may evidently appear, according to Mr. Grisdale's own Observation."[23] Yet, despite so sweeping a condemnation and so trenchant a denunciation, nothing was done to deal with the terrible abuse. More than thirty years later Jonas Hanway described the same kind of thing as still going on. " An acquaintance of mine," he wrote, " once solicited a parish officer for 2/- a week for a servant during her lying-in, and nursing her child ; alleging that a common parish nurse had at least that sum if not 2/6. ' Yes,' says the officer, ' it is very true ; but the young woman in question will most probably preserve her child, whereas in the hands of our nurses after 5 or 6 weeks we hear no more of them.' "[24] The Committee of the House of Commons which considered the question in 1767 also reported that " It appears that the Children are kept in the several workhouses in Town, or in the Hands of Parish nurses in Town, only a small portion of them being sent into the country to be nursed ; and the Price of 3/- and 2/6 per week first paid, is often reduced so low as 1/6 or 1/-, that cannot be presumed to be equal to the necessary Care of the Infants."[25] The same committee also repeated the condemnation of the parish nurse which the earlier committee of 1715 had presented as part of their report. And it was not until this date that any real attempt was made to grapple with so terrible an evil, though its existence had been known to authority at least from the beginning of the century.

The surprising thing is that, in those parishes where both the adult and the infant poor were provided for by the grant of weekly pensions, there should have been so little variation in the standard, since, owing to the lack of any central authority to set or enforce a common scale, each parish was free to pay whatever it pleased. It is, therefore, possible to say with a fair degree of accuracy, that round London the great majority of pensions were from one and six to two shillings a week, and that they ranged from a shilling to one and six in the south, and from sixpence to a shilling in the north. This differentiation of area corresponds roughly to Arthur Young's dictum that the cost of living varies according to the distance of a given place from London. These pensions were by no means ungenerous, for until the close of the seventeenth century there were few labourers who could earn more than six shillings a week on an average, and few single women who could earn more than 3s. 6d. or 4s., out of which sums they had to provide food, lodging, and clothes. Therefore, since the parish usually provided house room and clothing for such of its poor pensioners

as were dependent on it, the standard of life enjoyed
by those who received the higher amounts cannot have
been markedly lower than that of the ordinary labouring
part of the community. This remained true until the
latter part of the next century ; the cost of living
tended to be lower during the first part of the eighteenth
century, while the amounts granted as pensions retained
their traditional level. This tendency for the weekly
payment to remain stationary became, however, a
source of hardship to the poor, when prices began to
rise in the seventies, for in the lists of weekly payments
quoted by Eden in 1797 there is no very marked increase
on the old figures, the majority still averaging from 1/.
to 2s. 6d. a week for a single person. This remained
the case even when those parishes which farmed out
their poor were paying three and four shillings a head
to a contractor. It, therefore, seems true to say that
from the middle of the seventeenth to the end of the
eighteenth century there was very little increase in the
scale of payments made for weekly allowances to the
parish poor.

In many cases, however, weekly allowances were
given with the idea of supplementing existing resources
rather than of providing a complete maintenance.
Grants of 4d. a week, for instance, were common, though
anything under 1s. 6d. or 1s. in the south and midlands
must have been very much in the nature of a mockery.
It is of these smaller amounts that North wrote, " When
a poor Person or Family is maintained by the Parish,
it is done so grudgeingly by an extreme strait, that
life is scarce maintained by it. This Parish Poverty is
a condition void of all Comfort. For to be deprived
of Alms (as mostly upon that Acct. they are) and to be
left to Overseers' Allowances, and having no other
means to assist, is little better than a slow starving.
A short life with less Pain were to be preferred to this
pining Death with Parish Allowance."[26]

The smallness of the amounts granted to many of

their regular pensioners tended to defeat the aims of the
legislators, who had hoped by this provision to put down
the practice of begging and indiscriminate alms giving.
Firmin noted that the inadequacy of the parish pensions
was one of the chief causes of begging in London, for
many persons preferred to augment them by this easy
and lucrative trade, rather than turn to some industry
which, in all probability, was not nearly so remunerative.
Accordingly he proposed that all persons in receipt of
parish relief should be badged and forbidden to beg,
on pain of losing their allowance. As some slight compensation for this, it was arranged that the poor of
the parish should be permitted to go from house to house
at fixed hours to receive such broken meats as their
more prosperous neighbours had to give, who on their
part promised not to give anything to unauthorized
persons not wearing the parish badge.

There was nothing new in the device of badging the
Poor. It had been frequently employed by various
towns in Tudor times, as a means of distinguishing the
Poor of the town, who had a license to beg, from the
strolling vagrants. Firmin suggested that it should be
used to prevent persons who were receiving collection
from imposing on passers-by and asking for alms.
It was a method which found favour with many parishes
during the last part of the seventeenth century. In
1683 Tonbridge " pd to Thomas Johnson Taylor for
60 T.P. for the poor to wear on their arms..10s."[27] In
the October of 1694 the Middlesex Court of Quarter
Sessions, having been informed that a great number
of parish pensioners went abegging in other parishes
than their own, ordered the·churchwardens and overseers of the various parishes to provide badges or tokens
of some durable metal for all the parish poor."[28] These
badges were to indicate the parish from which the pauper
came and were to be worn " at the end of the left sleeve."
All poor pensioners, refusing to wear this badge, were
to be deprived of their allowances until they conformed.

That this was no idle threat is shown by an entry from the Brighton minutes, running : " At a meeting of the churchwardens and overseers held Aug. 27th 1696 an accompt was given that Susan Stone, the widow of Thomas, refused to wear the town badge upon which she was put out of the weekly pay."[29]

So popular did this expedient become that in 1697 it was incorporated in the 8 & 9, W. c. 11, which enacted that henceforth any person in receipt of parish pay should wear a large Roman P, together with the first letter of the name of the parish, made of red or blue cloth, upon the shoulder of the right sleeve. Anyone refusing to comply with this regulation was to be deprived of the relief, or committed to the House of Correction. After this date the overseers accounts regularly record payments for badges for the Poor, showing that the law was enforced. That it should be necessary to distinguish between the poor of each parish in so marked a manner is proof that the unit of the parish was too small for administrative purposes.

Such a law seems to have been fiercely resented, for many instances occur of persons refusing to wear the badge. It was an ordinance which would gall the deserving and undeserving alike, the first because of the humiliation imposed, the second because it was a hindrance to the popular trade of begging. Entries dealing with recalcitrant paupers are not uncommon. At Cowden in 1698 the overseers paid " to the Widow Stile that was kept back from her for neglecting to wear the badge..2–0."[30] In 1705 the overseers of the Liberty of Saffton Hill, St. Andrew's Parish, refused to pay Mary Edwards, a widow, an allowance which she received on account of her crippled child, because she did not wear the parish badge. She appealed to the Middlesex Quarter Sessions, protesting that such relief as she received was purely for her child and that it wore the badge in accordance with the law. Her explanation was accepted, and the overseers were ordered to pay the pension together with what arrears were due.[31] In the Gaol Calendar among the Hertfordshire Quarter Session papers is the name of a certain T. Omitt, of East Barnet, who was sent to the House of Correction " for assaulting Ed Hughes the churchwarden and not wearing the badge as act of Parliament directs."[32] In spite of the dislike felt by the paupers for these regulations, the Act remained in force until nearly the close of the eighteenth century. That it was finally repealed was owing to the new humanitarian movement when, since poverty was once more regarded rather as a misfortune than a fault, it was felt that such an act was degrading. In this connection it is interesting to notice that when this Act was first passed and put into execution there was not even a hint that such an Act was considered either degrading or humiliating by the writers of the day. The badging of the Poor as a class apart struck men as being right and even natural.

Besides the practice of badging the Poor, there was one other important administrative expedient, arising from the habit of giving monthly pensions, which must be noticed. This was known as the " allowance system," by which is meant the granting of a small regular sum of money by way of relief to a man who is himself in full work, but who cannot earn a wage large enough to support his family. This, to the Commissioners of 1833, was the central abuse of the Poor Law. For it had gradually come to mean the pauperisation of a very large section of the working class, particularly in the rural parishes. It is interesting to see that giving allowance in relief of wages was no new expedient adopted to meet the emergency of the French Wars, or to deal with the distress of the end of the eighteenth century. By that time the practice was at least a century old. It is difficult, indeed, to know why it arose, for it was not contained in the provisions of any statute. The overseer was ordered to relieve " the poor and impotent," not able-bodied labourers, however low their wages. Yet it seems to have been a responsibility which the parishes assumed at an early date. The reason for such allowances is to be found in the low wages which ruled for married labourers in many parts of the country. Overseers employed any means to get rid of married labourers without their gaining a settlement ; but once such a settlement was gained they seem to have conceded the necessity of granting some extra relief to labourers with large families. It was an expedient which serious writers condemned before the seventeenth century had drawn to its close. Thus Firmin wrote : " Nothing being accounted a better Argument for a large Pension, than that a Man or Woman hath six or seven small children unless they were all born at a time, or came faster into the world than ordinarily so many children do, it is very hard if some of them are not able to work for themselves." [33] In the same way Locke speaks of that class of poor persons with large families " whom they cannot or pretend they cannot support by their own labour." [34] Both these writers suggest methods of getting over the difficulty by finding some method of employing or otherwise taking the children off the parents' hands. Neither of them thinks of raising wages. The parish of St. Giles', Cripplegate, when it petitioned to be allowed to build a workhouse, stated that on its monthly pay list were " 126 Parents over burthen'd with children," who received between them every year the sum of £600-0-0. [35]

It early proved to be a method of relief particularly open to abuse. Roger North gives an instance of this kind at Colchester, where the management of the Poor was in the hands of the Bay manufacturers. He reported that the Bay manufacturers were very flourishing there, " And yet the Rates for the Poor are higher than in any other places around, viz., 25, 30, 35 per Cent. per Annum Revenue of Houses and Lands in the Town. Upon a strict Enquiry we, with much ado, found out that the Bay merchants, who set the Poor

on work, paid part of their wages by the Poor Rate
in the name of Collection. So that, if a poor Man could
earn Ten-pence a Day, they would give him but Sixpence for his Day's work. But then he should have
Four-pence per Day Collection. And, having Justices
among themselves, this is made good, whereby the
Landowners pay for the Bays making."[36] Doubtless,
frauds of this nature were easy of execution when a
small corporation of merchants had the management
of the Poor and the poor rates in their hands. By
1759 the abuses possible in such a method of relief,
and its unsuitability to the real needs of the case, were
acknowledged by one section of the community. On
the 30th of May the Committee of the House of Commons,
which, through the energy of Sir Richard Lloyd, had
been appointed to study the Poor Law, reported as
follows : " That the present method of giving money
out of the parochial rates to persons capable of labour,
in order to prevent such persons claiming an entire
subsistence for themselves and their families from the
parishes, is contrary to the spirit and intention of the
laws for relief of the poor, is a dangerous power in the
hands of parochial officers, a misapplication of public
money, and a great encouragement to idleness and in-
temperance."[37] Such a report was not in accordance
with the opinion of most people on the subject, nor
was it followed ; instead, in the difficult times ahead,
the allowance system was regarded, not as an abuse,
but as a remedy. This was in direct contradiction to
the remedy proposed by the committee of 1759, which
had advocated the confinement of such poor as could
not, or would not, find employment, in workhouses
where they might be set on work. In 1771 the Committee supervising the new workhouse at Parkhurst in
Hampshire decided, " That when it appears that Labour
in husbandry cannot be obtained at the usual wages
through scarcity of work, they may order any reasonable
sum not exceeding a quarter of the real earnings of the

such labourers employed by their consent to be paid
by the overseers to the different persons employing them,
so that such earnings do not exceed six shillings a week
for each man."[38] Gilbert, in his " Plan of Police,"
approved of much the same plan, for he definitely
stated, " It is not the object of this plan to have many
Persons capable of Labour kept in Workhouses ; it is
rather wished to have. them placed or hired out to such
Employments as they are most capable of ; and if they
cannot earn their whole Sustenance, the Deficiency to
be made up out of the County fund."[39] This was the
course which was afterwards widely adopted, and from
which sprang most of the demoralisation of which the
Commissioners of 1833 complained. It was a policy
very different from that proposed by Dunning a century
before. He, indeed, had advocated that the parish
should find employers for such persons as were unable to
find work for themselves ; but the condition attached
to this employment was that it was to be remunerated
at less than the current rate of wages, in order that
they should rather find work for themselves than depend
on the parish for employment.

Apart from the payment of a small weekly pension,
the favourite form of relief was the provision, in some
form or other, of house-room. In many cases persons
in receipt of parish pay had their house provided also,
whilst in the rural districts, at least in some parts of
the country, there appears to have been a considerable
shortage of houses, particularly of the type that would
be occupied by labourers. Since the reign of Elizabeth
it had been illegal to build cottages without attaching
four acres of land to each one. But with the growth
of the population and the gradual change that was
taking place in the status of the labourer, fewer of
these cottages seem to have been built. The Hertford
Quarter Sessions are full of presentments of cottages
that have been built without the statutory four acres
of land. In 1710 the parish officers were ordered " to

prosecute Will Brown of Walthamstow for erecting a cottage near Knight's Green in Leyton, there being not four acres, and warning given him to ye contrary."[40] Nevertheless, houses had to be found ; and as the overseers and churchwardens had certain dispensary powers, the onus of finding them, at least for paupers, fell upon their shoulders.

Throughout this period there still remained a considerable amount of waste, although enclosure was going on steadily. By the 43 Eliz. c. 2 the churchwardens and overseers were authorized to build cottages on the waste for paupers, without the statutory four acres of land being attached. Also in certain cases poor persons were allowed by Quarter Sessions to build themselves cottages on the waste. Thus, one man petitioned for leave on the ground that " his wife is distracted."[41] In all cases the consent of the Lord of the Manor had first to be obtained.[42] Such permission was quite freely given, and the use of the waste was one of the methods employed for finding houses for the labouring classes. Such cottages did not need to have the statutory four acres of land attached, and, being under the value of £10 a year, gave no rights of settlement. (In some cases they were owned by the parish, and inhabited by the paupers rent-free.). In the Lancashire Quarter Sessions, particularly in the late seventeenth century, the number of cases that deal with the housing problem is noticeable. Some of these are requests to be allowed to build on the waste, but the majority are orders to the parish officers to provide houses, such as the following : " forthwith upon notice hereof pvide some convenient place of habitation for Thomas Chernock, his wife and 3 poore children so that they be not starved by lyeing out of doors unless they show cause to the contrary at the next session here to be held or otherwise upon contempt."[43] This apparent scarcity may have been real, or it may have been caused by a desire on the part of the parish to prevent settlement. Some entries

PLATE IV

Drawn & engraved by J.T. Smith, Engraver of the antiquities of London, and its Environs.

ON MERROW COMMON, SURREY.

The residence of Dame Battey, aged 102.

A COTTAGE ON THE WASTE AT MERROW COMMON

[face p. 108

suggest that the overseers themselves were the trouble, for in October, 1666, the overseers of Shebington were ordered to find a dwelling for one Thomas Croston, " he paying some reasonable rent for the same,"[44] and in the same year a John Newnham was to be assisted to find " a place of habitation for his money,"[44] while in another case a house was to be found for one Lawrence Breares, " he paying for the same and having had a legeall settlem[t] in the said towne."[44] In any case, the difficulty of finding houses appears to have been real, and the constant pressure of Quarter Sessions seems to have been necessary if any working solution of the difficulty was to be found.

In some cases the parish might own cottages, in which it allowed paupers to live rent free. These cottages may have been built as a miniature poor house, but for the most part they appear to have come into the hands of the parish through the death of paupers.[45] Thus, supposing an old person owned the cottage in which he lived, but had no other form of sustenance, he would be forced to apply for a weekly pension, and to re-imburse itself, the parish, on his death, would take the cottage. In many cases the cost of repairing houses is entered into the overseers' accounts, though whether they were parish property, or merely the dwellings of paupers, does not appear. Sometimes details are given showing the type of work done as : " Pd for Laths and Nails for Wm Lees House..0–9," or, " For eight sheaves of Straw to Repair Severall Houses..2–8."[46] From some entries in the Quarter Session books it looks as if the justices occasionally had need to see that the overseers performed their duty in this respect. In one case where a weekly pension of twelve pence had been granted to a poor woman, the overseers were ordered before the 1st of November to " well and sufficiently repare her house with thatch and daub,"[47] and again in 1700 the overseers of Lathom were " well and sufficiently to repaire ye Cottage wherein

Mary Latsome a poore woman of ye same towne now dweles so that it may be dry and convenient for her habitation."[47]

But the majority of parishes provided house-room for their paupers by the payment of their house rent, considerable sums being spent in this way. Stroud, when building its new workhouse, proposed "that all elderly women, who may be only chargeable to the parish for their house rent, should have convenient apartments here but maintain themselves as before by going out to work."[48] But after the establishment of the workhouse the vicar was able to write, " We have not one of the sort tho' before our house was built, that single article amounted to near £30 per annum and occasioned a great deal of trouble to the officers of the parish."[48] Liverpool, in 1723, purchased houses for its poor and directed " that the Overseers of the Poor doe speedily as may be remove such and so many poor persons and families as are chargeable to this Parish for whom they doe now or shall hereafter be obliged to pay a yearly rent elsewhere."[49] The vestry book of St. Mary's, Leicester, contains long lists of persons who had their rent paid by the parish, and it is worth noting that a large proportion of them are widows. For example, " To Henry Marshall for a halfe years rent of Richard Parson's his house due the 24th June 1681 by order..05–06. To John Marshall for halfe a years rent of Widdow Billingtons house due in August 1681 by order..10–06, Paid to Mr. Bellamy for a halfe yrs rent of Widdow Rowlands house by order dated Nov. 18th 1681..06–06."[50] This list is not complete, but it gives some idea of the amounts paid for rent in this way. Usually they varied between ten shillings and a pound per annum, though in some cases they fell below this estimate, and occasionally they rose above it.[51]

Sometimes, if a parish had no workhouse and wished to save its officers the trouble of paying weekly pensions and finding house-room for some of its old pensioners, it would resort to a method that was a mixture of farming the poor and boarding them out.   In some cases the transaction amounted to more than the lodging of a pauper who was old, and who needed attention, with another pauper.   In 1661, at a vestry held at St. Margaret, Lothbury, it was agreed, "And for as much as Edwin Bush a poore old Pentioner of this parish is at Michaelmas like to be destitute for a place for his lodging and that the said widow Twine hath a roome to let and is willing to intertaine him, it is agreed that shee be allowed and paid three pounds a yeere for rent of the said roome for the said Bush from Michaelmas by quarterly payments and shee undertaking to make his bed and to assisstant otherwyse unto him, it is agreed that shee be paid after tenn shillings per annum for the same to be paid as aforesaid."[52]   This was a fairly common arrangement, indications of which can be found in most parish accounts ; for example, " pd to Richard Hurst for house rowme and Lodging of Mat Rener 12 weeks..2–0."[53]   In other cases the arrangement resembled more a system of farming out, as when Cowden made a " M^m of a bargain made with Richard Austin to keep Elizth Skinner for 2s. 6d. by the weeke for a 12 month, to begin with the 14th of April 1687, if she be not visited with sickness."[54]   Where arrangements of this type involved more than one person, such cases may be regarded as definite instances of farming the poor, and are more properly considered under the heading of indoor relief.

Besides money payments and the provision of lodging, another favourite form of relief was the provision of clothes by the parish.   Clothes loomed large in a poor man's budget when they had to be purchased with ready money, for the household economy of the time expected the wife to spin a sufficient quantity of thread, both linen and woollen, to supply most of the necessariès which her family would require in this direction. But if this were impossible, because the family was too poor to be able to resist the immediate pressure of the need for the woman to work for wages, or if the wife lacked skill or enterprise, or her family took all her time, the clothing for the family had to be bought out of the weekly earnings. This meant that the parish officers had not only to lodge and to feed, but also to clothe, the poor of the parish. Generally such poor were the regular pensioners of the parish, but sometimes labourers, overburdened with children, might get a little relief in this way. In any case, the various parishes appear to have done a large trade in clothes, and garments of the most diverse kinds were supplied through its medium to the Poor. All Saints, Hastings, even went so far as to publish the notice that all poor persons who wanted clothes were to apply to the vestry : " This is to give notess to all persons be Longen to the Poore, that what Clothes or shoos they have occashon for, they must come and acquaint the vestry with it ; that they there may be soplyed and noe otherwise."[55] In this respect the parish appears to have acted as a kind of supply stores to the poor of the place, where everything from a suit to a shift could be obtained, if only the overseer were amenable.

Some parishes bought the raw material, had it made up, and doled it out as required. St. Austell in 1692 spent £10 4s. 3d. ,a large sum in those days, for " Wooling for the poor," and " for lynnen " they expended even more, namely £12 10s. 0$\frac{3}{4}$d.[56] Six years later comes the gruesome entry : " Flannings for shrouding ye Poor..£2-3-9." Apparently they decided that too much money was being spent in this way, for in 1747 it was resolved " That the Price of Linnen for the Poor is not to exceed 8$\frac{1}{2}$d. per yard and the Price of Woollen cloth comonly called Cape cloth for the Poor is not to exceed 1/0 per yd."[56] At Westbury the practice varied. The parish children appear, in some cases, to have had material bought wholesale for their use, and there is an entry in 1696 : " Paid for 11 Ells of cloth for the Parish Children..oo–11–oo, for makeing ye childrens shifts..oo–02–oo."⁵⁷ Again, in 1699, the overseer " Paide to cloth to make shifts for the Parish children and makeing of them..oo–13–oo, for woollen cloth to make them cloths..o1–o1–o1, for lining and Buttons..oo–o1–o2, for making the children's woollen cloths..oo–04–oo."⁵⁷ But the next entry, which runs, " for 3 yards and a halfe carsey to make Preston's child an upper coat and under coat..oo–05–06, for whale bone and canvas..oo–oo–10½, for makeing Preston's childs cloaths..oo–02–oo." shows that the Parish did not buy wholesale for all its children. Also, before the entries for 1696, the general manner of providing clothes was to have them made as the occasion required. Some entries merely state " Paid for clothers for 4 of Alec Dowles children and Hannah Taint.. 06–oo–09," but others go into considerable detail ; for example, " pd for a Coate & hatt & buttons for W. Smith..oo–08–05."

Shoes and stockings were important articles. At Westbury the overseers " Payd for shoes for Sarah Pullins boy she keeps..oo–o1–06, while, when the recipient was a grown person, they had to expend between three and four shillings per pair on their paupers' shoes. Stockings were commonly one-and-six per pair.⁵⁷ At Hawkshead cloggs took the place of shoes.⁵⁸ Sometimes less familiar articles were provided, such as " a shinn to forepart his Breeches "⁵⁹ or a " paire of lather Breekhes," price half-a-crown.⁶⁰ At Leyton-stone, in 1740, the overseer proved so complaisant as to provide Beck Mitton with money " to fetch hir stays out of pawn."⁶¹

From the end of the seventeenth century the question of fuel became increasingly important to poor families. Coal was largely used in the big towns, and the petitions in the Journals of the House of Commons during this

period, both from the coal men, who shipped from
Newcastle to London, against the Navigation Acts,
and from the wholesale dealers, show that the trade
done in this commodity was considerable. The country
Poor had been accustomed to cutting their fuel on the
waste or collecting it from neighbouring woods, but for
several reasons this source of supply was diminishing.
In the past, too, the great majority of the towns had
been so small that their size did not cut the poor off
from many of the advantages of country life. But in
the early eighteenth century severe laws were enacted
against persons who destroyed hedgerows or young
trees. In some places, too, the waste was beginning
to be enclosed, and even when it remained, the supply
tended to become exhausted and to be too small for
the needs of the community. Thus even country
parishes were beginning to feel the need of a larger
supply of fuel, but because coal was bulky and therefore
very expensive to transport to any place not on a
navigable river, its cost to them was high. As a result,
fuel was a fairly frequent form of relief, though in a
country parish it might not always take the form of
coal. At Hawkshead 3s. 6d. was paid to Elizabeth
Atkin " for her peats getting,"[62] and Wm. Bradwell,
a poor person of Swaffham Prior, received a thousand
of turf in 1734.[63] In both these cases, peat, owing to
the proximity of the mosses above Morecambe Bay and
the Fens respectively, would be the most available form of
fuel. In Warwickshire both wood and coal were near at
hand, so that both were provided ; thus in 1691 the
Lapworth overseers paid " for 6 hundreds of coals for
the Widd Parrie..04–06 " ; yet two years later they
paid " 2 loads of wood for Widd: Minas, she being a
poore woman with several small children..12–."[64]
At Herne in Kent Miss Stevens was paid for " ile and
a bushell of Cole..00–10½,"[65] and at Westbury John
Rider was given some candles.[66] But for the most
part, except in cases of sickness, though fuel might be

thought a necessity, illumination was not, and very few entries mention either oil or candles.[67]

Very many entries in the overseers' accounts deal with sickness. As far as one can tell, the parish seems to have done its best for any of its paupers who might be ill. The question of sick relief may be divided into two parts—actual relief and maintenance during the illness, and the provision of medical aid. It was customary for parishes to make an allowance during a period of sickness, such as " geaven to John Calee in his sickness..00–05–00,"[68] " geaven to William Cary in his lameness..00–12–00,"[68] " geaven to William Smith in his daughters sickness..00–04–00,"[68] and this entry is followed by " paid for a shroud and for buring of William Smith's daughter..00–08–00." Some entries go into greater detail as to the kind of relief given, Goody Hoskings, who died in 1681, was an expensive case; the parish paid " to Joane Web for tending of goody Hoskings fower month at 10s. a month..02–00–00, for milk for Goody Hoskings ..01–05–06, for candels and sope for her..00–06–00, coule & wood..00–04–00, a bed pan and other necessaries..00–04–06," and finally " for buring of her..00–10–06."[68]

Usually the cure of more serious complaints was not left to the individual, the parish being accustomed to call in professional or semi-professional assistance. In 1678 there was " paid toe Robert Wade for goin for a boneseter..00–02–00, spent the day that Edward bourne bones was set..00–05–06, paid to the bonesetter ..00–16–00,"[68] and in spite of all their trouble " paid for a chest and shroud for Edward Bourne..00–12–00."[68] An entry from the Ancient Account Book of Cowden " for drink to the people that helped to set John Wanner leg..00–02–00,"[69] suggests what became of the five-and-sixpence " spent the day that Edward bourne bones was set." In this case, however, the doctor's bill was £1 5s. 0d. Parish usage appears to have varied as to whether a bonesetter and the skill of the local goodwife were requisitioned, or whether the professional doctor were called in. For the less serious cases the former had to suffice in most parishes. At St. Mary's, Bourne, Farmer Serle appears to have had some local reputation as a healer ; in 1687 the overseers paid him " for curing Mary Hollen's leg and James Hoins boy..00–10–06," and in 1731 he was still being employed, this time for " curing the widow Goodall's legg..00–10–00."[70] In 1693 the Cowden overseers paid ten shillings " to Good-wife Wells for curing Elz skinners hand " ;[69] but the same parish also employed professional services, for in 1690 Dr. Willett received £2 for " reducing the arm of Elz Skinner and for ointment, cerecloths and journeys."[69] By 1714 they had changed their doctor, and Dr. Gamford got ten shillings " for curing John Humphies Legg,"[69] and another seventeen shillings for " curing Goody Rose's hand."[69] Sometimes really large sums were spent in medical attendance. For instance, at St Austell's, Dr. Williams was paid £6 15s. 2½d. " in part of his labour and charges about Jane Cornish (he must have a guinea more)," and later " more to him in order to cure Jane Cornish of a late scald shee rec^d and under which shee now laboures ..01–01–00."[71] In some cases the overseers appear to have been most accommodating, as when they gave Widdow Parrie nine shillings " to go to the doctor with her sore eyes and for a horse to carry her,"[72] while at Westbury three pounds was paid " for the curing of Ane Peacock's child," and " her diett when she lay under the chiurgery hands..00–17–00." In 1690 they paid " to Edith Bowerne to goe with her Daughter to Bathe..01–10–00," and " for her daughter at several times..00–15–00," but it was of no use, and finally the parish had to pay £1 2s. 0d. for her burial expenses.[73] Most of the Westbury entries of payment in cases of sickness appear to be followed by an account of the money laid out at the funeral. The reason is not obvious. Either medical aid can only have been called in at the last extremity, or it must have been very inefficient. Probably the true reason was a combination of both causes.

Very little is revealed by these accounts as to the nature of the malady from which the pauper in question was suffering. Small-pox appears to have been by far the most dreaded as well as the most prevalent disease of the period, and there are a good many entries dealing with payments in this connection.[74] One comes from Cowden, " Where Robert Still and family had the smallpox laid out by the overseers :—Paid to Mrs. Allice for cheese for Robert Still..1-0, for apples and shortning for him..3, for a breast of mutton..1-6, to Goody Everset for beer and milk for him..2-0, for ½ a lb. of butter do...2½, for 4 lbs. of beef do 8*d*., for 1 lb. of butter do...5, for 2 lbs. more of cheese do...10, for 1 lb. of cheese for the family..2½, for two pecks of malt for do...1-10, for 6 lbs. of chesshire cheese for do...1-0, for ½ lb. of butter for do...2½, for a neck of mutton for do...1-9, Mr. Cockmans bill for shortening, milk and butter for do...5.4½, For 100 faggots for Robert Still..7-0, for a peck of wheat for him..1-0, for going to the doctors for him..1-0, to John Case, for canary for him and his family..1.7½, to Goody Halliday, for nursing him and his family 5 weeks..£1-5-0, to Goody Nye, for assisting in nursing..2-6, to Mr. Hayler, for journeys and physic for Robert Still..£2-12-6." The following remark is appended by the justice who signed the account : " If, as I am informed, be true, it is most unreasonable."[75] In the same parish accounts there are numerous other mentions of small-pox.

Other diseases are chronicled at times, though not with such frequency. Thus one parish paid, " for Medicine for ye children with ye Itch..1-8."[76] Persons suffering from fits and kindred complaints received a certain amount of publicity. At Leyton the overseers " Pd for Robert King being lame and mad..5-15-0," or " Paid for a woman in fitts in Ladenstone..6.6,' or " To widow Brown to bleed and doe something for Alice Reason, having violent fits."[77] In 1727 comes an interesting payment to " Mother pricklove Daughter & Grand Daughter both Sick in Bed, for Mutton, bred, coales, Oate meal, salt & Drink..3.7 ; Gave to Mrs. Heart for curing a dangerous swolled face and Broak inwardly of ald picklove daughter..2.6."[77] Mention is sometimes made of the falling sickness, and one woman is placed on monthly pay " being troubled with the falling sickness,"[78] while in another case the justices in Quarter Sessions ordered 4d. weekly to be paid " to a poor sickly creature who is troubled with the falling sickness."[79]

But for the most part the overseers seem to have felt that neither the nature of the disease, nor the administering of the remedy, was any concern of theirs, as witness the delightfully vague entry : " Gave Matha Briggs to buy something that Dr. Richardson ordered for her..1–0."[80] It is only when the illness strikes the overseer as being particularly interesting that he enters up any details. Accidents always get their due share of prominence from this reason, as do fits and smallpox, but other diseases are usually entered up as " sick " without any additional description. Besides the type of entry illustrated above, which deals with burns and broken bones, a favourite accident was a dog bite. " Elnor Cook " received six shillings for curing Sarah Pullin, " she being very Lame and bad in her Legg by ye biteing of a Dogge,"[81] and at St. Mary Bourne, to take another parish, " Old Charter " was paid six shillings " for curing Laine children being bit with mad dogg."[82] Perhaps the. most peculiar accident comes from Camberwell, where Goody Dyer was paid fifteen shillings for " looking after a mad woman under cure for a hurt done by her a cow."[83]

One particular disability which the parochial officers were forced to notice was lunacy. If a lunatic had relatives who could do so, these were supposed to maintain him or her, since otherwise the burden fell on the parish. The treatment meted out to them was a scandal, but this was a fault peculiar not to the parishes alone but to the whole age. When society people could go to look at the lunatics in Bedlam, the great hospital for the insane, as one of the shows of London, it is not to be wondered that parish officers were not meticulous in their treatment of the lunatics for whom they might be responsible. There were several ways in which the officers could discharge their trust ; they could, if they liked, provide for his or her maintenance in the parish ; but this method was usually followed only until there was a chance of getting the unfortunate creature sent to Bedlam. In some cases, also, pauper lunatics were sent to the House of Correction, there to be provided for, although such places were entirely unfitted for their reception and in every way unsuitable. Sometimes the problem of disposing of a lunatic came up among the ordinary business of Sessions. The chief function which the justices performed, however, was to force unwilling parishes to provide for such of their settled inhabitants as might be insane and to restrain them from wandering round the country, as when the inhabitants of Andswell were ordered by the Court " to receive and take care of a man by reason he is distracted, and not to suffer him to wander about the country, by which he may do either himself or others harm, and also to repair to some able physician for the recovery of his health."[84]

Such persons were usually sent to Bedlam, if the parish were within accessible distance of that institution. To send paupers thither seems to have been an expensive business, when the parish had to pay for their removal and clothing, and also for their maintenance there. St. Bartholomew Exchange had a lunatic who was chargeable to them for years, and who appears to have spent half her life coming in and out of Bedlam. In 1662 they paid " To Katharin Rumney for 17 weeks pension at 18*d*. before sent to Bedlam..1–05–06, To ditto for necessaryes and people to watch hir and other expenses before she could be admitted..1–06–00, To ditto paid Mr. Lee the clerke for a bond and a warrant etc...00–06–00. To ditto for Carrying hir to Bedlam and given the keepers..00.05–06, To ditto Paid William Godbie Steward of Bedlam for xxi weekes and ii dayes for hir keeping there at 5s. per weeke..5–09–06, To ditto. for a Bedlam Gowne PettiCoates Wast Coates Neckclothes, Shifts, Porter, etc...1–01–06, To ditto. for a paire of Hose and shooes..0–04–06, To ditto. for Necessaryes weekly after she came out of Bedlam, beinge the 12th of March to this time..0–16–06." Payments of this kind went on intermittently until her death in 1673/2, by which time she must have cost the parish a considerable sum.[85] Such accounts give a very clear picture of the methods employed by parishes in sending their pauper lunatics to Bedlam, and the expenses sustained in keeping them there. In some cases the plans adopted to secure such insane persons before they could be despatched to Bedlam can only be described as utterly barbarous, as for instance, " Pd for digging a post Hole for E.W...6d., Pd for shaven her Head..6d., Pd for Bell and Grave for Child and altering her chain..1–6. Pd for two locks for E.W... 1–0. Pd for a post and mending the window for her ..2–0. Pd for Dipping her..1–0. Pd for Carring her to London..£3.3.0."[86] Such treatment seems almost inconceivable, but none the less it was probably not unusual.

This provision for the sick meant that the parish had to engage in considerable medical activities. For not only had it to pay poor relief proper to the sufferers while incapacitated from earning their own living by sickness, but it had also to provide nurses, or at least attendance of some kind, and to take steps to get the malady cured. This meant either employing a local wise woman or man skilled in healing, or calling in the local bonesetter ; and even, in the more serious cases, summoning the local medical man. All this was both expensive and troublesome, and parish officers, accordingly, endeavoured to devise some method by which the sick Poor could be attended to without their having to give personal attention to every case. The result was that during the eighteenth century parish after parish began to make its medical arrangements by contract. Just as they contracted for the farming of the Poor in workhouses, and for the conveying of vagrants, so parishes contracted for the medical attendance of their Poor. Throughout the century anything that could be done on a contract basis was so done. These contracts varied from parish to parish. Sometimes the doctor contracted to attend all cases, of whatever kind, and supply medicine as well. In others it was agreed that certain illnesses, which were in the nature of an epidemic, should be left outside the contract. Some of these agreements are rather quaintly worded and amusing. At St. Austell as early as 1712, Dr. Williams received £6 9s. 0d. " for labour and medicines administered to the poor," and in 1715 the accounts definitely allude to " Dr. Williams' salary."[87] That the parish effected a considerable saving by this arrangement is clear from the former large items entered for medical attendance. Camberwell, in 1718, paid " Mr. Dyson for physick for the poor to Easter 1720.. £1–7–6."[88] This looks like a contract to supply medicine. The Poor were apt to suffer through being farmed out to a doctor in this manner, for there was always the danger that they would be neglected, since it was to the doctor's financial interest to waste as little money as possible over them in medicines and time, once he had got his contract. This, indeed, was always the danger when the Poor were farmed out by a lump sum, for whatever purpose. Furthermore, the medical skill of the profession was not high during this period, though it was improving throughout the eighteenth century.

In many cases the aid of a doctor does not seem to have
been very efficacious. The overseers of Burton-on-Trent,
however, did not intend to waste the ratepayers' money
without any result ; hence the following entry in the
vestry book :

> " At a vestry meeting it was agreed to give Mr. Gilks
> the sum of £10 for the cure of Jacob Mossley the younger,
> in case he shall make him sound and well, so as to be able to
> work at his trade and get his living, to the judgment of a
> vestry or otherwise. No cure no pay. The money to
> be pd. at the end of three months after he shall be
> reported cured."[89]

The solemn caution of this entry is delightful ; it is to
be wished that they had stated at the same time what
was the disease which had afflicted " Jacob Mossley the
younger."[90]

If medical aid could not save him, and the pauper died,
the parish had to bear the cost of the funeral. Accounts
for funerals will be found in every overseer's book.
Usually they are entered up laconically, as : " payd for
Buring of Edward Landsdown..00–09–01," but in 1693
an interesting statement of the expenses connected with
a pauper's illness and funeral is entered up. It runs
as follows :

> " Gave to Joane Jones in sickness..00–12–06, Paid for
> drink and Biskett for those yt carried her to ye Grave..
> 00–01–00, Paid ye Clerk and Sex-stone..00–03–08, Paid for
> a shroud for her..00–02–06, Paid to them yt Laid her out..
> 00–01–00, Paid for a coffin for her..00–07–00, to ye minis-
> ter..00–02–06, for Coles..00–02–00, to two women yt made
> oath..00–01–00, to woman to looke to her in her sickness..
> 00–02–00."[91]

It is a strange collection of items, but there is nothing
about it to suggest that particular unloveliness of a
pauper funeral which, according to literature, became
its distinguishing mark at a later date. In another
case, Coddenham paid " To Mr. Wynne for the Burial

of Girl Standard..1–0, Do the Affidavit..6d., To Sexton
for Digging Grave and Tolling the Bell, Do for laying her
Forth..2–0, To Cash to her Father for Beer..1–0."
The last entry is distinctly curious, but at least they paid
her the respect of tolling the bell.[92] Toppesfield, after the
habit of the time to do everything by contract, even
" agreed at a parish meeting by the parrishioners with
John Gall for fowr shillings and sixpence for all the
Coffens he makes at the parish Charge for men, women
and children agreed to by us." Again, in funerals as in
other things, a clear line of demarcation must be drawn
between the large towns on the one hand, and the country
and small town parish on the other. Probably the
former displayed to the full the inhumanity and callousness always attributed to the poor law in this respect,
but in small places, where the local business was easily
known and the majority of people on the rates were either
old and past work, or too young to start it, their condition
was no harder than the lot of other persons of the same
social class, who were not dependent on the rates.
Probably a child in a poor home, or an old man or woman,
living with one of their married children, fared as hardly
as the aged pauper or the child who was boarded out.

From these details it is evident that many parishes
managed the business of outdoor relief with a fair
measure of success. The technical skill displayed may
not have been very great, but in the smaller rural
parishes, where the number of those dependent on relief
was low, the poor were provided with house room,
clothes, fuel, medical attendance, and a weekly pension
that in all probability was not inferior to that which a
labourer in work could have procured for his family.
The doctrine of less eligibility, as set forth by the Commissioners of 1834, appears to have been unrecognized.
But the success of the overseers went in inverse ratio to
the size of the parish. Where the number of poor
parishioners was large, the difficulties were increased.
In the first case the overseer had neither personal know-

ledge of those needing relief nor the time to make adequate inquiries, and secondly, if the standard of wealth among the parishioners was low, then the amount available for relief was also limited. Consequently individual pensions were too small to sustain life, and hence arose the practice of begging, and the tendency was for the noisy pauper to be relieved at the expense of his more modest fellow. Thus as the eighteenth century progressed, and town parishes became more crowded with the labouring Poor flocking there for work, the administration became at once more inefficient and more corrupt. But on the whole the parishes, to the end of the century, proved at least as capable as their modern counterparts of managing the details of out-door relief.

CHAPTER IV

THE FAILURE OF THE PARISH TO EMPLOY THE POOR

THE real aim of the 43 Eliz. c. 2 had been " to set on work..all such persons, married or unmarried, who have no means to maintain themselves, and use no ordinary and daily trade of life to get their living by." Accordingly the chief activities of the Privy Council, before the Civil War, had been directed towards the compelling of parishes to provide a stock for the Poor. But for work of this character the organization of the parish was totally unfitted, and as soon as the constraining hand of the central government was removed, the parishes began to flag in their exertions ; and by the time of the Restoration there were very few parishes that made any pretence of employing the Poor. Occasionally, during the last part of the century, Quarter Sessions reprimanded the slackness which the parishes displayed in this direction, but even their reprimands were more formal than earnest. For instance, the North Riding Quarter Sessions, as late as 1693, issued a series of general directions to the Chief Constables for transmission to the petty constables ; and among them was the injunction, " That they also give notice to the Overseers of the parish to see that a convient stock of flax, hemp, and wool and other ware and stuff be provided towards the setting on work of such as are able to work but cannot otherwise find employment."[1] Such incidents, however, were not general, being but the relics of a disused custom.

If the parishes made any effort at all to employ the Poor, they contented themselves with supplying individual persons with the implements of their craft. Thus

Coddenham bought " Two Spinning wheels, one for ye Boy Bay one for Rose Cook girl..3-8,"[2] while at Batley the overseers expended sixpence " for 2 Cards for the Lass at Walkers."[3] In 1713 the feoffees of the parish land of St. Giles, Northampton, " paid to Goody Curtis to buy her son John a Loom..1-0-0."[4] Very occasionally a parish would make some trifling grant of money to put poor people in the way of employing themselves, as when St. Giles, in 1713, paid " To Goody Samwell to buy cattle to help support her family..1-10-0."[4] On another occasion they " Gave John Baker to buy seed to sow some land he rents, but was not able to pay for seed this hard winter..0-3-6."[4] The overseers of Burton decided " That John Wakefield hath 5*d.* given him to buy hemp to supply by his labour his present necessities,"[5] whilst the officers of Leyton " Paid Theodorus Smith by order of the vestry to put him in a way to live..0-10-0."[6] But with some few exceptions of this character parishes appear completely to have avoided their responsibility for setting the Poor to work by the methods indicated by the 43 Eliz. c. 2.

Contemporary feeling, however, was by no means prepared to let the matter drop, for it was fiercely and resentfully felt that, given the opportunity, any able-bodied person was capable of earning his or her living, and that only the idleness and laziness of all concerned prevented this desirable consummation from being achieved. Accordingly the parishes were driven forward to engage in enterprises for which they were unfitted, and after the Restoration new and more ambitious methods of employing the Poor were attempted. At first the overseers contented themselves with making arrangements with some manufacturer to employ the able-bodied poor of the parish, as when St. John the Baptist in Chester entered into an agreement with Peter Daniel and Richard Leigh, cotton spinners, that they should employ all the poor persons who were willing to work. The parish was to supply wheels, cards, and reels for the

PLATE V

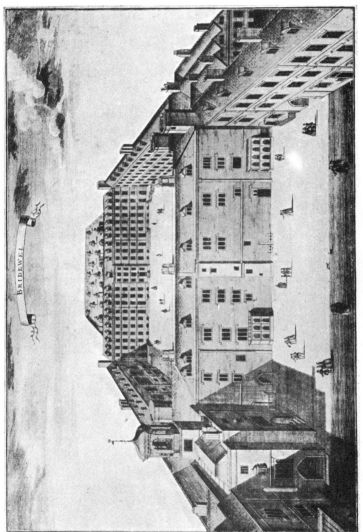

BRIDEWELL

A VIEW OF BRIDEWELL

[face p. 126

spinners, and to allow weekly relief to learners ; the profits of the adventure were to go to the contractors, and the parish promised to set up no other workhouse for the spinning of cotton for three years.[7] But such arrangements were foredoomed to failure ; when trade was good an average workman had no difficulty in obtaining work, while when trade was bad, such contract labour was merely a drug in the market, producing goods for which there was no sale.[8] Accordingly, the parishes soon discovered that if the Poor were to be employed some other method must be invented, yet the problem of how fully-occupied overseers were to find remunerative occupations for the odds and ends of their able Poor, was even then dimly felt to be beyond the capacities of the individual parishes.[9]

Towards the end of the century an interesting experiment was started at Bristol, under the guidance of William Cary, by which all the parishes within the town incorporated themselves by special act of Parliament, for the express purpose of a better administration of the Poor. The main plank in their programme was to pool their resources and equip a suitable workhouse where the Poor might be employed. Most of the power was taken out of the hands of the overseers and entrusted to a body composed of four guardians elected by the ratepayers of each ward, together with the mayor and aldermen. The idea of such a workhouse was not new, the first germ appearing in the establishment of Bridewell in London, where poor children and sturdy vagrants were to be taught a trade before being turned loose on the world again. In imitation of this, other Bridewells were built in various parts of the country, but as time went on these places became more and more akin to gaols, and began to be called Houses of Correction. They were not workhouses, but places of confinement for the unruly, their inmates being expected, however, to maintain themselves by their labour. The idea of collecting all the able Poor within one building and setting them on work was not embraced with any enthusiasm, until the experiment at Bristol fired men's imaginations, and within the next few years several towns obtained acts for building workhouses under a corporation. Within two years Tiverton, Exeter, Hereford, Colchester, Kingston, and Shaftesbury all obtained private Acts, and before the end of the next reign King's Lynn, Sudbury, Gloucester, Worcester, Plymouth, and Norwich had followed suit. In all these cases there was the frank recognition that the unit of the parish, at least in the towns, was too small to employ the Poor, and the writings of social reformers all urged the adoption of a larger area.

The early eighteenth century saw a slow but steady growth in the number of workhouses dotted up and down the country. In 1722 a new act dealing with the Poor was passed, which, from one of its provisions, came to be known as the Workhouse Test Act. This Act, following the approved opinions of the time, gave parishes permission to join together to build a common workhouse, if they so desired. It also empowered overseers in places where there was a workhouse to withhold relief from all persons who refused to enter the workhouse. In this way it was possible for a parish, or several parishes, to build a workhouse and concentrate all the business of poor relief in it. At one step it rendered possible the abolition of all weekly pensions, the payment of rent, and the boarding out of children. The sanguine might hope, also, to make something from the work of the Poor. This Act marked the importance of the workhouse movement, rather than started it. Indeed, it is almost an axiom of the poor law legislation throughout the period that nothing was made legal by the authority of Parliament until it had become an established practice in a considerable section of the country. Thus, in the case of workhouses, it was evident that they were an expedient sufficiently popular to be adopted in many places, and, as this was so, Parliament set about providing legal machinery to facilitate their establishment.

Whether this succeeded is more a matter of doubt. Before the Act, the smaller poor houses were built with the consent of Quarter Sessions ; the more important ones under private Acts of Parliament. After the Act there was certainly a great increase in the number of workhouses, but the more important continued to be built under special Acts. The Act of 1723 made special provision for two or more parishes to join together to build a common workhouse, and for such a union the consent of the justices alone was necessary. But in the majority of cases parishes do not seem to have availed themselves of this offer, the greater number of workhouses built under this Act being the property of separate parishes. In some instances parishes united ; thus at Chester there was a general poor house to which all the nine parishes in the city could send their paupers on the payment of an annual sum ;[10] likewise at Carlisle there was a workhouse for the four wards of the city to which neighbouring parishes also could send their paupers on the payment of so much rent per year.[10] The parish of Gilcrux reserved the right to send paupers to the workhouse at Cockermouth by a payment of £2 a year,[10] but such a provision was merely *in terrorem*, and deserving paupers were never sent.[10] When rural parishes reserved the right to send their paupers to a workhouse in another parish, this was usually done, not with any intention of availing themselves of the privilege, but with the idea of using it as a threat if their paupers proved troublesome. But where parishes actually formed a union under the 9 Geo. I. c. 7 for the maintenance of their respective poor, there seems to have been continual friction in the working. In order that the conditions of union should be clearly understood, when the parishes of a town of any size decided to erect a common workhouse, they usually went to the trouble and expense of getting a private act, whereby they might be incorporated as the governors of the Poor with all the rights and privileges of a corporation. Thus the Act of 1723

K

appears to have encouraged the building of the smaller type of parish workhouse, but not to have had much effect in inducing parishes to form unions for this purpose. Perhaps, as will be seen later, its most important clause was that which gave a legal sanction to the habit of farming the Poor out by way of contract.

When a parish decided to erect a workhouse it was usual for the whole vestry to deliberate over the matter and to arrange all the details as to the best site, the raising of money, and the placing of the building contracts, while a special committee would be appointed to draw up rules and regulations for the new house and see that they were followed. At Stroud, for instance, it was decided that "Twelve Governors be appointed to direct the Affairs of the Workhouse for one whole Year ; and to report the state of it at a vestry, to be held once a Quarter."[11] Thus it was not intended to leave the administration of the house to already over-burdened overseers, though they retained an ex officio interest in the matter.[12] This Committee had to decide what procedure should be followed for admitting paupers to the house, what time they should rise and retire, how they should be employed and fed, how they should be punished for small offences, and even what improving literature, as, for instance, *The Whole Duty of Man*, the master should read to them.[13] The actual management of these houses was entrusted to a master and mistress, directly responsible for the administration of the house, who themselves appear to have been drawn from the labouring class. At Leicester there was a master "who has the immediate care of the Poor, to keep them in order, and to employ them in such work as they are capable of, and to see that their food is duely prepared and given to them. He has two apartments assigned to him, his Diet and Washing, and £12 per Annum, beside maintenance."[14] In most cases a married man was appointed to act as master, with the idea that the domestic side would be managed by his wife. Judged by the salaries paid, the average master cannot have been much above the status of a labourer or a small shopkeeper, which in many cases led to bad or partial administration, when the visiting guardians were careless in the execution of their office.

In many cases parishes appear to have felt that they were incapable of exercising even so much supervision over the running of the workhouse. Accordingly many of them solved the whole troublesome question of the management of the workhouse by farming their Poor out to a contractor. The legal basis for this practice was the clause in the Workhouse Test Act which enacted that any parish, with the consent of the major part of the vestry, might contract " with any person or persons for the lodging, keeping, maintaining and imploying any or all such Poor . . . as shall desire to receive Relief or Collection from the same Parish." As a result of this permission various types of contracts arose. The most simple of these was when the overseers merely made arrangements with a manufacturer to supply the Poor with work, but, as has been said, such contracts were rarely successful. The second type was when a man agreed to receive, at a fixed price per head, all the poor whom the parish officers sent to him. The details of such contracts varied.[15] Sometimes the contractor had the use of the parish workhouse, sometimes he provided the premises himself, while in addition to the fixed weekly payments he had the right to any profits which might accrue from their labour. The third type of bargain was an even greater confession of failure on the part of the parish, for the covenant was that the contractor, in return for a given sum per year, should assume the entire responsibility for the poor of the parish. The difference between these last two types lies in the fact that in the former it was to the interest of the contractor to have as many poor in the house as possible, since he was paid by the head, but in the latter it was to his interest to keep them out of the workhouse by the payment of pensions, which were less than the cost of their upkeep in the house would be. Therefore this method was to hold the workhouse over them *in terrorem* in order to force them to accept the smallest possible allowance.

Such methods of providing for the poor were very popular, especially with the small City parishes in London, since the number of paupers per parish was not great enough to justify the building of a workhouse. Examples of both variations of these contracts often occur among parish papers. The following entries from the vestry book of Tooting Graveney show clearly the steps which a parish would have to adopt in making such an arrangement. In 1760 it was decided,

> " That Mr. Arnold and Mr. Hart churchwarden and overseer have leave to agree with Mr. Angier of Mitcham to receive the poor of our parish and maintain them all sent to him at his own proper cost at the rate of Two shillings and ninepence p^r head p^r week ; being first sent to him Cloathed in new apparel. He afterwards to provide each in sickness and in health with Meat, Drink, Washing, Lodging, Clothing and every Thing else necessary for a decent support of Life free from all other Expences to the Parish except the Two shillings & ninepence per week above mentioned."[16]

The next entry dealing with the subject said, " The Mitcham authorities declining to allow Mr. Angier to take in our Poor, It was agreed that he Take them to his own House in Coleman St., London, on the terms aforesaid.[16] The next entry recorded the fact that the poor had been taken to Coleman Street, and gave orders for the old parish house to be cleaned up in order to be given back to the landlord by November.[16] Three years later the parish came to a new agreement with Mr. Angier, viz. : " That the parish allow Mr. Angier after the rate of ninety pounds per year for which he is to take the whole care of all the poor of the said parish also all the casual poor."[16] After Midsummer 1764 another £5 was voted, and it was also decided that " Every person in the parish having serv'd Overseer and Churchwarden as also the Present Overseers and Churchwarden be of a Committee at all times to inspect the condition of the poor of this parish under the care of Mr. Angier at Streatham, and particularly, that the overseer and Churchwarden will a few days before the determination of every quarter make it their business to go and take an account of them in order to lay it before the Vestry, which shall be then held, and at the Vestry Mr. Angier shall be ordered to attend."[16] These contracts are interesting as marking two different stages, which have been mentioned previously, in the farming out of the Poor. The first arranged for the Poor to be maintained by a contractor in his own establishment in another parish, but only included such Poor as the churchwardens liked to send, at a given sum per head. The second agreement is for the contractor to farm all the Poor at a lump sum and to make what he can out of it. The first kind of agreement was particularly common among the parishes within the Bills of Mortality, many of which had no workhouses of their own, and preferred to farm their Poor out to contractors who lived in the suburbs. The report of 1776 gives particulars of the terms of these contracts for the years 1773–5.[17] St. Alban, Wood Street, farmed out its Poor with a person at Hoxton at 4s. 3d. a week, the parish providing them with clothes ; All Hallows the Less also farmed its poor out to Hoxton at a charge of 4s. 2d. and clothes. St. Augustine let out its poor on the same terms for three years, as did St. Clement's, Eastcheap. St. Dionis Back Church got slightly cheaper terms, namely 4s. including clothing. St. Edmund the King had a contract on the same terms, but the paupers were in the first case clothed by the parish.[17] This method in of dealing with the problem, by putting the Poor out with contractors who lived in another parish, and who provided the accommodation, was largely confined to the parishes within the Bills, though it was not unknown elsewhere.[18] Many parishes which farmed out their Poor had workhouses of their own, which they loaned to the contractor.

In 1724, Hemel Hempstead made a contract with Mr. Math. Marryot, for £40 per annum and a coat worth thirty shillings, to manage their workhouse. The agreement was for three years. Luton, too, made a contract with the same person, who here employed the people in making hats. Sometimes these contracts were made at so much per head, as at Hertford, where the parishes of St. Andrew's and All Saints' agreed, " to pay the master of the workhouse erected in St. Andrew's Parish June 1724, 1/10 weekly, for every poor Person that shall be sent into the said workhouse, till June 1734 · · · the Master to have all they earn and to employ them in or out of the House, as he pleases." In this case the House belonged to the Parish, and the contract referred solely to their maintenance ; the same conditions prevailed also at Cirencester.[19] The following is an example of the details of such a contract. It was made between the parish of Tonbridge on the one hand and Wm. Parker, yeoman, and Ashdowne, gardener, on the other,

" to lodge, cloath, keep, maintain and employ all the Poor the Parish do now or shall think proper for 2/- per week, to be paid on the 2nd Sunday of each month. They are to have the benefit of their labour and the use of the present Workhouse, outbuildings and appurtances and use and ordinary wear of the household furniture. The Churchwardens and Overseers are to provide a man skilled in midwifery and medicines and pay the cost of the burialls of those that die under their charge. For the sum of £20 to read, knit, sew plain and instructed in the knowledge of the Bible. The Churchwardens and Overseers to provide spinning Wheels for those under their care and that all poor persons towards whose support and maintenance a sum of 1/6 is paid shall be put under their care and they be paid the same rate."[20]

In cases of infectious disease the overseers were to remove all such persons so afflicted within seven days, or forfeit £1 1s. 0d. a day. On leaving the House, or at the expiration of the agreement, the Poor were to have as good clothes as when they entered it—and then comes rather an interesting list of clothes thought necessary.

" For men and boys 1 hatt, 2 woolen caps, 1 coat, 2 waist-coats, 1 round frock, 1 pair breeches, 2 pair stockings, 1 pair shoes, 3 shirts. For women and girls 1 hatt, 4 linnen caps, 2 handkerchiefs, 2 gowns, 3 petty coats, 2 linnen aprons, 2 scuffling ditto, 1 pair stockings, 1 pair shoes, 1 pair stays or bodices, 3 shifts."[20]

Opinions as to the advisability of farming the Poor varied according to whether the writer in question had regard to the theoretical advantages to be derived from it, or to the practical results which ensued. Speaking of the difficulty of running workhouses, one anonymous writer declared that " To prevent any Excess upon this Article (diet) as well as obviate Abuses and Partialityes too frequently practiced, there seems no surer Method than of contracting with the Best Bidder, for the main-tenance of the Poor, at so much a Head for those who shall become chargeable, after publick Notice given to all who shall be willing to bid."[21] The usual contention was, that under the care of a contractor the Poor would live a life of frugal activity, good for their morals and not unduly hard on their bodies. It was supposed that it would be to the interest of the contractor to keep the persons under his charge at the highest pitch of efficiency, for " Industry and Sobriety are for the Advantage of every man who practises Them ; and They bring the same Benefit to Those who have the Profits of his Labour : The Drunkard will be preserved Temperate, the Hale healthy, the Sick be attended, and the Lazy be compelled to work, for this Reason alone, because it will become the Interest of Those, who have them under Their Care, that They should rather be employed than lie idle "[21] Workhouses, on the other hand, if run by the parish officers or a corporation, led to nothing but jobbery. It is to be feared that there was more truth in his latter than in his former contentions.

The case against the habit of contracting for the farming of the Poor was, however, stated forcibly by many writers who took the trouble to see facts as they were, and not as by theory they ought to have been.

" The patrons of the practice of farming the poor," said John Scott, " will undoubtedly pretend that it is not injurious to the poor ; but, on the contrary, greatly conducive to their advantage : on such supposed advantages they will probably expatiate ; and endeavour to amuse with descriptions of the regularity, industry, plenty and contentment of their little communities. But the reverse of the picture will be found the semblance of the truth. Good fruit cannot be produced from a tree that is evil, right consequences cannot proceed from premises founded upon wrong principles ; yet, from indolence and avarice only can this iniquitous custom derive its origin. The lessors of the workhouse poor can have no rational inducement for their conduct, but the avoidance of trouble to themselves, and the procuring the support of their poor at an easier expense than it could be procured under their own inspection."[22]

He then goes on to prove how absurd and opposed to practical considerations is the contention that it is to the interests of the contractor to do his best for the Poor under his charge.

" If," he says, " the contract be at a certain price for every individual, that price is fixed at the lowest sum for which it is supposed a human being can retain a miserable existence : if for a certain annual stipend for a whole number of paupers which the parish contracting can furnish, the exactest calculation that can be produced from the experience of past facts, or speculation of future probabilities, is formed previous to agreement ; and the haazrd of unexpected contingencies must still be run by the contractors : yet evident it is, that no one would undertake a business so productive of trouble and so obnoxious to ignominy, without a prospect of ample repayment. If then he who engages to maintain the poor cheaper than they can otherwise be maintained, has still a profit from their maintenance ; to discover whence this profit must arise, requires no remarkable share of penetration : the power of oppression is in his hand, and he must use it, the gains of oppression are within his reach and he must not refuse them."[22]

The trouble was that, as it was no longer possible to employ the Poor with any hope of an adequate return for the time and capital expended, the only chance of profit for the contractor was to cut to the absolute minimum the amount spent on their maintenance, and this was the course adopted. It could hardly be otherwise.

It is very difficult to obtain specific details of the way in which this system worked, apart from the testimony born by the pamphleteers, because the fashion in which the contractors treated the Poor under their charge was nobody's business. The sole check was provided by the right of the justices to authorize the contract, which by the 9 Geo. I. c. 7 required the signature of two justices. Thus at Sedbergh, in Yorkshire, Eden reported that the Poor had been farmed there for many years, but that some years back, " upon the Contractors not allowing them sufficient victuals, the justices refused their acquisance."[23] As Scott says,

> " A thorough acquaintance with the interior economy of these wretched receptacles of misery, or rather ' parish prisons,' called workhouses, is not easily to be acquired : in these, as in other arbitrary governments, complaint is mutiny and treason, to every appearance of which a double portion of punishment is invariably annexed : particular incidents, shocking to humanity, may sometimes have transpired ; but the whole mystery of iniquity perhaps never has been or never will be developed. One thing is too publicly known to admit of denial, that those workhouses are scenes of filthiness and confusion ; that young and old sick and healthy, are promiscuously crowded into ill-contrived apartments, not of sufficient capacity to contain with convenience half the number of miserable beings condemned to such deplorable inhabitations and that speedy death is almost ever to the aged and infirm, and often to the youthful and robust, the consequence of a removal from more salubrious air to such mansions of putridity.[24]

Testimony to the wretched internal conditions of the houses under a contractor is general, and it is perhaps impossible to colour the canvas too darkly ; but it must

be remembered that the conditions under which the
majority of the inhabitants of a workhouse had lived all
their lives would seem to us unspeakably shocking and
filthy.   It was an age when sanitation was practically
unknown, when filth was allowed to lie anywhere in the
poorer districts, and when the Poor lived in mud hovels
under conditions of indescribable squalor.

Dr. Trotter speaks in the same terms of unmeasured
disapproval of the Act of 1723.

> " The 1 Edw. 6 wears indeed," he says, " a more ferocious
> air, but it is not more barbarous and oppressive to the poor
> than this statute, which empowers the overseer to cram
> them into a narrow, nasty workhouse, and to contract with
> any person to lodge, keep, and maintain them.   The fund of
> such House is not sufficient to redeem them from their
> filthy rags ; nor the capacity of it to furnish them with
> convenient, decent, and distinct apartments ; but the
> young, the old, the virtuous, the profligate, the sick, the
> healthy, the clean, the unclean, huddled together and inhaling
> a stagnant and putrid air, deplore their miserable existence ;
> which receives its utmost aggravation from their immediate
> servitude to the Contractor, some low born, selfish, surly
> ruffian, from whose sordid tyranny there is no appeal, no
> redress, until the unhappy sufferers repose in the grave,   If
> the Work House is under a better regulation, it is owing to
> the humanity of one or more Gentleman that directs its
> management, and not to any provision in the Act." [25]

Where the contract system of managing the Poor was
in vogue, the results appear to have been disastrous to
the Poor.   It is difficult to estimate how widely the
practice spread.   In some parishes the Poor were
regularly farmed, in others they were managed by the
parish officers, and in larger towns, where a special act
had been obtained, by statutory corporations.   Thus
local practice might vary to a considerable degree.
Where the parish kept the management in its own hands
the reason might be, either that there was an active
committee of gentlemen, who were willing to undertake
the oversight of the Poor, or that the officers wished
to have the patronage of the workhouse at their disposal,

in order that they or their friends might have the right
to supply it with provisions. But to farm the Poor
appears to have been the cheapest way of dealing with
them, and there can be no doubt that the practice was
very extensively followed. Some persons appear to have
been contractors in quite a large way. Thus, just after
the Act of 1723 was passed, a certain Mr. Mayyriot figures
in the history of several of the new workhouses as having
contracted to farm the Poor of the parish for a certain
number of years. And still later, in 1752, the author of
" A Letter to the Author of Several Considerations,
etc.," who wrote upholding the system, said that there
should be no difficulty in finding sufficient contractors,
as " There are now Contractors for Parishes. And I
have been lately informed of one Contractor who hath
thirteen Parishes committed to his Care."[26] That a
pamphlet should be written as late as 1752 in favour of
an extension of the practice of farming the Poor shows
that it was not of universal application even by this time.
These contractors, who farmed several parishes and
received the paupers from the respective parishes into
their own private workhouse, appear to have been the
worst of all so far as their treatment of the Poor went.
The following story comes from John Scott.

> " I have been informed by a substantial householder that
> a parish with which he was connected, once contracted for
> their paupers with a certain noted farmer of the poor ; at
> sixty pounds per annum ; he had forgot the number sent,
> but it may reasonably be supposed it was something ade-
> quate to the sum paid to the contractor. The place they
> were sent to was near twenty miles distant from the parish
> contracting ; and so sensible were the officers of the impro-
> priety of their conduct, that they sent the poor by night in
> order to elude the public observation and censure. They
> were treated with so much rigour, that, after a few years
> had elapsed, the overseers thought proper to make inquisi-
> tion into the affair ; and my informant, who was then in
> office, assured me, that they found the number, by death and
> escapes, reduced to eight only, and those mostly children
> who bore evident marks of injury from disease and hunger ;

one of the elopers was said to have perished under a hay-stack. The parochial workhouses are commonly bad enough managed ; but the management of the extra parochial ones is worse beyond comparison."[27]

Thomas Ruggles, writing at the end of the century, bore the same testimony to the state of the workhouses under the contractors. He says :

" The want of room and the bad management of that which they possess, occasion similar inconveniences ; the cloathes, or rather the covering of the inhabitants ; the improprieties arising from the two sexes of all ages, and dispositions, long kept together ; the ignorance and filth the children are brought up in ; the general spirit of rigid economy which the contracting master of the workhouse produces, as well in diet as in cloathing, lodging, cleanliness, to scrape from misery, as soon as possible, a property which may enable him to retire from his disagreeable avocation, give propriety to the opinion and expression that a parish workhouse is a parish bugbear, to frighten distress from applying for relief."[28]

According to Eden, a large number of parishes were still farming their poor in 1795, though many of them were then considering the advisability of resuming the responsibility themselves.

As has been seen, the effects of the contractor system were thoroughly bad, but the workhouses under parochial management appear to have been very little better. One defect was common to both, and that was the unsuit-ability of the buildings allocated for the purpose. Many of them had not been designed for workhouses in the first place, but had been taken over and adapted to that use. At Norwich, of the two workhouses, one had been the Bishop's Palace and the other a monastery. Even where the building in question had been designed for a workhouse, it was often too small either for comfort or for effective organization. For one thing the unit of the parish was much too small to maintain an effective workhouse ; yet few appear to have availed themselves of the facilities for union afforded by the 9 Geo. I. c. 7.

It is true that in towns common workhouses were often erected, either under a corporation by a special act, or by the joining together of parishes, but in the rural districts, where there was a poor house at all, it was usually wretchedly small and insanitary. For example, in the Hundred of West Flegg in Norfolk, when it was desired to build a new hundred house, the following evidence was given as to the state of many of the small poor houses within the Hundred :

> " That if the Old and Infirm are put into the poor House, they are placed without proper Assistance, and have very poor support from their Parish ; that the Officers do not allow more than Three Shillings a Week for a Man and his Wife who are incapable of Work, but that the Parish pay for the House, Rent and Fuel ; that the Size and State of the rooms where they are placed is very bad ; that sometimes more than one Man and his Wife are lodged in one Room ; that he has known a Man and his Wife put into One Room with another Family with Children, some of whom were sixteen Years old, lying in the same bed with their Father and Mother ; that the Floor of the Rooms are brick, and sometimes only Clay ; that there are Twenty Parishes within the Two Hundreds and in most of them there are Houses for the Reception of the Poor ; that the Houses are all in a miserable Condition, but that some of them are better than others."[29]

Occasionally the evil housing of the Poor in these small workhouses was brought before the Justices of the Peace. In October, 1759, for instance, Jonathan Quine, of the parish of Little Maulden, labourer, master of the workhouse of the said parish, was indicted

> " for neglecting to provide sufficient sustenance and firing for William Carter, an infant at the age of 18 months ; for permitting William Carter the elder, labourer, then suffering from violent sickness, to lie in the said workhouse on straw and without covering and sufficient relief, and for placing in two rooms of the said workhouse, several men, women and children, promiscuously to the number of 18, being the poor of Maulden, to the great peril of their health."[30]

But more often these conditions were allowed to continue without any interference and with but little remonstrance. A terrible picture of dirt, vermin, and neglect is drawn by the curate of Damerham South, Wiltshire, as late as 1796. Having tried in vain to make the overseers apply some remedy, at last he took the matter into his own hands, hoping by the publication of his " A brief Statement of Facts, etc.," to draw public attention to the state of affairs prevailing here. The purpose of his visit was to see a poor woman about to have a child. He describes it as follows :

> " A few objects with squalid, emaciated countenances, were hovering round a wide extended chimney ; on the hearth of which were a few handfuls of half extinguished embers ; nor had they any fuel in the house, or any means of procuring any (did their health permit) as the snow to a considerable depth, completely covered the earth. . . . The glass, in the window, was entirely shattered, and most of it removed ; and the cold being too intense to be endured, without supplying the defect, the materials employed for that purpose, had nearly darkened the room, giving it such an air of humidity and gloom, as not improperly, enabled it to the appellation of the dark hole of Damerham. The poor wretch, who was more immediately the object of our visit, was lying on a bedstead, wrapped in a piece of old rug, because she had no clothes, and because there was no fire . . . and although she had actually been in labour two or three times, there was nothing provided for her self or child."[31]

Yet the parish officers refused to do anything in the matter. Indeed, conditions of this kind do not appear to have been unusual, and overcrowding was general. Among the reasons given for the erection of a new workhouse at Barking was the fact that " Persons of both sexes, and of all Ages, lodge in the same Room ; and that there is no separate Ward, even for people who are sick."[32] Moreover it should be remembered that for one instance which comes to light, or which has been recorded, dozens remain unknown.

Nor does the state of the town workhouses appear to

have been much better. They, too, suffered from the prevailing curse of dirt and overcrowding, with all its consequences of ill-health and low morals. When, in 1733, it was desired to build a new workhouse at St. Mary's, Whitechapel, the following account was given of the state of the existing one :

> " Mr. Phillips said, ' That there is a Workhouse in the Parish, which will contain 200 Poor ; but is situated in a Back Street adjoining to a White Lead House, and is a dirty Place, there being no Yard, or any Room to erect a Warehouse to put Goods in . . . That at present there are about 30 Poor therein, who are not kept to work, but who go and come as they please, get drunk and are disorderly : That an Attempt was made to set them to work, but People would not trust them with their Goods."[33]

In view of evidence such as this, it is easy to understand the regulations that workhouse committees made, on the inauguration of a new workhouse, that " none of the Poor in the Workhouse do strike, abuse or give ill Language to one another, or spoil or daub their cloathes ; "[34] and that any Poor " found bringing into the House or drinking therein any Genevea, or other distilled Liquors,"[34] should be punished. In the same workhouse they were also ordered " not to presume to smoak Tobacco in their Beds " or to fight and swear, and prevent the other Poor from sleeping after lights were out. It was, however, one thing to make regulations of this kind, and another to enforce them, particularly on a dissolute, idle class confined in a dirty cramped workhouse. Thus :

> " Mr. Thomas Babington, master of the workhouse, (at Clerkenwell) being examined said ' That there are now 320 Persons in the Work House, which was built to receive only 150 ; by which Means it was crowded to such a Degree as to render it not only extremely inconvenient, but also highly prejudicial to the Health of the Persons residing in it."[35]

Where beds were provided, it was a common thing to find three or four paupers sharing the same bed. In

1770 the workhouse belonging to St. Martin's-in-the-Fields was reported to be " very ruinous and in Danger of falling,"[36] yet the Poor of the parish were still housed there. In the same year a similar report was made of St. Paul's, Shadwell, namely : " that the Workhouse belonging to the Parish is so old and ruinous, that it is absolutely necessary the same should be taken down and rebuilt."[37]

The internal conditions of all the workhouses in the country were not necessarily so bad as those which attracted public attention, and Eden, writing in 1797, reported that he found some of them in a very tolerable state of cleanliness. But clean or dirty the eighteenth century workhouse was an undesirable place, and among the abuses to be laid to its score must be reckoned the treatment which children received within its walls. Where a parish possessed a workhouse, children who would otherwise have been boarded out were sent there, with the most appalling results. The crowded London workhouses in particular were literally death traps, but it was not until Jonas Hanway started his campaign in the middle of the century that public opinion became alive to the evils of the system. He recites some terrible facts in his " Ernest Appeal for Mercy to the Children of the Poor." " Never," he wrote, " shall I forget the evidence given at the Guildhall, upon occasion of a master of a workhouse of a large parish, who was challenged for forcing a child from the breast of the Mother, and sending it to the Foundling Hospital. He alleged in his defence, ' We send all our children to the Foundling Hospital, we have not saved one alive for fourteen years. We have no place fit to preserve them in, the air is too confined.' "[38] And in another case, " Some years before the Foundling Hospital was opened, it appeared that of fifty-four children born and taken into the workhouse, not one outlived the year in which it was born or taken in. This seemed to be so incredible, that I went to the workhouse to inquire into the fact, and found it true."

THE FOUNDLINGS' HOSPITAL

[face p. 144

In another place he said, " It is confessed to be a rare thing for a child to be taken out alive except it be in the hands of the Mother."[38] The condition of children in the London workhouses as represented by Hanway is a terrible contrast to the idealized picture of their lot drawn scarcely more than thirty years before. But Hanway was not exaggerating facts in order to arouse the public conscience on the subject. In 1767, a Committee of the House of Commons was appointed to deal with the question, and on 24th of March made its report, which more than confirmed his assertions. The first two articles of the report were as follows :

" That taking the Children born in the Workhouses or Parish Houses or received of or under Twelve Months old, in the year 1673, and following the same into 1764 and 1765 only Seven in a Hundred appear to have survived this short Period.

" 2ndly That having called for the Registers of the Years 1754, 1755, 1761, 1762, of the Children placed out Apprentices by the Parishes within the Bills of Mortality, it appears there having been Apprenticed out the Number of 1,419 ; but upon examining the Ages at which the Children so placed out were received, in the Seven Years from 1741, till they grew up to be placed out, it appears that only nineteen of those born in the workhouses, or received into them under Twelve Months old, composed any Part of the 1,419 ; and even of Those received as far as Three years old, only Thirty-six appear to have survived in the hands of the said Parishes to be placed out Apprentices."[39]

Such an accumulation of evidence must show that by the middle of the eighteenth century the workhouse movement had failed, utterly and completely. For this failure there were two main reasons. One was the economic impossibility of making the Poor confined in these places self-supporting. The other was the jobbery and corruption which crept into the administration of the workhouses, as a consequence of leaving them to the management of unpaid officials or consigning them to unscrupulous contractors.

L

From an early date practical experiments illustrated the difficulty of organizing the work of the Poor in such a way as to obtain a profit from their labour. A certain gentleman, writing an account of the success of the workhouse at Leicester, affirmed that " The Product of their Labourers, one Week with another is about 14s., the Charge of maintaining them weekly is about 40s., that is about 26s. above their Labour."[40] In the year 1740 another experiment on a large scale was started at the Tiverton workhouse, with the object of employing the Poor to make a profit. A large woollen manufactory was started in the House to employ the Poor, £1,020 having been raised by public subscription to defray the cost of the initial expense. " It was, however, found to be so very disadvantageous, and so many losses were sustained by waste, and keeping manufactured goods on hand without an opportunity of sale, that, in the following year, the materials were sold, and the manufacture given up."[41] One gentleman suggested that the Poor even went so far as to spoil and waste what material was given to them, in order to discourage attempts to set them to work. His dictum was that " except the Person who is to overlook them understand the Work, and will be somewhat strict upon them, they will endeavour to spoil it, that they may have none."[42] The first reliable figures dealing with the expenses of the workhouses of the country, apart from those quoted in " An Account of several Workhouses," are provided by the schedules attached to the report of the House of Commons on the Vagrants and Houses of Industry made in 1776. These bear uniform testimony to the fact that in no case was a workhouse able to pay its way on the money earned by its inmates.

It was, indeed, very difficult to find any work with which to employ the workhouse poor.[43] For they were of various trainings, intelligences, ages, and strengths. This meant that whatever work was done had to be reduced to the common denominator of all their capacities, and such employment was generally unremunerative.[44]   Spinning was the chief work undertaken in a large number of workhouses.   It was an art known to most people, and was suitable both for old people, who could do little else, and for children.   Moreover, there was always a market for yarn.   But the prices were wretchedly low.   Even a generous estimate of the amount to be earned by spinning was " 6d. a day at least, if they spin well and are diligent at it."[45]   Since diligence from an eighteenth century point of view lay in working anything from twelve to fourteen hours a day, and since the majority of the inmates of workhouses were either old and impotent, or children still learning the art, it is not surprising that they did not produce much by spinning.   At Chelmsford we are told that the " Lusty and Strong are Tax'd according to their several Abilities, some to earn 5d., some 4d., some 3d. and the children some 1d., some 2d."[46]   And even when so tasked there were probably not many able to earn their keep. At St. Alban's the paupers wound cotton wick for the tallow chandlers, earning about 2d. a day.[46]   At Luton they made use of the local straw and employed the paupers in making straw hats, for which there was a fairly good market.[46]   In many workhouses oakum picking was the only industry carried on.

The report of 1776 gives details of the work carried on in the various workhouses.   At Monmouth it was spinning, at Preston " the Cotton Manufactury," at St. Andrew's, Holborn, " spinning and winding silk."   Christ Church, too, was employed " In various Branches of the Silk Manufacture," and St. George's, Hanover Square, " In making Linen and Plain Work, and in various other Things."   At Beverley the Poor were employed in " carding, knitting, and spinning wool and Yarn, and the infant Poor in Teasing Oakum," while at Canterbury the able poor were employed in " weaving Hop Bagging, making their own Cloaths, and beating Hemp ; the infants in Knitting, Sewing, and Spinning Linen and

Hop Bagging." At Kingston-upon-Hull the men were engaged in " teasing Oakum, and in the necessary Business of the House, the Women in Spinning Linen and Woollen Yarn, Washing, making up Cloaths, and other necessary Business, the Church Children above Eight Years of Age in spinning Jersey."[47] These are fairly comprehensive examples of the work done in the workhouses at the time. It does not differ in any material degree from the type of work done fifty years before. But in reading down a list of the various methods of employment adopted by the different workhouses, the great discrepancy between the expenditure and the earnings must not be forgotten. Thus, despite an imposing list of occupations, the total earnings of the Beverley paupers for 1772 were £6 0s. 0d., and of those of Kingston-upon-Hull, only £21 0s. 9d. The workhouse, as a place organized and run for employing the Poor and setting them on work, and as directed by the 43 Eliz. c. 21, cannot be considered as anything but a failure. Economic conditions were against it ; and had the organization of the contemporary workhouses been much less open to abuse than, actually, it was, they must still have failed.

The other chief cause of the failure of the workhouses to pay their way is to be found in the corrupt administration which prevailed in many of them. In still more, even where there was little actual dishonesty, there was much slackness and negligence. This was due to the fact that in the majority of cases the chief executive power, when not vested in a contractor, was in the hands of the churchwardens and overseers of the Poor. This was far from being the intention of the original founders. The ordinary course of procedure, when setting up a workhouse, was to arrange that the management of it should be vested in a board of elected Trustees, who were to exercise a constant supervision over the internal management of the place. With these the overseers and churchwardens were usually associated. So long as the

Trustees performed their function of oversight, inspected the weekly or monthly bills, and arranged for the buying in of provisions, they could exercise a real control over the affairs of the workhouse. But in time interest appears to have slackened, and in many places the Trustees grew careless of their duties, so that real control slipped into the hands of the parish officers and afforded them an excellent opportunity of indulging in jobbery for the benefit of themselves and their friends. One writer also observed, " But the chief Point will be, that some of the Substantial Parishioners constantly visit the House, and see that the Master and all of them keep up to those good Rules that shall be first agreed on."[48] It was evidently felt that it was not safe to rely too implicitly on the good faith of either master or parish officer.[49]

The consequence of this lack of oversight by the Trustees, was that much jobbery disfigured the management of many of these workhouses. This was the case, also, in parishes where the workhouse was managed by a vestry composed of local tradesmen, each of whom was apt to place his own private interests before that of an economical administration. For instance, at St. Mary's, Whitechapel, it was reported that during the first year after the establishment of the workhouse " it was regulated, and the Poor there in were maintained at 1s. 6d. per week each ; but, since the Vestry (an open one) have had the management thereof, the Expense is increased to 4s. per Week each ; and is occasioned by the Officers of the Parish, who are Tradesmen, and promote their several Trades, without having any Regard of buying Provisions, or other Necessaries, at the lowest Price."[50] Nor were they always particular as to the type of goods with which they supplied the workhouse. Sometimes the vestry roused itself and dispensed with the defaulting tradesman, as at Leyton (which seems to have been a well-arranged parish), when they sent a message to " Bray the Butcher who has hitherto supplyed the workhouse with meat that he forebear to send any more by reason that what he has several times sent us has been bad meat and not free from bones and the Churchwarden is desired to notify the same to him."[51] At Gloucester in 1751 the parishes protested that

> " One Cause of the growing evil of the Debts of the Workhouse is, that many Persons have procured themselves to be elected Guardians of the said House, with no other view than of serving their own Interests, by supplying, on their Own Terms the said House with Provisions, and other Necessaries and Materials, there used and wanting."[52]

When St. Leonard's, Shoreditch, got a new bill for the better regulation of its Poor, the two following significant clauses were added to the old bill, " A Clause was offered to be added to the Bill, that no Trustee shall be concerned in a Contract . . . that no Victualler shall be appointed an Overseer."[53]

The chief virtue which the workhouses possessed in the eyes of eighteenth century administrators arose from their aid in reducing the rates, by acting as a deterrent to people who would otherwise have asked for relief, the qualification for which was not so much absolute destitution as a very considerable degree of poverty. If a man had too large a family to support, he felt that he might legitimately ask for a little relief from the overseer, or a poor widow would ask that her rent might be paid. Legally, after 1723 (9 Geo. I.), if an overseer refused to grant the relief asked, the pauper had the right to complain to the justice, who was, in that case, bound to call the overseer before him to show cause why he had not given relief. And even if the pauper in question did not apply to the justices, he had plenty of opportunity for worrying the overseers. Sometimes a pauper could be very clamorous indeed when relief was refused, as witness the following incident from the Leyton vestry book :

> " Ordered that Mrs. Gibbon be sent to ye Petty Sessions at Ilford in order to be punished if she applys to any officer

or abuses or affronts any gentleman in ye Parish, she having this day applyed for to be taken into the workhouse & ye vestry having considered her, & think her well capable to get her living & that she has imposed on ye Parish in a very gross and impudent manner, and ye Constables be ordered to execute their duty accordingly."[54]

Evidently the parish vestry of Leyton intended to seize time by the forelock. Perhaps they already knew Mrs. Gibbon's tongue all too well. To save unpleasantness of this kind, together with the trouble involved in a visit to the justices, overseers often gave relief to the clamorous and impudent where it was not really deserved.

By the Act of 1723, and, before that, by special private Acts for particular places, any parish which possessed a workhouse might refuse to grant relief to any persons unless they first entered it. And because workhouses meant, at the best confinement and discipline, and at the worst dirt, semi-starvation, and misery, people kept out of them if they could. There were exceptions, of course, where the workhouse offered good food and a lazy life to all who were not too fastidious with regard to their company. At Leyton, for example, the vestry on one occasion found it necessary to pass the resolution that the workhouse was not to be used as a house for kept mistresses.[55] But, as a rule, the workhouse was detested by the Poor, and people who before had asked relief almost as their right, when a workhouse was built, preferred to manage anyhow rather than enter it if they could possibly make a living outside. This statement is corroborated by writer after writer. And because less people asked for relief the rates went down, even though the workhouse itself could not pay its way. One gentleman says:

"I must also acquaint you, that the principal Advantage to the Publick, by encouraging these Foundations, arises from the Spirit of Industry that is provok'd by it among the Poor. Many of our People, who before depended chiefly on what they could get weekly or monthly, by teezing the Overseer of the Poor, now buckle to Labour; and since they find they must give their Labour to the Publick, if they will depend on the Publick, they have exerted themselves, got Wheels and materials for Spinning, and work early and late to avoid coming into the Workhouse."[56]

And he goes on to say that, while in 1720 St. Alban's was rated at 6s. in the pound and disbursed £566 19s. 3½d., in 1724 its inhabitants were rated at only 2s. 6d. in the pound, while the disbursements were expected to work out at about £200 0s. 0d.[56] Instances of this were common wherever a workhouse was built. At Stepney there were more than seventy pensioners on the parish, but after the workhouse was opened, in 1725, all but six women " have chose at present to subsist by their own industry."[57] At Ware it was reported that since the completion of the workhouse " three-quarters of the Pensioners have left off taking their pensions."[57]

The threat of the workhouse was also used to reduce pensions and to force the paupers to take as little relief as was humanly possible. At Newport-Pagnell it was definitely stated that if a person could be provided for more cheaply out of the House than in it, then that person was to be given out-door relief.[57] The Chelmsford workhouse was built in 1716 ; before that, the rates had been 3s. 6d. in the pound, but by 1722 they had been reduced to 1s., including the churchwardens' rate. This was made possible because the Poor, rather than come into the House, " have made shift with a shilling where four before would not have contented them."[57] At Hanslope it is stated that " All who bee chargeable (and especially if they become noisy, and are not content with some small allowance, as a shilling per week at furthest) are sent to the Workhouse."[57] In this way workhouses were used quite definitely and consciously to frighten the Poor from asking for Collection, to force them to work for themselves, and thus to reduce the rates. While and where the " workhouse test " was adhered to severely, it does seem to have had the effect of reducing the rates, as the examples above quoted show. The system of management instituted in most workhouses, however, provided many opportunities for abuses to creep in ; and that, combined with the wave of humanitarianism which swept over the whole administration of the Poor Law in the last quarter of the eighteenth century, greatly impaired the efficiency of the workhouses in keeping down rates. Sir Frederick Eden's verdict was that at the time at which he wrote, 1797, there was very little to choose, in the matter of rates, between a parish with a workhouse and a parish without one.[58] Immediately after their inception, however, they do appear to have had the effect of checking the rise in rates.

But their importance as a deterrent was modified by three factors. The first was the lack in many parishes of a workhouse to be held over the paupers *in terrorem.* In these places the business of outdoor relief went on unchecked. Secondly, in many places the workhouse was not big enough to hold all the people who applied for relief, and therefore its effectiveness in this direction was limited by its size. This was particularly true of those places which had built workhouses in the early years of the eighteenth century without making any allowance for a growth in the population of the town. Thus at Barking, in 1774, it was reported that " the present workhouse is very inconvenient and so small, that it will not contain One Third Part of the Poor of the said Parish, and that there are now One Hundred and Eighty poor Persons, who are relieved by the Parish, more than can be received into the said workhouse."[59]

Lastly, even when a parish was equipped with an adequate workhouse, some of the Poor, through fraud or favour, would always contrive to receive relief outside. Thus, at Maidstone, it was reported that many of the poor of the parish, despite the establishment of a workhouse,

" find interest enough to receive their usual weekly Pay, and get themselves excused from living in the House. And this will happen more or less in all great Towns, where the Workhouses are left to the Management of Overseers Annually elected. And, from what I have seen at Maidstone, I conceive it to be a matter of absolute Necessity, that the Direction of a workhouse should be left to some single Person, to be chosen by the Parishioners, and not to a Number of Overseers who are more liable to a great variety of Application in Favour of particular Persons among the Poor, and more likely to act in an arbitrary way in the Management of the House, than any single elective Person will presume to do. By these means too, the Appointment and choice of the Work in which the Poor are to be employed, will be carried on in a regular and uniform Manner, and not left to the Humour and Interest of Annual Officers, to be charg'd and alter'd as they shall please ; for different Overseers will have different Interests ; and where the Direction is left to them, it will probably happen, as it has in Fact here in Maidstone, that the Poor shall be one Year employ'd in the Linnen, and another in the Woollen Manufactury, and this merely as it suits the Interests of the Managers."[60]

In all these ways the control of the workhouse by the parish officers appears to have offered opportunities for considerable abuse, of which, in many cases, they were not slow to take advantage.

The figures returned by the Parliamentary inquiry of 1776 show that even in towns and parishes which possessed workhouses various sums were still laid out every year for out-door relief. These returns are classified into " hundreds," " cities," " towns," and " parishes not under any particular act." The sums given in out-door relief by parishes which possessed workhouses varied greatly ; they might be but an insignificant fraction of the whole, and in this case the workhouse was evidently being made a condition of relief except in sickness and other extreme cases. Or they might be a considerable proportion of the whole expenditure on the Poor, in which event the workhouse test was obviously not being applied. In the majority of cases more was spent on the workhouse than on outdoor relief in the parishes or towns reviewed in the report of 1776, but the amounts spent on out-door relief were by no means negligible.

In the latter half of the eighteenth century the number of complaints caused by the failure of the parishes " to set the Poor on work " in an effective manner increased markedly.   Men had not abandoned the attractive hope of employing profitably the able Poor, but they were beginning to doubt, most seriously, whether the small unit of the parish would ever be able to achieve this end. In 1760 J. Tucker put forward a plan advocating the establishment of Hundred Houses, while a few years before Fielding had drawn up a plan by which all the Poor of Middlesex might be collected and employed at a central point.   In 1765, another scheme was put forward by an M.P., who suggested that each county should be divided into convenient districts for the purpose of Poor Law administration.   Indeed most of the tracts compiled about this time advocated some larger and more uniform area for this purpose than the historical organization of the parish.

Nor were these new theories and schemes merely confined to paper, for in East Anglia large Hundred Houses were actually founded, with the intention of replacing the small parish workhouses of the past. These houses were all founded by special act of Parliament ; for instance, the Hundred of Colnois and Carlford was first incorporated by 29 Geo. II. and in the year 4 Geo. III. the Hundreds of Blything, Bosmere and Claydon, and Loddon and Clavering, all applied to Parliament for similar powers, which were granted. By these schemes it was proposed to unite all the parishes in the Hundred for the purpose of managing the Poor. One House of Industry, as the new buildings were to be called, was to be built in every Hundred.   These houses were specially planned to meet the needs for which they were intended, and as a consequence were much more suitable for that purpose than the old-fashioned type of workhouse.   They were to be controlled by a board of Governors who were to appoint, pay, and supervise the salaried officers of the house. In them children and old people were to be well looked after, and employment was to be found for the able. The report of 1775 gives the work done in the House of Industry at Blything as follows : " Employed in spinning hemp, carding and spinning wool, weaving woollen and linen cloth for the use of the House, knitting stockings, mending shoes, etc., and in cultivating the land and garden." By such means the House earned £290 15s. 5d. in 1772 and £286 18s. 0d. in the year following. At Loddon and Clavering they had " 9 acres of land, 3 of which are used as a garden for raising greens and vegetables for the house ; the able women, most of them in for bastardy, are employed in washing, getting up of linen, nursery, etc." But by these means the House managed to earn only £101 17s. 8d. in 1772, while the total amount raised by the Poor Rates amounted to £2,132 6s. 5d.[61]

These Hundred Houses appear to have been started partly to ensure better provision for the Poor, and partly in the interests of efficiency. The petitions presented to the House of Commons asking for incorporation give about equal prominence to both objects. But each Hundred stresses the fact that the rates are increasing, and that better organized Hundred Houses would be likely to check them. Thus the Hundreds of East and West Flegg, in Norfolk, stated

> " That the Poor are considerably increased within the Parishes of the said Hundreds, that Seven Years ago he took an Account of the Average Expenditure of maintaining the Poor within the said Hundreds for Seven Years preceding that Time, which amounted to about £700 a Year ; that Two Months ago he took the like Account for the last Seven Years, and finds that the Expense is about £1,150."[62]

When Bosmere and Claydon petitioned to be incorporated, in 1764, they produced as one of their witnesses the Treasurer of the Hundred of Colneis and Carlford, the first Hundred to be incorporated, and he

" Produced an Account of the Money received from the several Parishes within the said Hundred for the last four Years (being a medium of their Assessment for the Relief of the Poor for the Seven preceding Years) according to the direction of the Act of Parliament for incorporating these Hundreds, amounting in the whole to the Sum of £6,686–4–7¾, out of which there has been a saving of £2,150–16–7½. And he informed your Committee, That the Poor are much better provided for now than they were before passing the said Act, being decently cloathed and well fed. That within this Period the Poor have earned the Sum of £735–10–11¾, being employed in the manufacture of Hempen Cloth and Twine Spinning."[63]

Another writer, a pamphleteer advocating the establishment of Hundred Houses, gives the following particulars of the House of Industry belonging to the Hundred of Blything.

" The expenses of building and furnishing the House at Bulcamp amounted to £10,000. The annual income of the House is £3,080. The House was fitted up for the reception tion of the Poor at Michaelmas 1766 ; it has saved and paid off £3,000. Here it appears that, though the Poor's Rates in the kingdom have in these years advanced nearly 1s. 9d. in the pound, the Parishes of the House of Blything have not advanced but have saved nearly 2s. 5d. in the pound."[64]

The same writer paints an enthusiastic picture of the internal conditions prevailing in these Houses of Industry.

" Let us now take a view of the Poor in the House of Industry. And here the assessment of every parish being precisely fixed and uniformly the same, precludes every possible advantage to penurious parsimony and obviates every inducement to injurious and oppressive treatment and this is the foundation of every advantage they enjoy. . . . . This care first discovers itself in an attention to their health. Benignity of air and soil first determined the situation of the House ; and the same idea directed its construction, thro' every apartment ; where spaciousness and continual undulation of the purest breath of Heaven remove the causes of vitiated air, and obviate the effects of nauseous and putrid accumulation. But as the human frame, not withstanding all precaution, is obnoxious to distempers, Infirmaries are provided at a proper distance, that the disease may not be communicated to others. . . . The happy effects of this care appears from hence, that on the 19th of December last in the House at Shepmeadow of 262 Poor not one was sick, on the 20th in the House at Bulcamp of 340 only one was slightly indisposed, on the 21st in the House at Heckingham of 252 not one.

" As soon as they are removed from their miserable cottages, and received into the hospitable mansion, they are stript of their filthy rags, made perfectly clean and decently habited, before they are admitted to join the family ; and ever afterwards cleanliness is indispensibly required. At breakfast, dinner and supper they are all assembled by the ringing of a bell, in the common hall, where they are provided with wholesome and well dressed food, and proper for their station in life and in liberal abundance. . . . Their beds are good, well covered and clean ; everything around them is clean. The house in every department and all its inmates neat to a degree that surprises. One circumstance in their lodging is worthy of notice. . . . Every married couple has a bed and room distinct and appropriated to themselves, which they have the liberty to lock up if they please, to retire to it when they please, undisturb'd, unintruded upon by others ; and their children, if young, are lodg'd in the same or adjoining apartment, under the immediate care of their parents. Of the aged no labour is required . . . to them the doors are always open, and whenever inclination and the weather tempts them abroad, and their strength permits, all proper indulgence is allowed. . . . In the Bulcamp House they manufacture every article of dress, hats excepted, and all the linen used in the House ; and to incourage their industry each receives two-pence in the shilling of what he earns ; and all more than sixty years of age one half. The children are at school from three to five years old ; from that age, during their stay in the House, they are allotted hours in the workroom."[64]

The language used in the above description is flowery, and everything is portrayed in the brightest colours. But the writer does not stand alone in his commendation of these Houses of Industry. Eden, who can usually be relied on to give an accurate account, also speaks favourably of the cleanliness, airiness, and general good management of these Houses. Certainly they appear to have marked a distinct advance on the former workhouses, even those belonging to large corporations.

They were, however, confined to East Anglia, and it is to be doubted whether they were of much assistance in checking the pauperisation of the district. As the same eulogistic writer says, " They are now as fond of the House as ever they were adverse to it but this may be carried too far ; prudence directs us to cultivate in the lowest minds a conscious sense of the superiority of honest industry, and a repugnance to any dependence but on the labour of their own hands." Their later history was not so satisfactory as the promoters of the enterprise had hoped ; the gentlemen of the Committee early lost interest in the management of the house, and failed to attend meetings. The result was that the conduct of business fell into the hands of the permanent officials, who, owing to a low rate of pay and a mean social status, tended to be unequal to the strain imposed upon them. Like the incorporation of the town parishes of an earlier date, the incorporation of the rural Hundreds also failed, and the fate of Colnois and Carlford was no better than that of Bristol, despite the hundred years of experience that divided them.

But this failure was still hidden in the future when, in 1782, Thomas Gilbert managed to steer an Act through Parliament, by which parishes were granted a permissive right to join together to build houses for the reception of the aged and for children. The able-bodied were to be found work outside the house, and if they refused to do it were to be sent to a House of Correction. In this Act also the real power was taken out of the hands of the parish officers and entrusted to a committee of the neighbouring gentry. This Act marked the beginning of a new epoch in several particulars. In part it was due to the new wave of humanitarian feeling which swept over England at the end of the century ; the idea of confining the aged and the very young in the dens of horror, which the pamphleteers revealed many of the workhouses to be, was repugnant to this new sentiment. Then again, after the seventies, prices began to rise and the value of real wages to fall, with the result that people felt that it was not idleness and a love of luxury, but real want that drove the Poor to the parish, and the result of this conviction was the desire to provide better accommodation for the deserving pauper. Eden, a little later, by collecting actual budgets, showed how few poor families were able to live on their earnings. Lastly this Act gave legal recognition to the unsuitability of the parish officer to manage the entire business of poor relief and employment. The intense parochialism which had reigned from the Restoration was nearly over.

Thus a hundred and fifty years of continual effort to evolve some scheme for employing the Poor produced no reward. Success sometimes crowned the endeavours of an individual parish for a period of years, but in the end slackness and corruption once more prevailed. For this failure contemporaries blamed the inertia of the parish officers, and we have seen that in many instances their strictures were deserved. But of all the problems that engage the attention of the social reformer, that of employing the unemployed so that their labour may produce an immediate profit, is, as this age knows well, one of the most difficult. Certainly it was quite beyond the capabilities of the untrained, annual, unpaid overseer. For the brutality with which the eighteenth century workhouse, with its promise of stench and starvation, was used to reduce the rates, and for the callousness which allowed the parishes to hand over their helpless Poor to the unrestrained mercies of a contractor, we can have only condemnation ; but for their failure to employ the Poor according to the 43 Eliz. c 2., there is no one in a position to cast the first stone.

CHAPTER V

THE EFFECT OF THE PAROCHIAL ADMINISTRA-
TION OF THE LAW ON THE STATE OF THE POOR.

THE continual difficulties and ultimate failure which
attended every parochial experiment to employ the
able Poor, left a heavy burden on the ratepayers. We
have seen that in the field of out-door relief the overseers achieved a qualified success, but the expense of
these activities, unbalanced as they were by any receipts
from the earnings of the able Poor, alarmed the body of
the ratepayers. The overseers and churchwardens
therefore, having neither the time nor the skill, nor
frequently the wish, to contrive the most economical
methods of administration, developed a fierce protective
instinct against any one who might " bring a charge on
the parish." This instinct for self-protection manifested
itself in different directions, all equally marked by a
callous disregard for humanity when the interests of
their parishes were involved.

That each parish should have some machinery for
defining its individual responsibility seemed to contemporaries highly reasonable. Hence, in 1662, the
Restoration Parliament passed the 13 and 14 Car. II,
c12, familiarly known as the Act of Settlements, which
proved the pivot around which the administration of
poor relief was destined to swing for nearly two centuries.
This Act gave to the overseers, with the consent of two
justices, the right to remove by justices' warrant any
" person or persons coming so to settle themselves as
aforesaid in any Tenement under the yearly value of
Ten Pounds," if they judged that the intruders were
" likely to be chargeable to the Parish." Such persons

were to be removed within forty days to " such Parish where he or they were last legally settled either as a Native, Soujoner, Householder, Apprentice or Servant for the space of Forty Days at the least." This practice of removing the Poor back to their own parish was by no means new ; it had been in operation at least since the 43 Eliz. c.2. had ordered that every Poor person was to be provided with relief or employment by his own parish, and in origin went back to the vagrancy laws of Richard II. and the early Tudors.[1] But though settlement cases were by no means unknown before 1662, they were not so frequent as they afterwards became, for while each parish could still find work and food for the greater number of its parishioners, there was not the same impetus to drive them to seek settlements elsewhere. The great difference between the old customary law and the new enactment lay in its scope. For where, formerly, individuals were frequently removed by Quarter Sessions, now the great majority of the working class were brought within its power by their financial inability to rent a tenement worth £10, as until the close of the next century the average rural labourer never paid more than £3 for his cottage. Also the shortness of the period which was required to gain a settlement left the overseer little time for discretion.

The eagerness with which parishes availed themselves of the right to remove strangers led to much litigation before Quarter Sessions, with whom, by the new Act, lay the right of appeal, and the ingenuity that was shown to circumvent the law forced Parliament to pass further Acts, stopping up the loop-holes that practice made evident. A favourite device was for a poor person to slip into a parish and there remain hidden until the forty days required for a settlement had elapsed.[2] Accordingly, by the 1 Jac. II, c. 17, it was enacted that the forty days " shall be accounted from the time of his or her Delivery of a Notice in Writing of the house of his or her Abode, and the Number of his or her Family, if he or she have any, to one of the Churchwardens or Overseers of the said Parish." In 1693, it was further decreed that the said notice should date from the time of its being read in the parish church at divine service. Consequently, after these two Acts, the gaining of a settlement by the publication of a notice in writing became impossible unless a man or woman could give security that he or she would not become chargeable, and the majority of settlements were gained in other ways. Children inherited their father's settlement until they reached the age of seven, when they might acquire one of their own ; women gained a settlement by marriage, while the Act of 1693 defined the other means of gaining a settlement in a given parish as being by apprenticeship, by being hired as a servant for a year, by executing some public parochial office for a year, or by the payment of parochial rates. Anybody who did not fall into one or other of these categories, and who failed to rent a tenement worth £10 per year, or to give security, might, at the discretion of the overseers acting through the justices, be removed. Other small legal changes took place early in the next century to prevent fraudulent settlements being acquired by the purchase of small parcels of land, since a man could not be removed from his own freehold ; but these were not of very general application. It is, however, interesting to note that already the parishes were using every means at their command to shuffle their chargeable poor on to other parishes. Such was the framework of the law as far as it was concerned with the settlement and removal of persons likely to be chargeable. Illustrations of the way in which it worked can be found in any collection of Quarter Session papers, or in the overseer's accounts of any parish.

The first question to be settled by the parish officers was, who were to be removed. Except in a very small country parish, it was manifestly impossible to move every intruder who rented a tenement worth less than £10 a year, for if this law had been exercised in its entirety, it would have been impossible for the labouring poor of England to have moved their place of residence. But this was not the case, and in practice there was a very considerable movement throughout the period. Accordingly, the overseers concentrated their efforts on securing the removal of these classes of persons whom experience had shown to be least capable of maintaining themselves without relief.

In a country district the type of wage earner most likely to fall into distress was the married labourer overburdened with children, because his wages, even with what his wife could earn, often proved insufficient to maintain a family of small children, if he had no other resources than his labour.[3] Next came the unmarried women, who had not gone into service, and relied on keeping themselves by spinning, or by day labour for the farmers. Many of these women were widows, or had dependent children to support. Unmarried labourers, however, if they had their health and strength, could always earn enough to support themselves without any assistance from the rates. Consequently, they were but little molested by the overseers. The Cambridgeshire Quarter Sessions records show that the parish officers of that county did, in fact, make some rough differentiation between the various types of poor who intruded into their sphere. Between 1699 and 1715 there were one hundred and sixty-two settlement cases entered in the books. Of these, sixty-three were married couples, with or without children, as the case might be, thirty-three single women, fourteen widows with children, and twelve unencumbered widows. Twenty-three were children, both bastards and orphans, and only seventeen were men. Therefore, sixty-three married couples and fifty-nine women of various descriptions were moved during these years, as opposed to seventeen single men. From 1716-32 there were two hundred and nine cases of removal recorded, of which eighty-one were married couples, forty-two women, twelve widows, forty-one children, and thirty-three single men. From 1736-1749 inclusive, there were one hundred and sixty-one cases, of which eighty were married couples, thirty-one women, twenty-one widows—the majority of whom had children—thirteen children, and only sixteen single men. So, out of a total of five hundred and thirty-two persons moved during these years, two hundred and twenty-four were married couples, one hundred and sixty-five women of all classes, seventy-seven children, and sixty-six single men. The warrants of removal which have survived among the Dunstable parish papers point to the same conclusion. Sixty-two warrants of removal, from 1692-1766, show that the same type of person was most frequently moved here, as well as in Cambridge-shire. There were twenty-four married couples, nineteen single women, ten men, three women with children, and six children. Here, too, out of a total of sixty-two, only ten single men were moved, and once again the number of married couples removed was greater than that of any other one class.

In districts where the population contained a greater urban element, the proportions were somewhat different. In manufacture the married labourer was rather at an advantage than otherwise, for he could draw on the labour of his wife and children to help him with the subsidiary work of his craft. It was the women following poor trades, and the young children, who were most likely to bring a charge on the parish. Consequently, they formed the group which received most attention from the parish officers. In Middlesex, where the influence of London was predominant, from 1690–8, out of two hundred and twelve persons moved, there were nine widows, forty-seven women with children, forty-nine women, fifty-six children, forty married couples, and eleven single men. From 1699-1709, out of two hundred and sixty-five persons moved, there were eighty-one childless women of various descriptions, fifty-nine others who were burdened with children, forty-seven children, fifty-eight married couples, and twenty men. In this case, too, the number of men moved was negligible, while the proportion of married couples is much less than it was in an agricultural area. Evidently the parish officers were most suspicious of the unattached women, whether they were burdened with children or not.

There is plenty of evidence to prove that the parish officers tended to leave strangers who intruded on their parish unmolested, if they neither attempted to gain a settlement by the delivery of a notice in writing, nor appeared likely to become chargeable in the near future. If, however, through accident or death the chief bread-winner of the family was rendered useless, the overseers awakened from their lethargy, and promptly removed the unfortunate family back to its legal settlement.[4] Such a practice was common, and is well illustrated by the following extract :

> " John Flye was last legally settled at Putney Parish, and that he afterwards married the said Frances at New Brentwood and died there but never gave any notice in writing of his abode and the number of his family as by law required ; it is therefore ordered that the said Frances and her two children be conveyed to Putney and left in the care of the churchwardens and overseers of the Poor of that Parish."

There must have been many cases where a man or a family, who gave no notice in writing and did nothing to gain a legal settlement, was tolerated until the husband died or fell on evil times. On the other hand, persons who might be expected to breed a charge on the parish were removed out immediately. A woman with dependent children was always likely to be removed as speedily as possible, as, for instance when, on 18th July, 1671, the North Riding Court of Quarter Sessions recorded, " for that it appeared that a woman and her 3 young children have lately come to Danby, and are likely to be chargeable, and that her husband's last lawful settlement was at Bilsdayle : Ordered that the Overseer of Danby do remove her and her children to Bilsdayle there to be settled."[6]

Besides the evidence drawn from warrants of removal and the reports of cases, contemporary writers bear witness to the same fact, though, for the main part, they deal with the more obvious case of the married labourer, and ignore that of the single woman. Even Howlett, who thought the operation of the settlement laws comparatively harmless, was forced to admit that once a man was married his period for wandering had come to an end, and that henceforth he would have to remain in his own settlement. Alcock says : " But the forced and expensive way of relieving the Poor has put many gentlemen and parishes upon contriving all possible methods of lessening their number, particularly by discouraging and sometimes binding poor persons from marrying when they appear likely to become chargeable, and thereby preventing an increase of useful labourers."[7] This he states, not as a matter of controversy, but as an obvious fact that would be allowed by everyone. He attributes it, moreover, solely to the working of the Poor Law. " When a minister marries a couple, tho' but a poor couple, he rightly prays ' that they may be fruitful in procreation of children.' But many of the Parishioners pray for the very contrary, and perhaps complain of him for marrying Persons, that, should they have a family of Children, might likely become chargeable."[7]

Therefore when a person belonging to one of these suspected categories came into a strange parish, or when the chief wage earner of a poor family which had no settlement either died or absconded, the overseers bestirred themselves to get a warrant for their removal. The first step was to take the potential pauper before the next two justices, in order that he or she might be examined on oath as to his or her last place of settlement.

Such examinations are interesting documents, often giving many details as to the past life of the person interrogated, as, for instance: " The voluntary Examination of Anne Slater as to her last legal Place of Settlement. Taken before us Two of his Majesty's Justices of the Peace for the sd County the 7th Day of May 1770. This Examinant, on her Oath saith she was Married about Two years ago to Robert Slater, and that She has often heard her sd Husband say his Settlement was in London in ye parish of St. Catherine's and she father saith That her Husband gained his sd Settlement by Apprenticeship to Mr. George, Wheeler of Red Cross Street, and that he served part of his sd Apprenticeship in ye sd Street, but That his sd Master removed unto ye parish of St. Catherine's near ye Tower, and That He ye sd Robert Slater served ye Latter part of his Time wth his sd Master in ye sd Parish of St. Catherine's. . . . This Examt further saith that her sd Husband has Run away from Her, and left her and her Child Elizth aged 9 Weeks chargeable to ye Parish of Dunstable in ye County of Bedford. And she saith That she don't believe her sd Husband has gained a Settlement Elsewhere than in St. Catherine's aforesaid."[8] Payments for taking persons before the justices to be examined, and for obtaining a warrant of removal, occur frequently in the overseer's accounts,[9] as when the parish of Westbury spent " goeing to the Justice with ye Widd:Barnet and removing her..oo–o3–oo." A removal to a distant parish was naturally more costly ; in 1686 the parish " disburst in Removeing a bastard child to Wales by order of ye Justice and for hireing man and A nurse to go with it besides myselfe and for horse and expences the whole charge I was out is—o2–o2–o6."[10] The whole transaction was then entered up in the Order Book of the Sessions, to the effect that the said pauper had been removed on complaint of the overseers and in accordance with the warrant made by two justices of the peace, and that the said warrant " not being appealled against is confirmed." The removal was then legal and complete.

The 12 & 13 Car. 2 c. gave the right of appeal to Quarter Sessions if any persons felt themselves aggrieved by an order of removal. This right was freely exercised, though, apparently, only by the parish officials, and not by the paupers themselves, who were seldom able to stand the expense of an appeal. Accordingly it was quite usual for a parish to lodge an appeal at Quarter Sessions, when the pauper was delivered back to his own parish, on the ground that a mistake had been made, and that it was not his last place of settlement, and was, therefore, under no obligation to receive him. Such appeals may be divided into two classes according to their motive. One type arose from the difficulty of deciding what the law was with regard to any particular case. The other arose from the habit of some parishes of removing persons, who were trying to obtain a settlement in their parish, to what they supposed was their last place of settlement, on very scanty evidence of the correctness of that supposition.

In some cases the law was so complex and involved that both parishes might have good grounds for thinking themselves right. Then the case would be brought before Quarter Sessions, where the Justices would do their best to interpret the law. Some cases, however, proved too knotty to be solved easily, and private letters would be exchanged before the Sessions met, or the leading man in the parish would write to a justice, who was a friend of his, to know if he could throw any light on the subject by way of precedent. Occasionally, when the justices were unable to come to any decision, the question was referred to the Judges of Assize to know their opinion. In the Cambridgeshire Quarter Session papers there are several instances of a case having been respited until the judges could be consulted in this way. Therefore it seems fair to say that in many cases appeals were brought before Quarter Sessions because, owing to the complexity of the law, parish officers simply did not know how they stood.

In other instances the parish officials appear to be trying to get rid of persons who had intruded into the parish, regardless of the question whether the parish to which they removed them had any legal responsibility for them. For in some cases as many as three different appeals were brought before Sessions over the same pauper. In instances where the same person was the subject of more than one appeal, such appeals were usually within the same county, and very frequently even within the same town. For example, at the 17th January Sessions of the Cambridgeshire Justices the parish of Freckenham appealed against a warrant granted by Sir John Cotton and J. Milliscent, Esq., for the removal of Thomas Cole, his wife, and children, from Lanwade to Freckenham as the suggested place of their last legal settlement. After a full hearing of both sides, it was decided that the warrant should be quashed and the Coles " sent back to the parish of Lanwade," there to be provided for according to law. Whether the parish of Lanwade thought it had been injured, or whether the Coles were an expensive family, does not appear in the record, but at any rate Lanwade made another attempt to shift them. In the entries for 1st of May, 1701, there is an appeal from the parish of Wood Ditton against an order granted by Sir John Cotton and Anthony Thomson for the removing of the whole Cole family thither from Lanwade, as the suggested place of their last legal settlement. The warrant was again quashed, and they were returned to the parish of Lanwade to be provided for according to law. Lanwade did not, however, give up the struggle, and at the next sessions, on the 17th of July, there is an appeal by the parish of Dullingham against a warrant dated the 3rd of May, for the removal of Thomas Cole, his wife, and family from Lanwade to Dullingham, as the suggested place of their last legal settlement. The warrant was again quashed, and this time the Court ordered that they " be sent back to Lanwade there to be received as a settled inhabitant."

It is in the various parish account books that the best account of the costs of these appeals or " Tryals " can be found. They appear to have cost a parish several pounds each, but, in Cambridge at all events, the general sum awarded for costs was about thirty shillings. The parishes, however, had to pay for producing witnesses and for the personal charges of the overseer, as well as for the lawyers' expenses.

Sometimes these accounts go into considerable detail as to how the money was expended, and in the poor accounts for Hawkshead, a village in a remote part of Lancashire, the following items appear under a neat heading : " An Acct w^h was spent ab^t Clarah Brampht setlem^t in Whitehāv.

" Impm 2 horses to Grarthw^t   1–0
      „   2   „   „ Whitehaven   ..   7–6
To Ad. Walker for her Entertainment   ..   1–6
To James Godfey „   „   „   0–6
Spent in our Journey to Whitehaven   ..   8–9
An horse 3 times to Graithw^t   1–6
Expences and repairing sadles   1–5
expences to Carlise   11–10
for conveying her to Whitehaven   9–10
Ent^rtainmn^t for man and horse at Carlise
      (and other lawyer expences filing bills
      affidavits etc.)   ..   ..   ..   £1–15–10."[11]

Accounts of a similar nature may be found scattered up and down in various parish books, and, as will be seen, they sometimes involved a parish in considerable expenditure. The parish of Dunstable, for instance, " being the Appellants from an Order of Removal of Wilson & Family obtained by the Parish of Bishop's Hatfield in the County of Hertford " were involved in expenses amounting to £29 12s. 9d., as a result of their taking a case to the King's Bench.[12]

The effect of these removals, and particularly of removals that were appealed against and perhaps quashed, must have been most harmful for the person involved. For not only was a person prevented from living where he chose, but if he could not rent a house over the value of £10 by the year, he was plunged into a state of miserable uncertainty in the event of an appeal. As has been seen, some cases of appeal between several parishes over the same pauper dragged on through three, or sometimes through four, sessions. In each case the pauper and his family and goods were moved by warrant, then sent back by order of the Court, then perhaps moved by warrant elsewhere, and in the end possibly moved back again. This meant that, though the person likely to become chargeable might not actually be so when the first removal was made, he was very often a pauper in the literal sense of the word before the Court had come to a final decision. For if he were to be thrown from pillar to post for half a year, what chance had he of attaining any material prosperity or of setting up any trade or business? There is a pathetic petition among the Hertford Quarter Session papers which bears witness to the miserable state of any person who was the subject of an appeal, and, also, to the difficulty of gaining any foothold in the parish to which such a person had been removed. William Piggot petitioned the Court on the ground that " it is not long since your petitioner was tossed to and fro from the parish of Bennington to Tewin, and from Tewin to Bennington att your petitioner's great charge and trouble although the town of Bennington is the place of nativity of your petitioner whose friends have formerly lived in good repute and creditt in the said parish of Bennington.

" Your petitioner did lately purchase a small cottage of one William Chapman, of Hadly, for the summe of £11–6s, and gave the said Chapman the forty and six shillings in part of payment, and when soe donn, one Daniel Mitchell of Bennington, went to the said Chapman and bought the house out of his hands, and moreover said that rather than your petitioner should inhabit and abide in the said parish of Bennington he would buy all the houses and lands in the parish, so that your petitioner and his wife and children must of force to lye in the streets and perish."[13]   It is, perhaps, not to be wondered that persons who had been removed sometimes wandered back, in spite of the parish officers and the justices, to a parish where they had some prospect of making a living for themselves.   In 1668, the churchwardens of Baldock petitioned the Court to the effect that John Fitzroy, being legally settled in Little Munden, " did privately and without the knowledge and consent of your petitioners, hire a house under the value of £10 per ann. in the said parish of Baldock, he being a poore man and refusing to give security for the discharging of the parish. And further more not withstanding that the said John Fitzroy, had been, by virtue of a warrant by two justices of the peace, removed to the parish of Munden, where he was last legally settled and had promised to abide and continue there, yet contrary to his promise hath returned againe to the said parish of Baldock and there indeavoures still to settle himselfe."[13]   What happened to John Fitzroy is not recorded, though probably he was once more returned to his parish.   There were many like him, who refused to stay in the parish where they had been settled, and wandered back to where their friends were, or whither they fancied their interest to lead them.[14] Accordingly, to return to a parish after removal was made an offence under the vagrancy laws, punishable with imprisonment.   In 1702 one Mary Cook was committed to the house of Correction in Cambridge by Sir Samuel Clark for returning from the parish of Decansfield in the county of Derbyshire, the last legal settlement of her husband, whither she had been removed by a warrant under the hands and seals of Sir Samuel Clark and William Russell.   It was ordered by the Court that she be sent back to her settlement, and that " the constables of Chesterton Convey her to Fennstanton in Huntingdon as the first stage of her journey."

There is a sufficiency of evidence to prove that this autocratic and enveloping machinery, which had so much control over the lives of the labouring Poor, was no dead letter. The records of Quarter Sessions, of the parish papers, of King's Bench and the current publications, all combine to show that the parish authorities did avail themselves of the right of removal, and that serious and continual attempts were made to obtain the advantages sanctioned by the 13 & 14 Car., c. 12. There is still more evidence to show that, though the Act inflicted considerable hardship on the least self-supporting branches of the community, it benefited the parishes not a whit, because, while each parish might prevent new persons from settling within its bounds, it was itself prevented from getting rid of its own surplus population. In short, the difficulty was to combine two objects that were incompatible—a settled Poor, and mobile labour. This problem, of allowing some persons to move, while nominally keeping the whole of their social strata to fixed places of abode, synchronized with the first attempt to put down wandering with a strong hand. It was a dilemma for which previous Parliaments had been forced to make some provision, and was a difficulty which, consciously or unconsciously, the parishes set themselves to solve. The method they evolved depended on the use of certificates or testimonials.

In so doing, they were only adapting to their own purpose the machinery suggested by the early vagrant statutes. When merciless laws were being passed by the Tudors against wandering, it was necessary to have some means by which poor, but honest, persons might travel safely upon their lawful occasions. The 5 Eliz., c. 2, had ordered all servants going from one place to another to equip themselves with a testimonial from their late master and the chief officers of the parish, testifying the cause and destination of their journey.

The 13 & 14 Car. 2, c. 12 itself had authorized movement
of a similar character. It had provided that " persons
may goe into any parish to work in time of harvest, or
at any other time so that he carry with him a certificate
from the minister of the parish and one of the churchwardens or one of the overseers that he hath a dwelling
and hath left a family and is a declared inhabitant there."
These provisions were to apply to persons who did not
rent a tenement of £10 a year, or qualify in any other
way for a settlement in the new parish. They were
merely inserted to meet the needs of persons who wished
to reside temporarily outside their own parish, but they
did not contemplate a whole family changing their parish
for a considerable space of time.

In due course, however, it was found that so con-
stricting a law of settlement brought many inconveniences in its wake. At times, whole families found that
their interests could be best served by removing into
another parish, where, perhaps, the demand for certain
types of labour was brisker than in their own. The
overseers of their own parish would have been content
to let them go, but it was feared, or found, that the officers
of the parish to which they wished to move were not so
complaisant. Accordingly, the practice grew up of the
parish officers giving such families a testimonial, acknowledging them to be settled inhabitants, and promising
to take them back at the end of a term of years, or in
the event of their becoming chargeable to the parish into
which they had removed. Such procedure was convenient, and it spread. It was easy, it saved law suits,
and, though it still left the entire power of the law with
the parish officers, could be used to give some flexibility
to the Act of 1662.

These testimonials might be granted permanently,
that is, until a person became chargeable ; or they
might be for a stated period of time. In their nature
they were private agreements between two parishes ;
they would not necessarily bind the granting parish

towards any other parish. Among the Sidbury papers for 1675 is an account, which the parish kept, of persons who were living there by virtue of a certificate. The title page runs, " An Account of the Testimonials Guien & Receiued By the Officers of this p'ish of Sidbury 1675. Rec a certificate for Mary Splat from Officers of the pysh of Honiton barring date ye 23rd of october 1675 & is general to receiue her at any time and is to be found in the Coffer . . . Thos: Pidgeon. Rich: Lecot. Churchwardens. Martha Addem Receiued A certificat for two years. Susanna Todd had A Certificat to Continue for a yeare." Many of the actual certificates still survive among the parish papers. In form they differ very much from parish to parish, some being simple statements of the fact of settlement while others are very elaborate, and have a legal flavour. Such was the practice of the parishes prior to 1697.

In that year Parliament adopted the same plan, and incorporated it in a statute dealing with the regulation and administration of the Poor.[15] It is an interesting speculation to conjecture to what extent it was influenced by the economic conditions of the last few years of the century. From 1693 to the end of the century, the price of corn remained high. During these years, too, the balance of trade turned in favour of England, and by 1697 our exports had reached £6,522,104 10s. 1d., exceeding our imports by £178,944 1s. 0d. Had this increase of trade, combined with the high price of corn, made men more than usually conscious of the inconveniences caused by the attempt to tie labour down to a fixed parochial basis ?

The Act did little more than provide a uniform method of procedure for the granting of certificates, which meant that after 1697, with the consent of the majority of the overseers and churchwardens, labourers could seek work in other parishes without the fear of being removed. For once a parish had received a certificate, no further steps were taken unless the persons actually became chargeable, in which case they were sent back to their parish in the usual way. There remained, however, some doubt as to whether the new certificates were binding on all parishes, or only between the two parishes immediately concerned. Now that it had been made more difficult for a certified man to gain a settlement, the question was important in that the only two ways remaining open to him were to rent a house of above £10 per annum, or to execute some annual parochial office.[16] Also, by a later Act, the apprentice or hired servant of a person residing under a certificate, was prohibited from gaining a settlement.

These restrictions made it important to know exactly to what extent they applied in parishes other than that to which the certificate was given, particularly as it covered all the children of a given family, including those that were born at a later date. Even though the father in the meantime might have gained a fresh settlement for himself, yet the parish which first granted him a certificate would be responsible for the relief of any of his children, provided they had not gained fresh settlements for themselves elsewhere. Such a certificate did not, however, extend to the grandchildren.[17] If a parish certified two persons as being man and wife, and it was afterwards discovered that they had never been married, so that the children were bastards, the certifying parish must provide for them, since a certificate once given was judged to commit the parish that gave it as to all the facts therein mentioned. If, however, a certificated unmarried woman had a child while residing under a certificate, the child was settled where it was born, as was the common rule for bastards, and was not covered by the certificate because "bastard children cannot be considered as the children of the certificated person : they are nobody's children ; they are filii populi."

By 3 G. 2, c. 29 two further alterations were made in the law with regard to certificates. Section Eight orders that the witnesses who attest the execution of such

certificates shall take oath before the justices, who allow
the same that they saw the parish officers sign and seal
the certificate, and the justices shall certify that the said
oath was made before them ; and such certificates shall
be used as evidence without further proof.

Other modifications were also introduced into warrants
for the removal of certificated persons, should they
become chargeable. It was provided that the overseers
and other persons removing a certificated person should
be re-imbursed, by the officers of the parish to which they
were removed, of such reasonable charges as they might
have incurred. These charges, having been first ascer-
tained by a Justice of the Peace of that county to which
the removal took place, were to be levied by distress in
case of default. By means of these precautions, a
parish which received a certificated person was absolutely
protected against the danger of incurring any expense
whatsoever over such a person. Moreover, a certificate
was now an unimpeachable witness in any contested case.
Some parishes were more alive than others to the desir-
ability of keeping down the number of their chargeable
Poor by demanding certificates from all new-comers.
In such parishes regulations, to the effect that " all
Housekeepers be for the future prosecuted who receive
inmates without certificates of their several parishes,"[18]
were common. At Burton it was ordered that " whereas several persons have lately come into this town not
having given to the officers certificates as the law ap-
points, that the officers shall bring for every of them a
warrant of removal."[19]

Such a device, if it were used frequently, was capable
of modifying the law of settlement to a considerable
extent. It is difficult, however, to estimate its influence
in this direction, because there are no means of knowing
to what extent parishes availed themselves of this
liberty. But there is enough evidence to show that the
clause authorizing their use did not become a dead letter.
In an old parish chest, where a number of papers have

survived, sometimes as many as fifty of these certificates
may be found, their dates stretching over a century. At
Northampton the parish officers kept a " Book wherein
the certificates brought and del: to the churchwardens
and Overseers of the Poor of the parish of St. Sepulchres,
in the town of Northampton, touching the settlement of
poor persons, are entered in alphabetical order."[20]
These entries extend from 1702 to 1792. At Dunstable
there is a list of a hundred and forty names, dated the
28th December, 1769, and labelled " Certificates." But
it does not say whether they are certificates given or
received, neither does it say whether it was a complete
list up to date, or whether they were all granted or
received at the same time. The former appears the
more probable. Nor is there any lack of examples of
certificates from other parts of the country. Where the
parish papers have survived at all, there copies of certificates are usually to be found.

Furthermore, in the cases tried before the Court of
King's Bench, the certificated person is a prominent
figure. In all these ways it would appear as if certificates were quite freely granted, at least during the first
part of the century. Eden reports in many places that
in 1796 and 1797 certificates were seldom or never given,
but that was at the end of the century, only a year or two
before all the Poor were put on the footing of the certificated man, and not removed until they were actually
chargeable.

In spite of the fact that they were probably used
fairly constantly, it is doubtful whether these certificates
had much influence in making labour more mobile.
The reason for this was that in many cases the movement
licensed by them was purely local. By virtue of certificates men moved from one parish to another in the same
county, but they rarely went far afield. The majority
of these certificates to be found among the parish papers
record the movement of labourers or petty craftsmen
from one neighbouring parish to another. In many

instances such movements can have done nothing to release more labour for the expanding industries. Probably the workers who went to the growing towns depended more on their ability to earn good wages than on certificates. For where work was plentiful and wages steady, parish officers tended to be less insistent in their demands that every new-comer must have a certificate. Moreover, it was easier for a person intruding into a town to avoid the notice of the overseers than it was in a country place, where each man knew everybody's business. North commented on this fact early in the seventeenth century.

By the end of the seventeenth century, therefore, the parish had procured a complete legal protection against the danger of being swamped by strangers against its will. All those whose economic position was not satisfactory were either forced to produce certificates or were driven forth. But this in itself did not content the instinct of self-preservation, which the theory of parochial responsibility for the Poor had called forth, and overseers adopted other and less legitimate ways of restricting the numbers of their poor parishioners. Since hiring for a year gave a settlement, ratepayers were warned, and sometimes threatened with a fine, against hiring servants for so long a period.[21] The practice grew up of hiring instead for eleven months and three weeks, with the deliberate object of preventing a settlement within the parish. In the same way, since a woman took the settlement of her husband, parishes encouraged marriages between their own pauper women and men from another parish. The other parishes were naturally very reluctant to have women thrust upon them in this way, and if possible they tried to avoid the charge. Thus, " Mr Daly & Mr Bruges went to Knightsbridge to search the Register wither Buxton Fruin was maryed to his new wife that was put upon us and we are like to have her..oo–o2–oo."[22] Where the complicity of the parish officers could be proved the injured parish might sue them for conspiracy, but in many cases it was not necessary for the overseers to implicate themselves directly. It was enough that men should know that such an action on their part would not go unrequited. The Tooting vestry minutes record that " Joseph Wilson of Ratcliffe Highway applied to the vestry for a donation of 40s. in consideration of his marrying Ann Hobert a Widow of this parish which was agreed upon on his producing proofs of his Marriage."[23]

Such methods of reducing the settled inhabitants of a parish were open to severe criticism, even when they were not a legal offence, but, not content with these devices, the overseers regularly victimized the most helpless of their charges, namely, the poor children who for one cause or another had been left to the care of the parish. The lot of poor children in the seventeenth and eighteenth centuries was no easy one at the best, since little was understood of hygiene, or of wholesome diet or childish ailments, while every child over six was expected to contribute something towards its own maintenance. In the worsted manufactory at Norwich " even children earn their bread," while in the candle industry of Frome " children of seven and eight could earn half a crown a week,"[24] and Defoe obviously thought it desirable that little children should " work by the Loom, winding, filling Quills, etc."[25] To assist the children of the Poor to attain an economic independence had been one of the foremost responsibilities laid on the parishes by the 43 Eliz., c. 2. Yet the history of the parish apprentice, like that of the workhouse movement, serves as a further illustration of the way in which the parishes sacrificed the tradition of providing work to the necessity of keeping down the numbers of the poor, and so lowering their poor rates.

Since the Elizabethan statesmen had decided that the best method of dealing with poverty was by a series of preventive measures, it was natural that they should turn to apprenticeship as being the best way to equip poor children to face life. For at this date the greater part of the industry of the country was still under the regulation of the gilds, and so it was necessary for a workman to be free of his particular gild before he could legally follow his trade. The chief, though not the only way of obtaining this freedom, was to serve a seven years' apprenticeship under a recognized master. If a man had to work for his living without having done this, he would be handicapped all his life. On the other hand, it was generally felt that if a person were free to follow a trade, having duly served an apprenticeship to that, there was no reasonable excuse on his part for failing to maintain himself. Accordingly it was natural that the 43 Eliz., c. 2 should make due provision for the apprenticeship of such children as might otherwise, through lack of funds or the idleness and depravity of their parents, go unapprenticed. The Act empowered the

> " Churchwardens and Overseers or the greater Part of them, by the Assent of any Two Justices of the Peace aforesaid, to bind any such children, as aforesaid, to be Apprentices, where they shall see convenient, till such Man-child shall come to the Age of four and twenty Years, and such Woman-child to the Age of one and twenty Years, or the time of her Marriage ; the same to be as effectual to all Purposes, as if such Child were of full Age, and by Indenture of Covenant bound himself or herself."

By such methods it was hoped that every child would be provided with a decent means of earning its living, and that as a result poverty would be confined to the sick, impotent, and aged, or to children too small to maintain themselves.

Such a scheme might have been carried out by the parish officers with very little difficulty, had it been to their interests to do so. But, unfortunately, by the Act of 1662, to serve an apprenticeship in a parish was recognized as being one of the authorized means of obtaining a settlement there. Originally no more had been intended by this clause than that a child should have the right to settle and follow a trade where he had received his training. Such a provision was looked upon as being only reasonable, but its results were unexpected, and perverted the whole intention of the law. Once parishes discovered that they could rid themselves of the settlement of a pauper child by placing it out as an apprentice in another parish, they found in this expedient the chief uses of the apprenticeship clauses. To secure this end meant the sacrifice of nearly everything that the Elizabethan legislators had hoped to obtain. Yet this was the road taken. Nothing so clearly marks the great gulf between the Elizabethan conceptions of the functions of the Poor Law and those commonly held from the Restoration onwards, though in theory, on the statute book, the law remained the same; if anything, it was better defined in the latter period. But whereas in the first place its objective had been the prevention of poverty, its latter aim was to prevent a rise in the rates.

The success of this attempt to check the growth of poverty by binding poor children apprentice to various trades depended not only on the way in which the obligation was interpreted and carried out, but also on the place that apprenticeship in general continued to hold in the economic organization of the period. For what was the best method of dealing with a problem in the year 1601 might be completely and utterly out-of-date, and therefore useless, after a hundred or two hundred years. It is therefore necessary to look briefly at the state of ordinary apprenticeship during the same epoch. With the growth of capital, and the spread of industry from the small boroughs and market towns to the country districts, together with the growth of the middleman, the power of the gilds was sapped. Miss Dunlop sums up the position in a phrase. " From 1660 onwards," she writes, " the gilds slowly but perceptibly began to lose ground in the fight." The collapse, however, came more rapidly after 1720. In the sixteenth century, general economic opinion supported the idea of apprenticeship, and the government of the day, working through the Justices of the Peace, was as eager to uphold it for the general good, as were the gilds for their private interests.   But after the Restoration not only were economic conditions different, but ideas, too, were changed, and men were questioning the right of gilds to prohibit a man from exercising a trade, unless he had first served seven years' apprenticeship.   Hence apprenticeship became more and more a distinctive part of the gild machinery, losing its importance as the power of the gilds weakened.   This does not imply that apprenticeship was dead, for the law that required a seven years' apprenticeship was still on the statute book ; and, what is more, the fact was still popular knowledge.[26] If a man tried to establish himself, without having served an apprenticeship, he did so at his peril, the danger being that he might be presented at Quarter Sessions by a man already following that trade, who feared his competition. Presentments of this character are sprinkled up and down the records of any Quarter Sessions ; thus, in 1675, John Warren was charged with " following the trade of a carpenter and not having served as an apprentice seaven years."[27]   But as the eighteenth century wore on, the number of these cases grew less.   Accordingly, apprenticeship was only valuable in so far as it taught a child a trade, by which he could get his living.   Throughout the period, the efficiency of parish apprenticeship as a means of coping with poverty, depended on the way in which it was carried out, and if in actual fact, it did furnish every child so apprenticed with an adequate training in some trade by which it was possible to make a fair living.

There were two methods of effecting such apprenticeship.   One was voluntary on the part of the master, and took the form of a business deal between him and the overseer and churchwarden.   The other was compulsory, the master being forced to take the child if it were bound by the officers of his parish.   These different forms both existed at the same time, and it was a matter of local custom as to which was in force in any particular locality. Generally speaking, compulsory apprenticeship was more common in the rural districts, where there was less opportunity for binding out, than in town parishes, which preferred the voluntary method, although, of course, many exceptions to this rule occur.

With compulsory apprenticeship there was no question of juggling with the law of settlement, since an overseer could only force one of his own parishioners to take a poor child. It was, however, a very unpopular method of providing for such children, and worked with a great deal of friction. If a person to whom such a child was bound could see the faintest hope of release from the burden, he would appeal to the justices at Quarter Sessions, or even refuse flatly to receive the child.

In order to make the law more effective, and to deal with persons who proved contumacious in this respect, the 8 & 9 Wm. III. c. ordained that if anyone refused to receive a child so allotted to him, " Oath thereof being made by one of the Churchwardens or Overseers of the Poor, before any Two of the Justices of the Peace for the County, Liberty, or Riding, he or she shall for every such offence forfeit the sum of Ten pounds." According to the report of the Commissioners of 1834, this practice of fining rather than taking a parish apprentice was still in vogue in many places, even at that date. In many places, indeed, the fines for refusal to take a parish apprentice were regarded as a definite form of revenue. This method of obtaining parish money by appointing persons to offices which were irksome to them, and then levying the statutory fine on their refusal to hold the said office, was not uncommon, especially in the more corrupt parishes. Defoe refers to the practice under the cant name of " birding," that is, picking up fines. It was not extraordinary, therefore, that, given the statutory sanction for levying a fine for refusal to receive an apprentice, such a method should have been used quite deliberately and consciously to raise money. Thus, in 1789, a Mr. John Ellis of Little Sheffield paid to the Overseers of Ecclesall, in lieu of accepting a parish apprentice, £10, which payment in this case was to absolve him from a like necessity for the space of twenty-one years.[28] J. D. Tweedy, the assistant-commissioner for Yorkshire, speaking of the general practice of the county, said,

> "The power of binding parish apprentices, upon an unwilling rate-payer, is very capriciously exercised, and is in many places the ground of just complaint. In several towns it is made a means of raising considerable sums annually, in the shape of fines for refusing to take apprentices. In Leeds one thousand pounds has been raised in this way within the year, and in several places one apprentice has been the means of raising thirty pounds, forty pounds and in one instance fifty pounds."[29]

It is obvious, when legal compulsion could be used in this way, both that the system had become very corrupt, and that the objection on the part of better class persons—such, for instance, as could pay the fine of ten pounds—was very keen. As in most cases the children whom the parish overseers wished to bind out were either workhouse children, who had a reputation for idleness and general undesirability, or the children of paupers and therefore brought from ignorant and often depraved homes, this dislike of receiving them can be easily understood.

How wide an area this compulsory binding covered it is difficult to say. The Commissioner of 1834 shows it to be much more prevalent in some districts than in others. Thus C. H. Maclean, Esq., Assistant Commissioner for part of Middlesex, Surrey, and West Sussex, found it so infrequently practised that he could give but little information on the subject. In Yorkshire it still persisted, but appeared rather to have been continued by the overseers for the sake of the money that the fines for refusing to take a pauper apprentice brought in, than for the sake of the apprenticing of the children. On the other hand, Captain Chapman reported that

> " The practice of binding children at nine years of age compulsorily, that is to say, without consent of child, parents or masters, was very general, and still prevails in many parts of Cornwall, Somerset and Devon, so as to form a leading characteristic in the county."[29]

He also adds that

> " The farmers in general appear adverse to having it done away with . . . and in strictly agricultural parishes the overseers generally consider it in the same light and appear utterly at a loss to advise any expedient for the employment of the children in case the practice was discontinued."[29]

How far this report represents the state of things in the previous century it is impossible to judge accurately. Rural districts are, as a rule, the slowest to change ; and where the Commissioners found compulsory apprenticeship in 1834, there it most probably existed in much the same form in the earlier period. In agricultural districts such apprenticing was definitely a means of providing for a child until it was able to hire itself out as a labourer, and the farmers for their part found such children useful and cheap about the farm. But agricultural and industrial apprenticeship were in reality very different things. In all probability the pauper apprenticed to a farmer had a much better time than the child apprenticed by a premium to a petty craftsman. In towns, however, the burden of a compulsory apprentice would be more felt than by a farmer, who could usually feed and provide for an extra mouth without being unduly oppressed. On the other hand, in towns there would always be more small craftsmen, who for a premium would take a parish apprentice from the next parish, and this method would be less troublesome to arrange, as well as much more popular with the ratepayers, who would not only not be forced to take a child themselves, but who might also hope that all responsibility would be permanently removed from the parish, by the said child gaining a settlement elsewhere.   Accordingly, the tendency would be for compulsory apprenticeship to drop out first in the towns, and to persist longest in the more remote country parishes.

The system of voluntary apprenticeship was much more popular with both the overseers and the ratepayers, for in this case great care was taken to find a master who lived in another parish, with the pleasing result that forty days after the child had gone to its new master its old parish was relieved of all further responsibility for it.   This, and not a desire to provide a training for the young, was the real motive that made the overseers zealous to place out their poor children.[30]   Indeed, as much was commonly stated in the vestry minutes, as for instance :

> " It was Agreed y^t Tho : Kemble uper Churchwarden should dispose of Jno Michaell a nurse Pish boy to a Master y^t should giue bond to discharge ye pish from him & to bind him apprentice to Learne his Art & trade of a painter and that he should Agree with the said Master as cheape as hee could for his soe doeing not exceeding seuaen pounds."[31]

Many details concerning pauper apprenticeship can be gleaned from the indentures themselves, and from the various items recorded in the parish accounts or vestry minutes.   The amount which it cost a parish to put out an apprentice varied greatly both in different parishes and also with different apprentices in the same parish, according to the trade to which they were apprenticed.[32] At Tooting Graveney, near London, the average amount paid was five pounds, though this was not a fixed sum Thus, in 1759, £5 was paid for apprenticing Joseph, son of Sarah Akam, to John Hastings, collar maker, of St. Benet's, Paul's Wharf ; and £5 for John, son of Robert and Elizabeth Gibson, to Johnson, Peruke maker, George Yard, Lombard Street.   In 1739, Walter Bignal was apprenticed to John Lucas, butcher, of Leadenhall

Market, with a premium of £5 ;[33] and two years later another poor boy was apprenticed to a blacksmith of Wimbledon with £5.[33] In 1757, as much as £7 10s. 0d. was paid to apprentice Anne Butler to a ginger bread maker,[33] though five pounds of this premium was found by the Bateman Gift for apprenticing poor children, and only the remainder by the parish from the rates. In 1731 Jonas Smith was apprenticed at a cost of £8 to John North, a carpenter of Little East Cheap ;[33] and in the same year another boy was put out to a farmer with a premium of nine guineas, a really large sum. But the highest premium to be given was £18 " for putting Henry Barmister a Lame Boy apprentice to Wm Deacon Cordwainer of Epsom."[33] Probably on this occasion the boy was put out, and the large premium given, in order that he might get another settlement in a different parish, and so remove all fear of his future chargeability from the parish of Tooting Graveney. On the other hand, Goddard's son, who was apprenticed to a waterman in 1732, was put out with a premium of only £3, which was to be paid within twelve months.[33] Another boy, bound out to a shoemaker of Mitcham, was given the same amount. Thus even in a small parish the sums expended on the putting out of different apprentices might vary considerably, and there appears to have been no hard and fast rule, though in each case a parish would be mainly guided by the demand for labour which existed in the neighbourhood. In this instance the majority of the poor children were put out to some trade in London.[33]

The premiums given in country parishes were, as a rule, less than those paid by parochial officers in towns. At Dunstable, in Bedfordshire, for instance, £3 was the usual sum paid with apprentices, who were not compulsorily bound.[34] When Thomas Meal was placed out with Edward Houst, of Frampstead, husbandman, £3 was paid with him. In the same way £3 was paid with " Cornelius White aged abt twelve yrs " when he was apprenticed to " Richard Porferd of Charter House lane in ye parish of St. Pulkrord wth out " to learn the art of " a tayler." Among the same papers there are also receipts for similar sums, as, for instance,

> " January ye 12th, 1711, Rect then by the hands of Tho Cripps the Summ of Three pounds being in full payment of what I was to have with John Huggins my apprentis I say Recd by me. John Rauen."

In some cases the sum given did not amount even to £3, for another receipt bears witness that

> " Recd. then of Mr. Christopher Oliver the sume of fforty shillings the same being given to me upon the accompts of my takeing Martha Becmon apprentise for six years by Indenture I say recd."[34]

This document is signed 17th June, 1706. Masters who would accept such low premiums must themselves have been unprosperous in trade. In the rural parishes and townships of the north the sums paid out were also small, it being no uncommon thing for less than £2 to be paid out. At Skelmersdale, in Lancashire, out of nineteen parish indentures which survive, from 1728–81, the highest sum given was £5 12s. 0d. to a fustian weaver in 1778. Of the rest £5 was given with a boy apprenticed to a cotton weaver in 1781, and the same sum with a boy put out to a joiner in 1759; in 1748, £4 10s. 0d. was expended in putting out a boy to a Linen weaver. The remainder of the premiums given in no case reached four pounds, while the usual sum was £2 15s. 0d., or even less, particularly with girls bound to " the trade or occupation of a Housewife." Thus one girl was placed out with a premium of fifteen shillings, while another had nothing beyond " one good suit of apparel both Linnen and Woollen," which on the back of the Indenture was described as follows :

" To one Woman's hat ..	..	..	1–0
" To one handkercheff ..	..	..	6
" To one Gonne & covering for stay's		..	5–0
" To one Quilled Coat ..	..	..	2–2
" Stockings ..	..	..	1–0
" To Shoes ..	..	..	3–4
" To 3 yds Yardwide linecloth ..		..	2–3
" To one Yardthick ..	..	..	1–1
" To thread and tape ..	..	..	2

$$16–8^{35}$$

The child in question was " aged twelve years and upwards " and was bound for four years, obviously for the sake of her labour.

Some parishes, by only paying the premium in parts, strove to see that the master did not treat a child so badly that it ran away or died. At Skelmersdale the practice varied. Thomas Abrahams, for example, took a poor boy apprentice for " the sum of One pound Fifteen shillings of lawful Money of great Britain . . . well and truly paid . . . at and upon the Execution hereof." That is, he signed the indentures, received his money and the apprentice at the same time, and went away. In other cases some months were allowed to elapse between the signing of the indentures and the payment of the premium. When Mary Clitheroe was placed out to service, it was arranged that the money, " £2-15-0 of Lawful Money of Great Britain," was to be paid on the 25th day of December, now next ensuing," though the date of the indenture was the second of February. Whether this provision was made to ensure that the child should be decently treated by its new master, or to make certain that it resided long enough under the indenture to gain a settlement in the parish in which it was bound, is not clear. But in several instances this provision for the payment of the premium in a lump sum, but at a date several months after the signing of the indentures, occurs. The majority of the indentures, however, provide for the payment to be spread over several years. Thus when Elizabeth Clitheroe was bound out to be a housewife, it was arranged that "£2-10 of Lawful money" should be paid "to the said Daniel Walsh in a manner herein mentioned, that is to say, the sum of £1-5-0 part thereof the first day of August now next ensueing, the further sum of fifteen shillings on the twenty first day of June now next ensueing and the further sum of ten shillings being the remainder thereof the twenty first day of June, 1751." The date of her binding was the 22nd June, 1749, and therefore the payment stretched over two years, which seems to have been the usual period at Skelmersdale. That this system of deferred payments was really carried out, and did not tend to become a mere formula, is confirmed by the fact that on some of the indentures there is the receipt for the last payment.[35]

Besides the actual cost of the premium a parish had certain other expenses to meet, when it bound out a poor child as apprentice, these being chiefly connected with its outfit. Expenses of this kind were entered up together with the other expenses for the poor in the overseer's accounts. Sometimes considerable sums were paid out for one child ; Westbury, for instance, spent £8 9s. 10d., over one Edward Hatter. This included his binding and outfit.

> "payd John Bramble ye Smith in money with Ned Hatter and expences when he was bound .. £05–05–00
> "Disburst for two suits of apparell, 4 shirts, A Hatt, two payre of shoes and 3 payre of stockings and other necessary for Ned Hatter when he was bound an apprentice .. .. £03–04–10[36]

Thus, though the premium would be the most expensive item of the apprenticeship, the payments for clothes were by no means negligible, and the whole business involved the parish in a considerable outlay.

It is very difficult to say how the system worked in actual practice. Its effectiveness depended on the thoroughness of the training which each child obtained. In so far as the parish apprentice was actually taught a trade it was beneficial and to be commended, while its usefulness varied with the craft to which the child was bound. It is, however, not easy to ascertain how far this was actually the case. The parish accounts and the indentures themselves give abundance of details with regard to the arranging of the apprenticeship, the sort of premiums paid, and the trades to which poor children were apprenticed. But once the premium was paid and the child handed over to its new master, it is difficult to know what happened, for in practice it was nobody's business to find out. This was especially the case when a child was placed out in a strange parish, where it was unknown. If the master took the child largely for the sake of the premium offered with it, he cared little what happened to it, while the overseer, once it had gained its new settlement, no longer felt the slightest responsibility for its future welfare. As for the wider aspect of the case—the need to train the youth of the country so that it should be able to cope with life—that was lost sight of by everyone but a few theorists, who still wrote of the need to provide an adequate training for the children of the poor. The fact that the poor law was run locally for local interests, without any broad national policy behind it, meant that there was no regular machinery to see that pauper apprenticeship was carried out to its intended conclusion, and so there remain no records from which we can see how the system worked. All the evidence that can be collected on this head comes from the tone of the parish papers, and from the minute and order books of Quarter Sessions, with sometimes a stray comment from contemporary writers.

The type of trade to which parish children were usually apprenticed is of the utmost importance when attempting to estimate the success or failure of the movement as

O

a whole. Here again a distinction must be drawn between urban and rural parishes. In the country the majority of the children were placed out with the neighbouring farmers for the sake of their labour, and when they grew up automatically went to swell the ranks of the labourers. Or if not bound to farm service the boys would be apprenticed to the local craftsmen, such as the carpenters, the shoemakers, the tailors, the blacksmiths, or the thatchers. The great probability is that such boys fared no worse than the sons of more prosperous labourers, who had been placed out by their parents. They were taken for the sake of their labour, rather than for the relatively small premiums offered with them, and when their master was in full employment they were worked unmercifully; but that was a fate common to the children of the seventeenth and eighteenth century. That they were often under-fed when times were hard, or went scantily clothed, is also true; but so did the children of the labouring Poor, and in all likelihood there was little to mark off the parish apprentice from the normal village boy. Moreover, once his time was up his knowledge of his craft would be sufficient to allow him to earn as good a living as his neighbours.

The case of the pauper apprentice in a town parish was very much worse. The higher and better paid branches of any trade were filled by the sons of shopkeepers and householders, only leaving those in which a man could earn " very poor bread " to be supplied by the sons of the Poor. As a result such trades tended to become overcrowded, so that the apprentice, even if he were carefully instructed in his craft and served out his time, which few of them did, was apt to find that even as a master he could earn only a bare subsistence. Tooting Graveney, which bound out most of its children with masters living in London, apprenticed its boys to watermen, collar makers, peruke makers, stay makers, press makers, printers, shoe makers, carpenters, tailors, butchers, and its girls to mantua makers, mantle makers,

ginger bread makers, framework knitters.   But most of
the girls were bound out to learn the art of a housewife,
which in practice meant that they became household
drudges.   For what could a girl bound out to a " Linen
Weaver," who probably occupied one or two rooms, learn
that would be of use to her in getting a better place later ?
It was from this class of poor parish girls, who were
thrust at the most impressionable age into poverty-
stricken, and, only too often, degraded surroundings,
that the class of street walkers and pick-pockets was
recruited.   For it was very seldom that such poor girls
were placed in respectable families, since no one, who
could afford any other kind of domestic help, would take
a child who had been brought up either in a workhouse
or in the house of a habitual pauper, because of its
lack of training in habits of industry and obedience.
Other trades to which poor children were apprenticed
were so unpleasant that a supply of labour for them
could be drawn only from the most unfortunate section
of the population.   One of these was catgut spinning,
" a very mean, nasty and stinking trade,"[37] while
another was the notorious trade of the chimney sweep.
For this purpose children were bound out as young as five
and six, so that, being small in person, they could climb
the narrow and constricted chimneys then in use.

Another class of pauper apprentices were those who
were placed out to what may almost in some respects be
looked upon as pauper trades.   Wherever the gilds had
any power left they used it to limit the number of
apprentices a brother might take ; in many cases a
member was not allowed a new apprentice until his old
one had completed four or five years of service.   In this
event it was impossible for a master to take, merely for
the sake of the premiums offered with them, more apprentices than he could train, or than he had work to employ.
But in many of the handicrafts the power of the gilds had
either broken down or had never been fully exercised,
particularly when the manufacture had spread from the

towns to the country districts. Such in several places were the weavers, the various branches of the silk trade, and the stocking makers. When this condition held, there was no power to prevent a poor master from taking as many apprentices as he wanted for the sake of the premium offered, irrespective as to whether he had work enough to do, or whether the trade were already over-crowded. There was the temptation, also, to employ only apprentice labour, which was cheap and easily replaceable, with the result that the trade was over-stocked with journeymen whom nobody wanted to employ. Further, in times of good trade there was the added temptation to a master to accept more appren-tices than he could possibly employ in a slump. As a result of this disorganization, parish officers could always find in these trades masters who, for a premium, would take their pauper children off their hands, and conse-quently pauper labour was poured into those manufac-tures without any regard being paid to the over-stocking of the market, so that eventually it became hardly possible to earn a decent living in such a trade, and the whole trade was slowly pauperized. Many children were apprenticed to weavers with small premiums of four pounds or less. A large number of the boys placed out by Skelmersdale were apprenticed to linen, fustian, and cotton weavers in or near Wigan. In the area round London poor children were bound out to the silk weavers at Spitalfields. As early as 1681 the author of the " Trade of England Revived " speaks of the silk industry of Spitalfields as a pauper industry by reason of the great number of poor children that are apprenticed to it. This trade was very over-crowded, he wrote, " because there hath not been for a long time any other but this to place forth poor men's children, and Parish Boys unto, by which means the poor of this trade have been very numerous who can do nothing else almost having been bred up to it from their youth."[38]. In trades as poor as this, masters who needed money were not hard to find, and they did not demand large premiums. Sarah Palmester, for instance, who was bound by the overseers of Tooting to one David Doctor, a weaver of Spitalfields, had a premium of only £2 10s. 0d. given with her.

Perhaps one of the worst of the pauper trades was that of the stocking-framework knitters. This industry had been centred in and around the same area as that of the silk workers, and had had a charter granted to it in 1663, incorporating it as a company, and thereby allowing it to limit the numbers of apprentices whom a master might take. Its regulations were, however, persistently ignored, and the result was a serious riot, about 1710, in the neighbourhood of Old Street Square, Bunhill Row, and St. Luke's, Shoreditch, where the rioters broke about a hundred frames. Hence some of the masters, notably one Fellowes, moved to Nottingham, where they proceeded to ignore the rules of the company. Fellowes is reported to have had at one time as many as forty-nine apprentices at once, of whom, writes Mr. Felkin," many were bound by their parishes to him ; the practice being to pay at least £5 each to the master on thus getting rid of them." " This system," he continues, " of apprenticing by parishes to the weaving trades throughout the country, besides causing much suffering and demoralization to the oppressed and friendless youths of both sexes, gradually so overloads the trade with wandering unemployed journeymen, as to cause serious riots in various manufacturing populations."[39]. In short, the tendency was for parish children to be apprenticed only to such trades as were already semi-pauperized, or else to some blind alley occupation, such as milk selling or button moulding, which was carried on entirely by this legalized form of child labour, and where there was no possible opening for them when they became adults.[40] Parish apprenticeship, therefore, can only be said to have been effective in so far as it made children self-supporting at an early age, and provided them with maintenance in return for their labour.

Unfortunately the practice, everywhere followed by the overseers, of apprenticing children to masters living in other parishes, left no guarantee that the master would make any effort to teach his apprentice his trade, or even that he would supply him with the reasonable necessaries of life. The only method by which indentures could be discharged was by appeal to Quarter Sessions, and from this source alone come well-nigh endless complaints from apprentices that they are being forced to act as errand boys and drudges instead of being taught their trade, or that they are denied enough food and clothing, and that their lodgings are unspeakably dirty and overcrowded. Numerous, too, are the actual cases of cruelty reported. By law the master was empowered to give his apprentice needful correction, but the limit of what was considered reasonable correction, even in that age of flogging, was repeatedly exceeded by brutal masters. In some cases the ill-treatment which apprentices received was due to deliberate cruelty, but still more often it arose from the habit of masters taking apprentices when they had neither the work for them to do nor the means of providing them with an adequate maintenance. The cause of this behaviour was twofold. In the first place, when trade was good there was the temptation to take more apprentices than could be trained, or even provided for in normal times, for the sake of obtaining cheap labour. In the second, the premiums offered by the parish were very often more than an insolvent craftsman could resist, particularly as it was well known that the parish would make no further inquiries, once the apprentice had gained a settlement elsewhere. When an apprentice had friends who were able to give him some help he might appeal to Quarter Sessions to be discharged from his indenture, and it is from these appeals that our knowledge of the various ills from which the class as a whole was apt to suffer, is drawn. For instance,

" Order discharging James Callender from his apprentice ship with James Owne, tailor, of the parish of St. Andrew's

Holborn. Callender had been apprenticed by the church-wardens of St. Pancras to Ownn, who had received him with £5 in money and two suits of clothes. During the last year Owen had very little work and the apprentice was not provided for. Owen had undertaken to find another master for him, but he had been taken to the Compter, and was now a prisoner in the Fleet Prison."[41]

But until a discharge could be obtained such an apprentice would be condemned to range up and down the streets, begging or pilfering or doing odd jobs, in order to keep himself from starvation. Such cases were mere commonplaces, especially in London, where the uncertainties of life were greater than in the small provincial towns.

Our actual knowledge of the pauper apprentices is scanty, because an ignorant child of twelve, separated from its friends and absolutely at the mercy of its master, had no real chance of making its wrongs known. Hence, while there are appeals in plenty for the cancellation of indentures, very few of them deal with parish apprentices ; yet these latter being more defenceless and often apprenticed to poorer trades, it is not reasonable to suppose that they were better treated than the ordinary child who was apprenticed by his friends, on whom he could rely in time of necessity. These cases record many instances of neglect and cruelty to children who had been bound out by their friends. Thus one Henry Harding,who had been bound apprentice to Thomas Norman, of Tring, scrivener, deposed before the justices that his master, " had dobbed him on the breast with his cane and almost beat the breathe out of his body for answering him the question which he had asked him," and on the following day he " gave him a box on the ears almost ready to beate him down because he asked him leave to go and see his father who was at that time very sick and like to dye."[42] Even this was comparatively mild treatment, compared with that meted out to some apprentices. Young girls were always particularly defenceless, and were the victims in some of the worst cases. For instance one Richard Price, a tobacco pipe maker, was accused by " His apprentice Anne Tutchbury, who upon her oath accuses him of tyeing her with a line by the wrists and thumb upp to a beame and there unreasonably beat her." Even to appeal to the justices was not always to secure a discharge, for the Court was apt to take a broad view of what constituted reasonable correction. In one instance that came before the Middlesex justices a silk stocking frame worker, who was stated to have barbarously ill-used and assaulted his apprentice, and "then and there beat him cruelly and in a manner exceeding the limits of true chastisement so that his life was dispaired off," was merely fined 3s. 4d., which he paid in court ; but the indentures were not cancelled.[43] In another instance, however, a boy who had been apprenticed to a surgeon of Clerkenwell was discharged of his indentures upon proof that he was not taught the said art, but compelled to be " a rope dancer, tumbler, and jack pudding."[44] When children who had friends to protect them, and the right to appeal to the justices, were subjected to such callous treatment or to such a perversion of the aims for which they had been apprenticed, it is not likely that the lot of the parish apprentice was a particularly happy one. In the majority of cases they would be so helpless that unless the overseers who apprenticed them actually did supervise the way in which they were treated, or unless they were not sent out of the parish where their friends lived, there was little likelihood that they would ever have the knowledge, the money, or the courage to appeal to Quarter Sessions. To run away was the easier course. Therefore it is not surprising that the pauper apprentice figures so little in the Quarter Session records. Nor does this absence mean that all was well with the child. But where the ordinary system was subject to so many abuses, pauper apprenticeship, robbed for the most part of even the usual restraints, must have been worse ; in an age when a woman who had murdered her apprentice by beating her immoderately received a pardon, public opinion was not easily stirred.[45] Thus in many cases the sole refuge of the unfortunate apprentice was to run away. It is impossible to conjecture, even roughly, the number who never served out their bondage, but it was large, and the runaway apprentice was a common eighteenth century figure. Very often the master made no effort to recover the truant, and indeed in some cases he seems to have adopted deliberately a policy of cruelty, with the idea of driving the helpless child away, so that having received the full premium, he might no longer be troubled with its maintenance. Moreover, when business was slack the apprentices of poor men were forced to wander up and down the streets picking up what sustenance they could, and it needed but little persuasion to turn these boys into regular vagrants, or into confirmed thieves.

Another cause which helped to swell the numbers of the runaway apprentices was the length of the period for which they were bound. The provision that a girl should be bound until she attained the age of twenty-one or married, and that a boy should serve until he was twenty-four, dated from the time when compulsory binding out was the usual method of disposing of parish children. When a ratepayer was compelled to take children which he did not want, and at an age when their services were of little value, it seemed only just that he should be recompensed by retaining them when they were most useful to him. But to be kept in what approximated to a form of slavery, when old enough to earn his own living, was intolerable to an apprentice, whose master had received a premium in the first case, who for years had had the benefit of his labour, and to whom he was bound by no debt of gratitude. As a result many apprentices ran away just when their services were of value to their master. In this case an attempt was usually made to recover them, and advertisements for this purpose were common. If caught the apprentice was liable to be imprisoned in the House of Correction ; the following warrant gives a vivid picture of the treatment he might expect there.

" Whereas complaint hath this daye beene made unto me, Edward Wingate, Esq. one of the king's Majesty's justice of the peace in the county abovesaid, that Ralph Pearte, an apprentice to William Rolf of Upper Holloway, in the parish of Islington, county Middlesex, butcher, being putt out by the overseere of the poore of Wheathamstead, and by indenture bound unto the said Rolfe for seven years not yet expired. And that he the said Ralphe Pearte remaines an idle dissolute fellow now at Wheathamstead, being run away from his said master, and also guilty of severall other greate misbeehaviors both against Sir John Garrett, knt and bart., Edward Christmas of Wheathamstead, brewer, and others, in taking their wood and selling it. All which offences the said Ralphe Pearte being brought before me by the Constable of Wheathamstead stands charged with. These are, therefore, to will and require you to receive the sayd Ralph Pearte and hym safely to keep in your house of Correction untill that hee shall be thence delivered by warrant. . . . And in the mean time to hold him to such workes and to give him such punishment by putting fetters or gyves on him and by moderate whipping him, as in good discretion you shall find cause, yielding him for his main-tainance so much as he shall earn or deserve by his worke or labour, and that at the next quarter sessions you shall have the said Ralph Pearte there together with this warrant."[46]

By a later order of the Court the said Ralph Pearte was duly returned to his master.

Apart from the views of a few isolated pamphleteers, public opinion appears to have occupied itself very little with the subject of pauper apprenticeship. It seems in most cases to have been taken for granted that appren-ticeship was the only way in which to deal with the training of children to play a useful part in the world, and to its very obvious defects people shut their eyes. For, however ideal the workhouse schemes might be in theory, in practice writers could not but know that they left much to be desired in the treatment which they afforded even to adults, quite apart from children, for whom in their present state they were impossible as a training ground except in the practices of deceit and vice. Within their walls many a child like poor Richard Monday must have been,

> " Sad, silent, supple ; bending to the blow,
> A slave of slaves, the lowest of the low ;
> His pliant soul gave way to all things base,
> He knew no shame, he dreaded no disgrace ;
> Him, might the meanest pauper bruise and beat,
> He was a foot stool for the beggars feet ;
> His were the legs that ran at all commands ;
> They used on all occasions, Richard's hands ;
> His very soul was not his own ; he stole
> As others ordered and without a dole ;
> In all disputes, on either part he lied,
> And freely pledged his oath on either side."[47]

Consequently there seemed no adequate substitute for the present apprenticeship system, convinced as some people were of its general undesirability.   Richard Burn, who as a justice of the peace had ample opportunities for observing the way in which it worked, wrote a strong condemnation of the attitude of the parish officers towards their chargeable children.   Other writers who discuss the subject regard it with almost unqualified disapproval.   Bailey's opinion was that

" The present method of putting out poor Children Apprentices is very well-known to be attended with great Inconveniences, as it lays an Encumbrance on Estates and Families.   Few of those poor Children now serve out their time, and many of them are driven, by neglect and cruelty, into such Immoralities as too frequently render them the Objects of Public Justice.   Many of those who take Parish Apprentices are so inhuman, as to regard only the pecuniary consideration ; and having once received that, they, by ill usage and undue severity, often drive the poor creatures from them ; and so leave them in a more destitute Condition, and at a riper Age for Mischief, than they were in when first they became the care of the Parish Officers."[48]

The minister at Stroud also bore witness to the same thing. He had started to re-organize the administration of the Poor Law in his parish, and for this end, had persuaded the parishioners to build a workhouse, of which he was very proud, and which at first appears to have been exceedingly well run. He wished parish children to be well trained and looked after in the work-house, as an alternative to early apprenticeship ; he was confident that such a system would work better than the existing one. He wrote that

> " This Proposal, as it takes place in Market Towns and populous Parishes, will, I hope, save many a poor Orphan from being ruin'd. We have now Parish Officers too eager to get rid of them ; and they place them out so young with little money (two guineas a Common Price) to sorry masters, and 'tis little better than Murdering them. But when Children are put in a way of Contributing to their own Maintainance, and may be kept in these Houses at little or no Charge to the Parish, till they are old enough for Trades or Services ; it can hardly be Supposed that Officers will then be so monstrously cruel, as to go on in the old Road of Sacrificing them."[49]

Towards the middle of the century some attention began to be directed towards the abuses from which the parish apprentices suffered, and in 1747 an Act was passed by which an apprentice, with whom not more than £5 had been paid, might complain of ill-treatment or failure to teach a trade to a single justice, who was empowered to call the parties before him, and, if he thought fit, to discharge the indenture without the payment of a fee. But any real interest in the subject dates from the efforts of Jonas Hanway, who during his investigations into the condition of the pauper children in London, and during his connection with the Foundling Hospital, necessarily came into contact with the con-ditions of pauper apprenticeship. The result of his exertions was embodied in an Act of 1767 which, as far as London was concerned, dealt with two outstanding abuses. Henceforth no parish apprentice was to be bound with a premium of less than £4 2s. 0d., half of which sum was to be paid at the end of seven weeks and the remainder at the expiration of three years. By this means it was hoped that masters who took parish apprentices would find it to their interest to treat them in a humane manner, whilst it was also hoped that a larger premium would secure a better type of master. By the same act it was also decreed that parish apprentices should only be bound " for the term of seven years or until they shall attain their respective ages of twenty-one and not longer." In 1778 these provisions were made universal throughout the rest of England, on the grounds,

> " that it has been found by experience that the said term respecting men children is longer than is necessary, and that, if such man child was bound only until he came to the age of one and twenty, all the benefit intended by the said Act, would be preserved, and all the hardships brought on such parish apprentices by the length of their apprenticeship would be avoided, and the good harmony between master and apprentice would be better maintained."

Despite the rosy prospects painted by this preamble, the commissioners of 1834 were of the impression that the period of apprenticeship was still too long.

Thus, by the end of the eighteenth century, social reformers were making a serious effort to grapple with evils which had been long existent, and their efforts began to arouse public opinion on the employment of the children of the Poor, particularly on that of those who were left as a charge upon the parish, and had therefore no one to protect their interests. But it was not until the evils of such indentured child labour were concentrated before people's gaze in the cotton factories of the north, that public sentiment became really active on the subject, and it was felt that the nation as a whole had no moral right to leave so important a matter in the hands of individual parish officers.

Nothing illustrates more completely the tremendous

gulf which yawned between the Elizabethan conceptions
of poor relief and the practices of the eighteenth century
than the history of pauper apprenticeship in this period.
In no sphere were the original intentions of the Act so
subverted to the need of keeping the rates down, or the
reactions of the law of settlements more disastrous. The
lack of a central authority was never more fatally
displayed than in the selfish action of each parish in
thrusting young children into overcrowded trades or
among brutalizing surroundings where temptations were
rife, and so increasing the class of casual labourers, of
vagrants, and eventually of criminals, in the next
generation. If for no other reason than its management
of the parish children, the parochial administration of
poor relief in the eighteenth century would stand self-
condemned.

The overseers, however, remained impervious to
blame, and continued to regard the marriage of a poor
labourer as a menace to the rates, because of the large
family which might result. It was to avoid this contin-
gency that the parishes removed so drastically any
married labourer who attempted to gain a settlement
within their boundaries. But, not content with this
legal protection, the vestry actively encouraged the
demolition of cottages, with the intent to debar marriage,
even among the settled Poor. By the end of the
seventeenth century North could write,

> "It is another very great Destruction of People, as well as
> an Impediment to the Recruit of them, that Gentlemen of
> late years, have taken up an Humour of Destroying their
> Tenements and Cottages, whereby they make it impossible
> that Mankind should inhabit upon their Estates. This is
> done sometimes bare faced, because they harbour the Poor
> that are a charge to the Parish."[50]

Nearly a hundred years later Young confessed that
" Marriages are very frequently obstructed," and he
further declared that the settlement laws provided " a

strong and effective motive for many people to do everything in their power against population, by raising an open war against cottages."[51] The result was a great increase in the number of illegitimate children born, for where the dice was weighed so heavily against matrimony men preferred not to marry[52]; and the upshot was perhaps no more than might have been expected. As Mr. Greaves said in an address to both Houses,

" Young men, intimidated by such cruel treatment, are unwilling to marry ; and this leads them frequently to debauch young women and then leave them with child in a very helpless condition."[53]

Such was the result of the attempt to expel Nature with a pitchfork.

Bastardy as such is not an offence against the laws of England, but to have an illegitimate child, who was actually, or likely to become, chargeable to the parish, was early recognised as an offence against the Poor Laws, with definite penalties attached to its commission. Like so many poor law provisions, the first important statute dealing with the question goes back to Elizabeth. By the 18 Eliz. c. 2 two justices of the peace were to examine the causes and circumstances and to make an order for the punishment of the offender and the better relief of the parish, by requiring the mother or reputed father to pay so much weekly or monthly to the overseers of the parish. Any one failing to conform with the order was to be committed to the common gaol until he or she gave security for compliance. It was found to be easier to pass an act of this character than to enforce its provision, for the reputed father, with the intention of evading his legal responsibilities, often absconded, leaving the parish to bear all the charges in connection with the child. Accordingly, a clause in the Act of 1662 gave the churchwardens and overseers power to seize as much of the property of the absconding father as would indemnify the parish.[54] Unfortunately the man in question seldom had any resources beyond his labour—in which event the parish was left without a remedy. Resort was therefore again made to Parliament, and a new Act, whose provisions speak for themselves, was obtained.[55] Henceforth it was enacted that if any single woman came before a justice and on oath charged any person with having gotten her with child, then the justice, on the application of the overseers, was to issue out his warrant for the immediate apprehension of the person so charged.[56] When the arrest had been effected, the man was to be forced to give security to save the parish harmless or to enter into a recognizance to appear at the next Quarter Sessions.[51] If, through unwillingness or lack of means, he neglected to fulfil these conditions, he was to be committed to the common gaol or house of correction. If, however, the woman " shall happen to die, or be married, before she shall be delivered or if she shall miscarry of such child, or appear not to have been with child at the time of her examination," then the man is to be discharged from his recognizance or released from gaol as the case may be. The sole protection given to the man against a revengeful woman was the right of appeal to the justices, who were, in that case, ordered to call the overseers before them " to show cause why such person should not be discharged." Moreover, " if no order shall appear to have been made in pursuance of the said act of Eliz. c. 3 within six weeks after such woman shall have been delivered, such justice or justices shall and may discharge him from his imprisonment in such gaol or house of correction to which he shall have been committed." Under this act, a perfectly innocent man might be charged by any single woman as being the father of her child, and if he were poor, or had no means of proving his innocence, he might suffer a sharp term of imprisonment before the truth was discovered. Or he might be compelled on the oath of the woman to pay for the maintenance of somebody else's child. That such a law could be passed at all shows how inadequate were

A WOMAN SWEARING A CHILD TO A RICH MERCHANT

the measures then in force to deal with the question. Even before the act was passed, it was not unknown for women to threaten to accuse men with having rendered them pregnant, for the sole reason of extorting money from them. Thus at the Middlesex Quarter Sessions in 1691, Elizabeth Dunban was convicted for conspiring with Eleanor Dick to accuse falsely John Oiliteer with being the father of her child, with the intent to extort £3 from him.[58] After this Act, nothing was easier than to threaten to swear that a certain man was the father of a bastard, the victim in these cases being chosen solely because he was judged able to pay hush money. The Commissioners for 1834 report this as being a common method for women to extort money. At Royston in Cambridgeshire it was reported that " Many girls have got as much as £20 or £30 from different young men not to swear children to them.[59] On one amusing occasion a certain George Brockhall, grocer, fled panic-stricken to the justice. and there deposed that a certain Elizabeth,

" In revenge and malice, upon no other occasion than an ordinary falling out betwixt her and the said Informant, most slanderously and unjustly say him the said Informant to be the father of the said child and also hath spoken other words leading to the damage and prejudice of his trade, threatening also that, if either swearing or saying would doe it, she would torment the said Informant to eternity, or to any other neighbour ; and further sayth that she is a person of ill reputation and behaviour ; and further sayth not. Capt. coram me. Rich. Graham."[60]

Such were the main laws by which Parliament strove to protect the parish against the charge of having to provide for children born out of wedlock. But despite these, in many cases the overseers appear to have been left with the children on their hands, and without much hope of pecuniary redress. Bastard children continued to be a most chargeable section of the community. Moreover, the laws which regulated their settlement were different from those governing the settlement of legiti-

P

mate children. Bastards took, not the place of settlement of their father, nor even that of theirmo ther, but
that of the parish where they were born. Therefore, by
every means within their power, overseers prevented
women from being delivered of illegitimate children
within the bounds of their parish, and where such births
took place, enforced as actively as they could the law,
which enabled them to claim maintenance from the
father.

The treatment accorded to pregnant women varied
considerably. If the woman were a settled inhabitant,
then the overseers made what arrangements were needed,
and attempted to get their outlay refunded from the
father of the child. It was customary for a woman,
living in another parish, to be returned hastily to her
place of settlement, when the time of her confinement
was near, in order to avoid these expenses, as in the
following case :—

"Charges that Grace Peerson hath put the parish of
Aspenden to, since we received her by virtue of a warrant from
the justice :

For her lodging and living at 1s. per week ..	11–0
For her lying in for beer candles soape diet firing and other necessaries	1–3–4½
The midwife for delivering her of her child ..	1–6
For 3 weeks for her nurse	15–0
For the use of linen at her lying in	2–0
For necessary things to put the child in ..	5–1"[61]

Yet, though a parish provided for the confinement of a
poor parishioner, even when it was common knowledge
that the child would be illegitimate, it only did so when
there was no other possible way of ridding itself of the
burden. Often the overseers tried to smuggle the
woman in question into another parish, when the time
of her delivery drew near, in order to alter the settlement
of her child. To counteract this behaviour the case of
Twing v. *Twing* decided that, in cases where fraud could

be proved, the child should take its mother's settlement. Despite precautions of this character, however, many women were turned adrift when the time of their delivery drew near. One man was bound over to appear at the Hertford Quarter Sessions and answer the charge of turning one Sarah Whitty out of doors, when in such a condition, with the intent of forcing her to become a vagrant.[62] The accounts of St. Bartholomew, Smithfield, for the year 1697 give a very clear picture of the way in which parish officers exerted themselves to get rid of women who might give birth to an illegitimate child likely to be chargeable to the parish. " 20th May pd about Lydea Hardy past upon us bigg with Ba. Child ..00–1–00." Then on August 19th " Mr. Webb & Mr. Burges & I went to My Lord Mayor's about Lydia Hardy bigg with a bastard child. It was prity sport how we banded the Drs. Comm[s]. fops too & again but it cost .. 00–2–6." Two days later they had another meeting on the question of Lydia—" We had a great fateage about Lydia Hardy to get clear of her. Burges, Gascoyne, Webb and myself workt our witts bout her, but I paid & spent (the beadle came in for a snack)..00–6–4." Then we get a picture of the last meeting—" Once more about Lydia Hardy, by the help of strong stout and good bottle ale we basshed the poor churchwardens and overseers of Doctors Commons but thank old Rozin for that but I was paymaster so farewell Lydia..it cost (the beadle came in for a snack)..00–2–6." On the 24th September he wrote, " And now begins more trouble. Mrs. Cooper's maid was big with a bastard child. Mr. Webb & I had a long discourse with her & Mrs. Cooper. It cost..00–2–0." Next day he " pd at Mrs. Cooper's about her maid in order to get the parish clear of her..00–3–0." On 9th October came the final entry, " Mr. Burges & another by threats drove away Mrs. Cooper's bigg bellied Maid so that you shall hear no more of her. But it cost..00–1–3." By the beginning of November he had another case on his hands, for on the First he " pd at Mr. Burges & Mr.

Lamb's about Lucey Shipman big with a bastard child..
00–1–2." Under November 2nd comes the following
entry, " Mr. Burges & myself was 2 days about this
Lucy & at last found out the true father. It cost me
3s. 9d. & a 1s. the warrant we turned her going & saved
the parish of a greater charge (there was a great many
words to get it out of her)..00–4–9."[63] When responsible parish officers adopted these tactics, it is no wonder
that the roads were thick with wandering women in a
pregnant condition.

No other word than brutal can describe the treatment
which these women received from the parishes through
which they strayed. The following are some typical
examples, taken from parish accounts. " Gave a
travelling woman big with child to depart the place
1–0."[64] " Itt geaven to a poore woman that was in
labor carrying of her away..2–0.[65] Or, " For getting a
great belly'd woman with Child out of the parish " ; or
from the same parish, " paid Wildbore the Warder for
Removeing a great bellied woman..00–01–00."[66] The
next set of entries is taken from one parish, and shows
the typical nature of such occurrences. " 1723 for
removing of foure bige bellyd woemoen out of ye parish
when like to bee chargeable..16–00 ; 1724 Gave hir to go
off with hir Great Beley..16–00." " 1731 for maintaining a Poore woman found in the forest in Labour
who afterwards Died..2–0–0." " 1733 To Cost for
nursing ye woman Delivered at the stocks..2–0–0."
And finally an entry which sums up in a few lines the
utter brutality of the period. " 1722 To a big bellyd
woman several days & nights at nursing at Robinsons, &
conveying her to Chigivell after she had gathered strength
to prevent her lying in here, she fell to pieces in 2 or 3
days there..17–7."[67] Nor was treatment of this kind at
all unusual. In the Hertford quarter sessions books are
many cases of women being moved from one parish to
another when they were so near their confinement that
the removal caused their death.[68] Another entry from

Mr. Laming's account shows the promptitude with which women judged to be near their labour were driven from the parish, as witness, " I was called out of bed 12 o'clock at night to take care of a big bellied woman that Lay in ye close.   I sent her away in a chair and it cost in money and drinks (I question whether I shall have thanks)..00–2–6."[69]   In the execution of the bastardy laws parochial officers appear to have been bereft of both humanity and decency, and nothing in the old poor law presents a more disgusting spectacle of callous inhumanity.

When the culprit was a parishioner and it was inadvisable to take any of the steps outlined above, the overseers concentrated their attention on finding the reputed father and forcing him to pay for the maintenance of the child.   When the mother went to ask for relief the overseers had the right to take her before the next justice and make her declare on oath the name of the man involved.   Once that was known, the justice issued out a warrant for his apprehension, and when caught he was forced to give security to perform the affiliation order which was drawn up by the justice, or go to gaol. The amounts of these orders varied a good deal in different parts of the country.[70]   In the south and east a shilling to one-and-six a week was a common sum. Thus James Incasole, the reputed father of " a male bastard child borne of the body of Mary Wilks in the parish of Great Abbingdon " was ordered to pay 1s. 6d. per week so long as the said child should be chargeable. In another case a certain John Hein of Little Eversend had to pay one shilling per week and £2 18s. 9d. for lying-in expenses.[71]   Sometimes the father was forced to apprentice the child, and in these cases five pounds appears to have been the usual sum asked.   In the north the amounts of the affiliation orders were less.   For instance, as late as 1750 the folllowing payments were prescribed :—7d. weekly and 15s. for lying in ;   30s. yearly and 10s. lying-in money, the mother having to provide for it with that money ; another for £2 6s. 8d., with 12s. 6d. for lying-in, the mother maintaining it and both parents giving security ; another of 9d. a week and 20s. towards lying-in charges, the mother to pay 4d. a week also to the overseers or take the child.[72] Such orders were to remain in force for varying periods, generally " so long as the said child shall be chargeable." Occasionally, however, a definite age was mentioned, such as " until the child is fourteen " or until it could maintain itself.

If the putative father thought the amount in the justices' order excessive, or if he wished to protest that he was not the father of the child sworn to him, then appeal lay to Quarter Sessions. The Middlesex Quarter Sessions are full of appeals of this nature, and though in the majority of cases the order is confirmed, the appeal is sometimes successful, a proof that the woman in question did not always swear to the right man. Thus Thomas Blemfield, of Gonville and Caius College, B.A., appealed against an order judging him to be the reputed father of a bastard child born in the parish of Horingley of the body of Ann Reves of that parish. When the Court had heard " what could be said on either side," it decided that " This Court doth allow the appeal and sett aside the order made aforesaid and doth discharge the said Thomas Blemfield from the said Bastard Child." When no appeal was made against the order, then the transaction was recorded in the Order Book at the County Sessions, and that was the end of that particular case.

How great a proportion of their expenses in this direction the parishes recovered it is very difficult to say, because of the secrecy which the overseers preserved over their accounts. According to the Commissioners of 1834, the overseers were very lax in this respect ; at Clifton, for example, it was reported, " Money is not obtained from the putative father in one case out of six. The usual order of maintenance made on the father is 2/–

a week. The mother, even when she is in service and the child maintained at the cost of the parish, never pays her order. As far as the Mother is concerned it is, under all circumstances, a dead latter."[73]   And at Bedminster it was likewise reported that " The annual expenses of Bastardy are £300, and of this sum the parish does not on an average recover more than £100 per annum." It is difficult to know how much money the parishes of an earlier date recovered. The first set of official figures available on this point comes from the schedules attached to the report of 1776,[74] and is for the years 1773, '74, '75. They are, however, very incomplete and imperfect. The questions asked were, How much money did the parish receive, and how much did it expend, on account of its bastard children ? But whereas the remaining columns, devoted to other matters, appear to have been filled up with a fair degree of accuracy and detail, the columns dealing with bastardy are very often blank ; even when they are not absolutely empty, figures are only given for one year, or else the money received, but not the money expended, is quoted. For instance, the only figure quoted for St. Bartholomew, Exchange, is for 1774, when £6 4s. 9d. was received, while St. Mary, Aldermanbury, spent £4 0s. 0d. in 1775, but had nothing entered up under the heading of receipts. Such carelessness shows that parish officers must have been very lax—not only in one, but in many parishes—about the way in which they kept their accounts relative to this head. And where accounts are lax in the eighteenth century, it is not infrequently the case that they cover a certain amount of malversation. The practice of receiving composition fees for bastards became doubly open to corrupt uses if no proper record of such transactions were kept. Sometimes, indeed, all details were completely entered, at least for a certain period. But the entries are curiously uneven ; in some years a parish apparently received much more than it expended, while in others it was considerably out of pocket, though whether this represented its true condition, or whether it arose from bad book-keeping, it is impossible to say. The figures for St. Anne, Blackfriars, were :—1773, received £8 8s. 0d. and expended £39 0s. 0d. ; in 1774, received £3 3s. 0d. and expended £45 10s. ; 1775, received £52 12s. 0d. and expended £56 0s. 0d.[74] Thus for the whole period the parish was considerably out of pocket, though in the last year there is a surprising increase in the receipts. This may have been due to the practice, which from the beginning of the eighteenth century some parishes had adopted, of accepting composition payments of ten pounds from the fathers of bastards. Among the entries in the vestry book at Tooting is this, " Mr. Ridge to accept £10 from John Godman for the Bastard Child sworn to him by Elizabeth Best & that he be discharged for all expences of the said child."[75] Such sums were not equivalent to the cost of rearing the child, but perhaps nobody expected a child raised by the parish to live long enough to exhaust this sum, most of which, it was hinted, was soon spent on a parish feast.

In other parishes the figures given show a profit over bastardy transactions, presumably owing to the death of the children concerned. St. Leonard's, Foster Lane, in 1773 received £20 and paid out £5 ; in the following year it received £5 and paid out £3 1s. 6d. St. Margaret Patterns, in 1774, paid out £1 1s. 0d. and received £26 5s. 0d. in the same year ; St. Martin-within-Ludgate received £41 10s. 6d. and paid away £11 9s. 2d. St. James', Clerkenwell, received £75, in 1773, and spent £39 6s. 0d., whilst in 1775 its receipts were £97 10s. 0d. and its disbursements £50 1s. 0d., which provided for twenty-four children. Everything, in fact, appears to have depended on the individual parishes. The chief value of these figures lies in their revelation as to how very erratic was the administration of the bastardy laws. In some parishes little was recovered, while in others a profit was made ; never by any chance do the receipts and disbursements balance.[76]

Some parishes attempted to recover their due by imprisoning the reputed father until he should give bond to observe the order made against him. In the Lancashire Order Book it is quite common to find men sent to the house of correction till they give security to abide by the affiliation order served upon them. Thus :

> " John Brown of Woodplumpton weaver refusing to give security for maintaining of Grace his bastard by him begotten of the body of Ann Hardman in Clifton cum Sowich widow is by this Court committed to the house of correction at Preston there to remain till he give sufficient security for the same."[77]

On the same day another man was committed for the same offence. On April 30th, 1750, William Woodlate and Timothy Parkinson, who had previously been committed under the bastardy laws, were brought before the court a second time, but, " again neglecting to give security," were sent back, while on July 16th the court made an order to sell poor Timothy Parkinson's goods to pay for his going to Lancaster to the Castle there. Yet the amount of his order was only 15s. lying-in expenses, plus a weekly payment of 7d. Three days later Thomas Roydes was also committed to the house of correction at Manchester for the same offence, and in the following January John Dugdale, of Billington, weaver, was sent to Lancaster Castle for failing to give security.[77]

Nor were the Lancashire justices the only ones who sent the fathers of illegitimate children to the house of correction if they failed to give security. George Murfell, of Wilbratim, in the Isle of Ely, appealed against an order, which adjudged him to be the father of a bastard born of the body of Ann Abbis, of Kingston. His appeal failed, however, and the end of the matter was that the said George was committed to the county gaol for not finding sufficient security for the performance of the justices' order respecting the maintenance of the child. Three years earlier the Court had ordered that " Francis Luck is to remain in gaol till he shall give security to indemnify the parish of Swaffham Bulbeck in this county from the maintenance of a base child by him begotten of the body of Barbara Little " ; when discharged, he was to pay his fees.[78] In the eighteenth century it was the practice to make the unhappy prisoners pay certain fees to the gaoler out of their own pockets.

Sometimes these imprisonments lasted over a considerable period. At a court held on the 14th of April, 1686, it was ordered that " James Wade of Rendle now prisoner in the House of Correction for bastardy wherein he has lyen for one whole yeare shall bee discharged." And on another occasion it was recorded that :

> " it appeareth that the said Heawood hath lyen in prison for the space of one year and upwards and is a poore man and not able to doe anything towards the maintenance of the said child and that information is given to this court that both the mother and the Child are gone out of the kingdom and soe that the child is never likely to become chargeable to the towne where it was borne."[79]

In these circumstances the court decided to release the said Heawood. This was how one man obtained his release on a charge of bastardy :

> " Whereas Lawrence Martin was committed to the Castle in Cambridge for begetting Elizabeth Carpenter with child and refusing to give security and upon examination Martin seems very willing to serve his Majesty as a soldier therefore the Court do desire Christopher Jefferson to enquire whether West Colvill is willing and to report to the next Quarter Sessions with a certificate from the churchwarden and overseers of the poor and two of the chief inhabitants signifying their consent thereto."[80]

In these cases, certainly, the overseers did not get much pecuniary recompense for the money expended on rearing the child in question ; but at least they made it desirable to pay the security, if possible. It is probable that the great majority of those represented as failing to perform the order were men who could not raise sufficient security. Failure on the part of a parish to collect the money due to it usually arose when the men involved were too poor to pay, or when they managed to create enough influence with the overseers and church-wardens to avoid payment. Sometimes, when the man obviously had no money, the court was puzzled to know what to do, as when, for instance, on dealing with an affiliation order, it discovered " that the said Long hath not any estate real or personall and is a day labourer. This Court doth think fitt to adjourn and respite the further hearing thereof until the next sessions."[81] An interesting case of a man who vowed that a child had been sworn to him falsely comes from St. Bartholomew, Exchange, though whether Robert Charles acted out of an obstinate conviction of innocence and a love of fair play, or whether because he could not afford to do otherwise, does not appear. On the face of it, Robert Charles was apparently a man to stand on his rights. This is the incident :

" At the same vestre was A petico brought by the wife of Robert Charles her husband being in Nugate for that he Refused to keepe a Bastard Childe laide to him he saith Roungfully & his goods was seized one bt vertue of an Execution & his wife & three children like to com to be a parish Charge, soe it was ordered that Som of the Overseers of the poore with the Churchwardens should gooe and spake with Charles to see if he could putt securitie to saue the parish harmless then they were to help him out of prison and dow something for him."

In the margin was the following note :

" Ald webb Mr Bruer Cap Sauage Mr Mastin Mr Bishop & the 2 churchwardens & took the child and putt it forth to nurse, it was agreed upon then that the pish had better to keepe one than 3 or 4 & to take the Charges of the Basterd Child & pay the Charge."[82]

There is something very refreshing about the emphasis lent by the wrongly-placed capitals ; evidently it was felt that all the important words needed capitals.

As the eighteenth century wore on, an alternative course to sending the man to the house of correction, if he did not find sufficient security to save the parish harmless, was often followed. This was to force the man to marry the mother of the child, and so make him responsible for the maintenance of both. It was evidently found that this method was more likely to save the parish the charge of the bastard, while the man had less chance of escape—since, if he ran away, there were laws which might send him to the house of correction for deserting his wife and family. These marriages were generally forced, as the following entries illustrate :

" Expences of taking Thos. Webb for a child sworn to him by Hannah Chitty..9–6. Midwife..5–0. Expences at Sessions..5–0. License to marry Webb and Chitty.. £1–6–6. Expences of attending the marriage of ditto.. £1–2–6."[83]

And also, " Expences of apprehending and marrying Tho. Green to Elizabeth Betts..£5–15–0." Judged by the cost, this was a difficult marriage to arrange.

Evidently, if the prospective husband objected, he was committed to gaol until he changed his mind, as witness the following items, " To Expences att Lowestoff when took List—11–11, To do att Beccles getting him to gaol..8–0 ; To do when married him & charges for ye wench..8–4 ; To ye marriage..1–7–0."[84] In the same way the Cambridgeshire justices ordered that William Taylor, a prisoner in the Castle at Cambridge, where he had been committed on the charge of getting Sarah Haslewoods, of Brinkley, with child, should be discharged out of prison on his marrying the woman upon application made to the mayor by the parish officers of Brinkley.[85] The parish officers certainly seem to have done what they could to enforce the bastardy laws, and evidently, unless they could arrange matters with the overseers, there was always an element of risk for the parties concerned.

Nor do the bastardy laws appear to have been a dead letter where women were concerned, as, we are told, they became later. By the 18 Eliz., c. 3, f. 2, it was enacted that any woman failing to fulfil her bastardy order might be sent to gaol. The 7 Jac. I., c. 4, was a stricter measure. It enacted that " every lewd woman which shall have any bastard which may be chargeable to the parish, the justices of the peace shall committ such lewd woman to the house of correction there to be punished, and set on work one whole year." If she offended again she was to be committed until she could find security to do so no more. Traces of women being sent to the house of correction for bastardy are not as frequent as commitments for vagrancy ; but they do occur, as witness the following example from the Lancashire Quarter Sessions, when Ruston appealed against an order settling Jenett Bradshaw and her bastard child there, saying that she ought to be settled at Huntcoate. But as Huntcoate failed to appear, the case was respited. When it was finally tried, Ruston lost, the woman and child being declared to be settled there. The woman was forthwith sentenced to be committed to the house of correction for a year and a day. In another case, after the affiliation order had been dealt with, the court committed the mother to the house of correction, and gave the child over into the hands of the parish. In a third instance a mother who failed to maintain her bastard child was threatened with imprisonment if she did not do so in future.

As has been seen, the parish officers did everything they could to check the growth of bastardy, a thing which they abhorred, not on moral grounds, but because it was likely to cost the parish money, and so raise the rates. Yet, despite the utmost stringency of the law and its brutal execution, it was found impossible to stamp out the evil. Even more, it increased to such an extent as to be an affair of special moment to the Assistant Commissioners of 1834, who report in place after place that bastardy is almost always the prelude to marriage, and how it is no longer a matter of the slightest shame, in the eyes of the labouring Poor, to be the mother of an illegitimate child.

In circumstances such as these it becomes a matter of importance to know why the practice was increasing at such an alarming rate. The eighteenth century is generally regarded as being coarse and of a low moral standard, but that in itself is not sufficient explanation of a state of things which, by 1834, can only be described as frankly appalling. There were, of course, some conditions which made for a low state of morals, whatever the attitude and administration of the law might have been. In town and country alike overcrowding was the rule among the labouring Poor. In the former the Poor lived in the cellars or attics, or were crowded together in rooms, where persons of both sexes and all ages lived and slept together. Quite apart from the usual supposed temptations of town life, it is not surprising that in these circumstances the proportion of illegitimate children born was high. The common lodging-houses were another factor which made for immorality. In these men and women could find a place of refuge against the parish officer if they had no settlement, and were likely to be driven forth ; in them beggars, and worse, found a hiding place against the police. The conditions which prevailed in these places, as described by Fielding, were such as to make ordinary morality out of the question. Nor, as has been shown, were the conditions in some of the workhouses much better, so far as overcrowding and the free intercourse of the sexes was concerned. In the country districts the cottages were generally small and insanitary and inadequate in number to the needs of the population. When throughout life many of the Poor were huddled and herded together promiscuously, it is little to be wondered at that the general moral tone was low.

These factors must all be taken into consideration, but it cannot be denied that the laws themselves deserve a great part of the responsibility for the state of affairs which prevailed. Perhaps the most fatal thing about the working of the settlement laws was the way in which they seemed almost to conspire to debase the moral tone of the people who came under their influence. By striking at marriage, though this was far from the intentions of the legislators at Westminster, they struck at an institution which tended to keep sane and wholesome the lives and outlook of the poorer classes, otherwise drab enough. But if a man is to be robbed of his fundamental instinct to make a home for himself, and a woman to be denied a lawful opportunity to become a mother, then their whole attitude towards life becomes warped and twisted. The substitution of fear for better instincts is not likely to be productive of good results. So when parish officers endeavoured to frighten people into being moral for no higher purpose than to keep the rates low, it is no wonder that they failed and that bastardy increased. This brought about the terrible state of things revealed in the Commission of 1834, when it was discovered that among a large part of the Poor, chastity and continence were no longer of importance. And for this they were inclined to blame the action of the overseers, who, since the terrible rise of prices at the close of the century, had become, under the influence of the new wave of humanitarianism, too slack in their administrative duties. Thus the Commissioners report that the mothers of bastards get greater allowance than widows with legitimate children, and refer to other scandals of the same nature ; to the advantage of having bastards they seem to attach the blame for the great prevalence of the habit. This is taking too short a view of the case ; it was not the allowance for the child, which, in any case was little enough, that had first sapped the chastity of the poorer women. It was the fact that on every side marriage was hampered by low wages, restricted settlements, and a lack of cottages, which made the Poor, in spite of what the overseers might threaten to do, take what outlet for their desires they could. And then, when the habit of disregarding marriage became common, the spirit behind the administration of the Poor Laws altered. Where before the incontinent had been threatened or punished, they were now helped and supported. But this was no longer any reason for remaining moral ; rather was it the reverse. In effect, what the Poor Law did was this : first it broke down the habit of chastity among the poorer classes, and then, changing its attitude, encouraged bastardy by a system of liberal allowances, having previously removed any disinclination for it. To have bullied the helpless, corrupted the children, and polluted the moral life of the countryside—such were the consequences of leaving to the parish a problem which it had neither will nor wit to solve.

CHAPTER VI

THE FAILURE OF THE ACT OF SETTLEMENTS

THE result of the failure of the parish to provide for the Poor contributed largely to the difficulties in the way of dealing with the question of vagrancy, for the administration of the Poor Laws had been perverted to such an extent, that those very laws which ought to have restrained wandering, encouraged it. The able-bodied labourer, who could find no employment at home and whose parish refused him a certificate, was forced to take to the road in his search for work. If his resources failed before he was successful he was forced to turn beggar, pilferer, and sometimes thief, rather than risk being returned to his parish, with the consequence that often, when the chance of steady employment offered itself, he had lost his desire for it and could not shake off the habits of his wandering life. Even if he were apprehended, punished, and returned to his parish, no reformation took place, for the overseers and parishioners did all within their power to induce him to take to the road again. In this way the parishes helped to encourage that restless, improvident spirit, which marked the eighteenth century. The evil of the apprenticeship system, for which there was so little practical redress, also made its contribution to the swarms of vagrants ; the runaway apprentices, liable to arrest if caught, comprised a sturdy and lawless element in the vagrant class. Then again there were women, who, having been seduced and deserted, were almost literally driven forth by the parish officers to wander and steal, and to this helpless class should be added the children, who were forced by their parents to beg, or who wandered deserted up and down the roads, like the poor little " vagrant beggar of low statare, browne-hair'd, about twelve years, [who] was openly whipped at Thursfield, for a wandering rogue."[1]

Throughout the period there is evidence in plenty to show that the scourge of vagrancy lay heavy on the country. The numbers of vagrants were composed of various classes. Apart from those people who had sunk to that condition through misfortune, there was the type that wandered up and down the country side with false passes, or who told fortunes, did a little legal hawking, played interludes, juggled, collected for charities which did not exist, and made up the rest of their living by robbing hen roosts, pilfering gardens, and poaching. Such an order as that made by the Buckinghamshire justices at the Easter Session of 1678 shows very clearly the official, and indeed the general, way in which such wanderers were regarded; it sheds a side-light also on their methods of picking up a living. After bemoaning that " the daily concourse and great increase of Rogues, Vagabonds and Sturdy Beggars is a great Grievance and Annoyance to the Inhabitants of this Country," it states that " they are now become so growne soe insolent and presumtious that they have oft, by Threats and Menaces, extorted money and victualls from those who live in houses remote from neighbours whilst theire Husbands and Servants have been employed abroarde in the Management of theire lawful Vocacons and have put the people into a General Fear and Consternation for feare that they will fire theire houses or steale theire Goods."[1] Accordingly, the Bench ordered that all suspicious vagabonds were to be " stripped naked from the Midle upwards and openly whipped till theire bodyes shalbe bloody."[2]

In 1703 the keeper of the county gaol of Hertford was ordered to receive Th. Ingroom, Margaret his wife, Easter Joanes and Susan Wood, the heads of a gang of about fifty Gypsies travelling about, telling fortunes and calling themselves Egyptians.[3] That such large bands of lawless wanderers should tramp up and down the country-side constituted a real risk to law-abiding persons. The vagabond class were chiefly feared for two things, besides the damage they might do by robbing and stealing. Firstly, they were suspected of carrying the plague or small-pox from place to place, and so spreading the danger of infection. Small-pox was the terror of the time, and the terrible outbreaks of the plague in London, and all over the country, had increased the habitual terror of these outbreaks of pestilent diseases. Vagrants were supposed to form one of the most common means by which such infection was spread ; and in the Hertford Quarter Session books convictions were common for dividing one tenement into two—" to the great danger of infecting the inhabitants with the pestilence," or for " entertaining of vagrants which hath brought diseases into the towne and prejudices severall familyes therein."[4] One important reason for all kinds of malignant distempers lay in the insanitary condition of the gaols and bridewells, frequent complaint being made that discharged prisoners infected the people among whom they went. It was in consequence of the state of the prisons, said John Howard, writing in 1777, that " at Quarter Sessions you see prisoners, covered (hardly covered) in rags ; almost famished ; and sick of diseases, which the discharged spread where ever they go. . . . At Axminster, a little town in Devonshire, a prisoner discharged from Exeter gaol in 1755, infected his family with that disease : of which two of them died ; and many others in that town afterwards."[5] Vagrants as a class might have been expected to know more about the insides of the Bridewells than most, and many a vagabond who was imprisoned for a short period and then whipped, and after paying his fees, discharged, must have been turned on the world with the germs of the infection in him. This fact, together with the cold, damp, and other rigours of a wandering life, would account largely for the unhealthiness of many of the

vagrants. Such fear of the vagrants as spreaders of
disease was justified, according to many scattered entries
alluding to some vagabond who is suffering from the
dread infection. In 1677, John Collupp, of Puckeridge,
in the parish of Stondon, was presented for " entertaining
of vagabonds at unreasonable hours, as also for receiving
one having the small-pox upon him, thereby infecting
the said town of Puckeridge."⁶ If they could, the parish
officers got rid of the infected person with more regard
for the pockets and safety of their own parishioners than
consideration for the public health. For instance, at
Towcester in Northamptonshire, the following item
appears in the churchwardens' accounts : " Gave a
woman & two small Children to Goe from Towne having
the Small Pox on them..6d."⁷ Such methods would
hardly appeal to the medical officers of to-day, and in
themselves must have done much towards spreading
the pestilence. Sometimes the victim was taken to the
local pest house, if there was one, as witness, " For
carrying a poor Rashed Traveller in my cart to the Pox
Officer owing to Mr Ewelles 2s. & 1s. I gave her to get
up my cart..3–0."⁶

The other great fear with which the vagrants inspired
the country dwellers was the fear of fire. At a time
when the Great Fire of London was fresh in the popular
memory, this was not strange, since the danger of fire
was very real when the majority of houses were still built
of wood and thatch ; in a dry season any small piece of
carelessness might result in a serious fire. In 1676 there
was a period of great drought, and in some places " the
country people had to drive their cattle from parish to
parish for water."⁹ At such times there was evidently
danger of fires. For instance, " fire at Tiverton last
week burnt down 32 houses, and it being occasioned by a
vagrant, who is said to begin it in an out-house with a
pipe of tobacco, makes the country full of fears that it is
designedly. The person was taken into custody."
Again, in the Isle of Thanet, a fire which consumed a

great barn of corn and cost the tenants between two and three hundred pounds, was supposed to have been caused by " a way going man, smoking a pipe of tobacco near the stable." [9] Sometimes the Session books record the petitions of persons who, ruined by a fire, ask for a licence to beg. Before the days of general insurance such a fire might often mean absolute disaster. Thus, in 1688, Bridget Ansell, of Ickleford, stated in her petition that " upon the 19th day of April last, one Lawrence ——, a vagrant beggar, set fire to the barns, outhousings and part of the dwelling house of your petitioner, which in the space of one hour was burned to the ground. Besides the loss of hay, wood, straw and household goods, with several implements of husbandry which were consumed at the same time, the whole loss upon the survey of able and substantial workmen amounts to the sum of £137, which is to the ruin and impoverishing of your petitioner, who has three small children to provide for." [10] She accordingly asked for a letter of request to beg within the county.

Sometimes a fear of fire is expressly stated as the reason why vagrants should not be harboured. In 1675, the vestry of Amwell laid the following complaint before Sessions,

" This is to informe that Edward Humerstone, of Amwell is a very evill liver, keeping a disorderly house, harbouring vagrants and theeves in his house night and day to the prejudice of the neighboroughood, suffering them to have fire and candle in a thatched barn night and day, to the great danger of the houses of the neighbours. Also keeping such company as aforesaid, drinking, revelling, singing and roaring on Sabbath days all day, yea, even in sermon time." [11]

Apparently the inhabitants lived in nervous dread that one day the vagrants, too far gone in drink, would set half the village on fire.

In 1689 this fear grew so intense that a general warrant

was issued for the apprehension of all vagabond, unknown, and suspicious persons, because

> " diverse fires have lately happened in several parts of the kingdom and that many Irish Papists and other lewd and vagrant persons dissaffected to the Government, are observed to wander up and down, to the terror of his Majesty's subjects, and have feloniously designed to burn several towns, as by the confession of some already apprehended doth appear."[12]

Thus the vagabond was anything but a popular person, quite apart from the general feeling that he ought to work and that he was a drag on society. He was distrusted as the kind of person who would pilfer, rob, and steal game, and help on the two great scourges of the age, pestilence and fire. A large proportion of the vagrants must have been of this type, getting their living somehow by wandering about and making themselves general nuisances to all law-abiding citizens. They were not, however, the only class of rogue and vagabond with which the authorities had to deal. In the majority of the books of the time it is the other class which looms larger. These were not vagrants in the sense of being wanderers but were regular town beggars, members of what was a profession in itself. It is against these town beggars that the average pamphleteer rails so bitterly. London was particularly infested with this type, which consisted of the off-scourings that a big city produces, link boys, boot blacks, loungers, persons who begged by day and most probably robbed by night, cripples both real and false, pick-pockets, and thieves.[13]

Of another class were the unlicensed itinerant vendors of small wares, who infested the streets crying their goods and making these an excuse for wandering. Sundry efforts were made during the latter part of the seventeenth century to put these hawkers down, both as being a nuisance and as encroaching on the business of the lawful shop-keeper, in consequence of which they were prosecuted as vagrants. For instance, on the 30th of September, 1687, a True Bill was found against

> "John Webb late of the parish of St. Mary-le-Savoy, county Middlesex, an idle vagrant, in the habit of wandering abroad and carrying with him drinking glasses and other glasses, wandered abroard with such wares crying out in a loud voice through the place and lanes these words, to wit, 'Will you buy any glasses?' in order to colour his said vagrancy and escape punishment for the said vagrancy."[14]

These people were suspected of getting as much by begging as by the sale of wares, and were in general considered undesirable, but the efforts to put them down do not seem to have been successful. Sometimes vagrants were prosecuted for "being common ballad-singers wandering abroad."[14] But all endeavours to suppress this floating, half-begging, half-criminal class that subsisted in the big towns, and particularly in London, were of no avail. The Mendicity Reports made to the House of Commons in the early part of the next century prove that the state of affairs respecting mendicity was nearly as bad as it had been a century before, through the danger of the roads at night, with regard to thieves and almost unconcealed robbery, appears to have diminished.

H. Fielding thought that the immunity of this class was due to the fact that poorer parts of the city offered so many ideal hiding-places where thieves and pickpockets could take refuge. For it was generally agreed that the vagrant class, in London at least, was for the most part criminal. In the lower districts there were numerous lodging-houses where such vagrants could avoid the law, and Fielding gives a graphic, if disagreeable, picture of one of these places. He says that—

> "In the Parish of St. Giles there are a great Number of these Houses set apart for the Reception of idle Persons and Vagabonds who have their lodging there for twopence a Night : That in the above Parish and in St. George, Blooms-

bury, one woman alone occupies seven of these Houses all properly accommodated from the Cellar to the Garret, for such twopeny Lodgers : That these Beds, several of which are in the same Room men and women, often strangers to each other lie promiscuously, the price of a double Bed being no more than threepence as an Encouragement to them to lie together : That as these Places are adapted to Whoredom, so they are no less provided for Drunkeness, Gin being sold in them all at a penny a Quarten ; so that the smallest sum of money serves for intoxication : That in the execution of search warrants Mr. Welch rarely finds less than twenty of these Houses open for the Receipt of all comers at the latest hours."[15]

With such places of retreat behind them the beggars of London could defy the badly-organized forces of the law, which were supposed to cope with them.

Complaints and descriptions in plenty of the London beggar appear in contemporary writings. Defoe in a well-known passage says quite definitely :—

" I am obliged here to call begging an employment, since it's plain if there is more work than Hands to perform it, no man that hath his limbs and his senses needs to beg and those that have not ought to be put in a condition not to want it."[16]

Joshua Gee at a later date bears witness to the same state of things :—

" Great numbers of sturdy Beggars, loose and vagrant Persons, infest the Nation, but no place more than the City of London and parts adjacent. If any person is born with any defect or Deformity, or maimed by Fire or other Casualty, or any inveterate Distemper, which renders them miserable Objects, their way is open to London, where they have free liberty of showing their nauseous sights to terrify People, and force them to give money to get rid of them ; and those vagrants have for many years past moved out of several parts of the three Kingdoms, and taken their station in this Metropolis, to the interruption of Conversation and Business."[17]

But besides the impotent beggars, as they may be called

PLATE VIII

DOMESTIC ARCHITECTURE.
HOUSES LATELY STANDING ON THE WEST CORNER OF CHANCERY LANE FLEET STREET.

SOME FAMOUS LONDON BEGGARS

[face p. 232

—that is, those who tried to get money by trading on real or sham physical disabilities—the town swarmed with sturdy vagrants of a more dangerous type,

> " especially those profligate Wretches called the running Camp, which every day pester our streets ; they are a People that one would think came from the Suburbs of Hell itself, a Dishonour to Human Nature, a Shame to the Government, and an intolerable trouble to all persons they come near, by their swearing, scolding, fighting, etc. You may easily know them also by their numbers, for they commonly go in companies, and will be present at all Solemnitys, but more especially at Feasts and Funerals."[18]

Writers complain repeatedly that it is not possible to stop to speak to a friend in the street without one of these beggars coming up and pestering for money and making all conversation impossible. At night they resorted to more violent methods, so that the streets were not safe for pedestrians. Altogether, the picture is not entrancing, for the problem was one which the authorities found it exceedingly difficult to tackle.

Like the relief of the poor, the suppression of vagrancy had been allotted to the parishes. To the parish constable was entrusted the task of apprehending all such wanderers, whipping them until their backs were bloody, and then and there either conveying them personally to the constable of the next parish or providing them with a pass, which allowed them to go the direct way back to their place of settlement. For work of this character the constables were singularly unfitted. Like that of the overseer, the office was annual and unpaid, and usually fell to the lot of a man who had his own living to earn. The more respectable or wealthy of the parishioners usually preferred to pay a fine than serve their turn, and the fines for constable brought considerable gains to the vestry. In all respects it was a most unpopular and badly-executed office. Yet it was on the constable that the chief responsibility lay for putting the vagrant laws into effect. As a result, though every statute made provision for levying a fine on constables who neglected their duty, writers are full of complaints against their slackness. Dunning was very bitter against them.

" The contempt, obstinacy, and neglect of Inferior Officers are in this Age as 'twere Treason, proof against all Authority, publick Interest, Common Reason and Civility, the Mare Lethi of all Laws."[19]

The position was, however, a difficult one, and Dunning was hardly fair to the constables, who were forced by circumstances to neglect either their own business or their official, but unwanted, duties. Hugh Hare, Esq., in a Charge given at a General Quarter Sessions for the County of Middlesex in 1692, expressed the same opinion.

" Gentlemen," he said, " we want neither good Laws, nor due incouragement from our Superiors, nor yet good Magistrates of the higher Rank ; but the Constables, Headboroughs and other under Officers, have so little Religion or Honesty in them, that their Negligence in Informing and Prosecuting, renders our pains as it were ineffectual for promoting a general Reformation of Manners,"[20]

Gee, on the other hand, took a more comprehensive view of the matter when he said :—

" I must confess I think the Error is depending on Constables ; for they are men of Business and have families to support ; none of them take office upon them but with Regret ; and if they can find money, rather buy off than serve in their own Persons ; if they are forced to serve, when the laws against vagrants should be put into execution the Constable is about his own Business and if possible will not be found. I therefore think that the Constable should not be depended on in this case, but that the whole care should be committed to the beadle of every Ward, and their under Beadles with an Augmentation of their Salaries, to make it worth their while to put the laws into execution against all such loose People."[21]

As things stood, there was no real force to prevent

people from giving alms to beggars, and therefore no real hope that begging could be put down without a strong and stern executive, which the constables could not provide. Consequently, in spite of the numbers of people who were actually taken up and whipped, or sent to houses of correction, very little impression could be made on the body of vagrants as a whole.

As in the case of the Poor Laws, Parliament tried to patch the sinking ship by a series of decrees which, by stating the law with more exactitude, aimed at reducing the leakage. The ease with which false passes could be forged, enabling their possessor to live at free commons on the parishes through which he passed, had actually encouraged the spread of vagrancy.[22] Even a cursory glance through the pages of any churchwarden's accounts reveals that the number of persons travelling up and down the country side with these passes was very considerable. Usually the entries recording the payments made to them were very vague, " geaven to a poore man with a passs ..6d." being a common formula. To reduce the amount of fraud by providing some scrutiny the 1 An, st. 2 c. 3 enacted that all persons with passes should be taken before the Justice. This measure, however, did not succeed in putting an end to the practice, and persons convicted of travelling with a false pass appear frequently on the gaol calendars ; for example, in 1749, in Cambridge,

" John Rivers and Tho: Bleckford, convicted of travelling with a false pass, are remanded to the House of Correction for two months and to be whipped at the Markett Cross in Cambridge to-morrow at noon and again that day month and again that day two months and in the meantime to be kept to hard Labour and then discharged and sent by pass to their respective habitations."[23]

In 1714 a determined effort was made to codify the law, and define more exactly what was meant by " rogue and vagabond." By 13 Anne, c. 26,

"All persons pretending themselves to be patent Gathers or Collectors for Prisons, Gaols or Hospitals and wandering abroad for that purpose, all Fencers, Bearwards, Common Players or Interludes, Minstrels, Jugglers, all Persons pretending to be Gypsies or wandering in the Habit or Form of counterfeit Egyptians or pretending to have skill in Physiognomy, Palmistry or like crafty science or pretending to tell fortunes or like phantasical Imagination or using any subtle Craft or unlawful games or Plays, all Persons able in Body who run away and leave their wives and Children to the Parish and not having the wherewithal to maintain themselves use Loytering and refuse to work for the Common Wage and all other idle persons wandering abroad and Begging (except Soldiers, Mariners and Seafaring men licensed by some testimonial or writing under the hands and seal of some Justice of the Peace setting down the Time and Place of his or their Landing and the Place to which they are to pass and limiting the Time for such their Passage while they continue in the direct way to the Place to which they are to pass and during the Time so limited) shall be deemed rogues and Vagabonds."

Any persons who came within this definition were to be taken before some Justice of the Peace of the same county or division and examined on oath as to their place of settlement ; and their deposition was to be taken down, signed, and filed among the records at Quarter Sessions. A good many of these depositions survive, and throw considerable detail on the ordinary life of a vagrant as well as on his cause or excuse for adopting that career. They show, too, that sometimes a considerable amount of wandering took place before vagrants were brought before any justice whatsoever. Anne Johnson, for instance, when taken up in the Parish of Wotton, gave evidence as follows :—

" She says that she does not know very well how old she is, but appears to be between 13 and 14 years of age. That her father and mother were named Richard and Sarah Johnson, and that her father was a miller and lived in the parish of Wirksworth, in the county of Derby, in which parish the deponent was born, as she had often been told by her father and mother. That her father owing more money in and about Wirksworth than he was able to pay and afraid of being thrown into prison, some years ago (but how many deponent cannot tell) together with his wife and deponent, left the parish of Wirksworth and went from thence to the City of London where after they had been some time deponent's mother died, and the same summer the father also died. Ever since his death she had lived by begging, and some times had earned some small wages by keeping of sheep and cows in the fields belonging to the several parishes and counties through which had wandered."[24]

The next important law to deal with the question of vagrancy was the 13 G. II., c. 24, which repealed all the former laws and attempted to comprise all the provisions for dealing with vagrants in one statute. It amplified the classification of 13 Ann c. 23 by dividing all vagrants into idle and disorderly persons, rogues and vagabonds, and incorrigible rogues   The first class was composed of persons who threatened to leave their wives and children on the parish, or who returned to a parish from which they had been legally removed ; of persons living without visible means of sustenance who refused to work, like one John Spencer, who was " an idle dissolute fellow refusing to put himself out to service, liveth and spendeth high, keeping many horses and not having any visible means to do the same,"[25] and, finally, of persons who begged in the parish where they lived. Such persons were to be committed to the house of correction for one month. The rogues and vagabonds were people who gathered alms on false pretences, who collected for hospitals and prisons, who were bearwards, fencers, all kinds of unlicensed players, jugglers, minstrels, and persons pretending to be Egyptians and skilled in their arts (this was very much the list of 1714, in fact). Pedlars without licenses were to come under this category, as were persons leaving their families, and persons wandering and begging, who could not give a good account of themselves. They were to suffer imprisonment with hard labour for a period not exceeding six months. The last class of incorrigible rogues comprised persons who

gathered ends of wool, so helping to defraud manufacturers; persons who had already been convicted as
rogues and vagabonds and had escaped; and, lastly,
persons who gave a false account of themselves. Constables not doing their duty in arresting such offenders
were to forfeit ten shillings. A privy search was to be
made four times a year. The examination on oath, and
the method of deciding the last place of settlement, were
to be as before. One alteration which was made in the
manner of passing was that, when the place to which
the vagrant had to be sent was a long distance away,
the vagrant was to be taken to the first house of correction in the next county and so passed from house of
correction to house of correction until the master of the
last house delivered him to the overseers of his parish.

Four years later another large scale vagrant law was
passed which was in many ways a recapitulation of that
of 1740. The three divisions into idle and disorderly
persons, rogues and vagabonds, and incorrigible rogues
are preserved, and the same classes fall into the three
groups. Any Justice shall order such persons to be
publicly whipped by the constable or his deputy, or to
be sent to the house of correction until the next session,
or for any less time as the Justice shall think fit. The
Justices may sentence any rogue and vagabond committed to the sessions to a further period of confinement
not exceeding six months, and any incorrigible rogue to
any period between six months and two years, during
which time he is to be whipped as they think fit, and
afterwards to be sent away with a pass. If he escapes
from his confinement and is recaptured, he is to be transported for seven years. Nothing more is said about
passing from house of correction to house of correction,
and the old method, by which each constable conveyed
the said vagrant to the first constable of the next county,
liberty, or place on the direct way home, was revived.
Persons who could not or would not find themselves any
service, were to be detained at the house of correction

until they or the Justices could find them a service either at home or in the colonies. In this, as in the previous statute, special provision is made to force masters of ships to re-convey vagrants to Ireland, and to prevent them from shipping poor Irish to England by means of a system of fines on those who are discovered so doing. The number of vagrant Irish in England seems to have been a constant trouble ; moreover, having no last place of settlement in England, they did not come under the provisions either of the Act of 1662 or any of the later Acts dealing with settlement, so that they could be convicted only under the vagrancy laws. Many of the rougher beggars in the towns were reputed to be Irish. There was also an important clause which dealt with the case of pregnant women who were vagrants. Formerly a bastard had been settled where it was born, and the chances were that any child born of a vagabond woman would have no legal father. In any case, that which had to be paid for her lying-in expenses, would have to go on the parish accounts. As a result, no parish gave any resting place to a wandering woman in this condition, if it could possibly avoid so doing. It was accordingly enacted that any vagrant woman who was delivered of a child, should, after her confinement, be sent to the house of correction until the next Quarter Sessions, where the Justices might, if they wished, cause her to be detained another six months and publicly whipped. Whatever money the parish had expended on her was to be refunded by the Treasurer of the County, and the child, if a bastard, was to take its mother's settlement. Altogether, the Act of 1744 provided a comprehensive, though somewhat involved code for dealing with wanderers of all descriptions.

Simultaneously with these measures, a new series of efforts was made with the hope of rendering the parish constable more effective in the discharge of his duties. The Act of 1662 had sanctioned the levying of a parish rate to reimburse the constable those sums of money

which he had been forced to spend in the execution of
his duty, but this had been a poor compensation for the
trouble he was forced to take, for in many cases constables were still trying to recover their money years
after they had left office.[26] To remedy this abuse the
11 Gul. III, c. 18 provided that :

> " to the Intent that every such constable and other officer
> may be fully paid and satisfied for his Losses of Time and his
> Expences in Execution of this Act : Be it enacted that the
> said Justice of the Peace shall tax on the Backside of such
> Certificate," *i.e.* which was to be given to the constable with
> the vagrant's pass, "such Constable a reasonable and sufficient
> Allowance for his Trouble and Expence which Certificate the
> said Constable shall deliver to the Chiefe Constable of that
> Division, who is thereby ordered forthwith out of the Sumns
> of the Gaol and Marshalsea Money he shall receive to pay
> such Constables."

The Marshalsea money was raised in every parish
quarterly, and paid by the churchwardens to the Chief
Constable for the relief of poor prisoners in the prisons
of King's Bench and the Marshalsea. This was one of
the provisions of 43 Eliz., c. 2. However :

> " in case the said Gaol and Marshalsea Money shall not be
> sufficient after having discharged the Purposes for which it
> was raised to reimburse the Expences and satisfy the
> Allowance as hereby required. It is hereby further enacted
> that the Justices of the Peace in their Quarter Sessions shall
> have Power to raise Moneys . . . in the manner as they
> raise it for County Gaols and Bridges."

After this Act, entries dealing with unpaid constables
give place to entries like the following : " Order for the
attendance of the chief constables of Ossulston, Edmon-
ton, and Gore, who are to bring their accounts relating
to the passing of vagrants."[27] Apparently the Marshalsea Money did not suffice, and money had to be levied
on the separate parishes, for we find entries in churchwardens' accounts like this : " Pd towards vagrant
money..£3–6–6."[28] In the Yorkshire North Riding

Quarter Sessions books it is common to find an order for £50 to be escheated for defraying the charge of conveying of vagrants and paid to the Treasurer.

Apparently this was not an unqualified success, for the constable claimed greater allowances, while the owners of waggons, horses, and carts demanded more extravagant rates for the use of their vehicles than was felt to be reasonable.[29]   Accordingly, by the 1 An. st. 2, c. 13, it was provided that in future the Justices, at the Easter Quarter Sessions, should be empowered " to ascertain and set down the several Rates that shall be for the year ensuing to be allowed for maintaining, conveying and carrying vagrants."   This clause appears to have been put in action as a piece of useful legislation, and many entries in the Orders Books of various counties gives the rates that were fixed by the Justices.[30]   At Middlesex the rates were fixed as follows in 1703 : sixpence for maintaining a vagrant twenty-four hours, sixpence for conveying a vagrant a mile by horse and carriage, or by cart ; and for conveying a vagrant by foot, less than sixpence a mile, at the discretion of the Justice.[31]   At Hertford, in 1719, the rates were : for a single person for one night, fourpence ; for a man and his wife, or for two men or two women together, sixpence ; and twopence apiece for children.   If the said vagrants were not to be lodged for the night, but merely passed straight on, the constable was only to have half these sums, except on extraordinary occasions.   They were also to be allowed threepence a mile for a vagrant conveyed by horse, and sixpence a mile for a cart with a horse and driver, in addition to one-and-six per day for their own labour.[32]   After the passing of this Act, the parish constable was by no means so free an agent in his treatment of vagrants as was the overseer with respect to the parish poor.   From this time, both in law and in practice, the suppression of vagrancy tended to slip into the hands of the county rather than to remain with the parish.

R

This became still more the case after 1739, when a general county rate was levied for all purposes, such as the repair of county bridges, gaols, etc., and it was enacted that the money for passing vagrants was to be paid into, and drawn out of, the fund so created. Considerable sums, of which it is difficult to obtain any account, were expended in this way. The first year for which we have any reliable figures is 1772, when, from the extracts of returns made by the clerks of the peace and other officers concerning vagrants, we find that Bedford was spending £164 11s. 6d. a year; Berks, £183 12s. 10d.; Bucks, £303 9s. 11d.; Cambridge, £114 10s. 10d.; Ely, £55 3s. 5d.; Chester, £482 12s. 10d.; Cornwall, £47 17s. 9d., for which it had to thank its geographical position; Cumberland gives no figures; Derby, £254 3s. 10d.; Devon, £340 10s. 10d.; Dorset, £43 6s. 7d.; Durham, £230 3s. 4d.; Essex, £311 16s. 9½d.; Gloucester, £697 9s. 2d.; and Hants, £120 0s. 4d., in passing vagrants.[33] The other counties were spending sums of about the same amount.

These figures, which represent considerably more in the value of the time, show that the business of passing vagrants was really too vast to be managed by the parish constables, requiring, as it did, most elaborate organization if it were to be carried on without appalling waste and overlapping. Accordingly, a new class of officer sprang up. He was not in any way a statutory person, being appointed and paid by the Justices of Quarter Sessions, acting through the county treasurer. This man was the vagrant contractor. After the beginning of the eighteenth century, references to such a personage are common in the quarter session books, and most counties seem to have adopted some such arrangement for the transport of vagrants through their confines.[34] In the case of Devon, the decision to employ a contractor was reached after " mature deliberation," because great numbers of vagrants were brought into the little town of Axminster, " to be received by the proper officers

of that place and by them conveyed unto the town in
the next county, and other remote places." The result
of the "great numbers of such vagrants and their frequent and sudden coming" was that the officers were
"disturbed and hindered in the managery of their
affaires, trades, and professions"—to avoid which,
Quarter Sessions made a contract with one, John Crosse,
of Axminster, clothier, for £40 a year, which was to
include his "Labour, care, pains, expences, and disbursements."[35] This contract was entered into in 1708,
and appears to have been due to the increased numbers
passed, owing to the vagrancy laws of the last reign.
In the same year, 1708, the Buckinghamshire Justices,
being suspicious of the accuracy of the bills presented
by the constables, contracted with two persons to convey vagrants for £80 a year.[36] It was usual for one
contractor not to take over all the vagrants of the county,
but only those who came, or had to be conveyed along
a certain route. For example, the North Riding
Justices ordered the Treasurer " to pay John Raper
of Langthorpe £20 per quarter for the conveying all
vagrants that shall come to Kirkly, to Nesame, or other
places according to the usual custom and John Raper
to give security to perform the agreement."[37] Two
years later it was agreed to reduce his allowance to £60
a year. The Mendicity Report of 1815 gives a very
clear picture of the duties of such an officer, and of the
way in which he carried them out. It had probably
been much the same in the previous century. Mr.
Davies, the vagrant contractor for Middlesex, gave
evidence before the Committee that he had contracted,
in consideration of £300 a year, to convey in and out of
Middlesex, all vagrants who were sent to him by the
magistrates with a pass ; hence he is often alluded to as
the pass-master, though he did not himself make out
the passes. He had a large house capable of holding
fifty to sixty vagrants at a time, and as these were released from Bridewell, they were brought to him there

by the constables. He conveyed only such persons as
had first been committed to Bridewell for seven days,
and had nothing to do with persons removed by ordinary
orders ; those were conveyed by the parishes. He
employed a man and a cart and two horses in his business.
When he had collected sufficient vagrants going one way,
he despatched a cart-load of them to one of his receiving
houses—of which he had four, acting as out-posts for
the county. Once there, they were delivered " To the
person employed to carry them on to the next county.
There is a woman at Egham, of the name of Meads, I
give her six guineas a year to take in the people that
are coming up ; and I go down and fetch them, and
what ever she pays I must pay her again, and the same
at Colnbrook." On being asked where they took them,
he replied, " They take them on to Blackwater, there
they deliver them to a person of the name of Munns.
At Colnbrook, the man only takes them to Maidenhead,
through the county of Bucks ; then the contractor for
Berskhire takes them on to Hungerford, that is fifty
miles." Thus, by this time, there was a definite net-
work of contractors for passing punished vagrants to
their settlements. Mr. Davies received nothing beyond
his salary, save sixpence a night for three nights for
maintaining the vagrants sent to him ; if he spent more
than that, the loss was his. He further said, " I imagine
I can prove I have passed as much as 12,000 or 13,000
a year," and added that he often passed the same person
several times a year.[38]

Until late in the century some counties continued
to leave the business of passing vagrants to the parish
constables, and in the Quarter Session Books one can
trace the transitional stage through which they moved
before deciding to leave the whole management to a contractor. But as a general rule it was freely recognized
by the end of the century that the problem of vagrancy
was too large to be left to the parishes, and the management thereof devolved on to the county authorities.

But despite improvements in this respect, the connection between vagrancy and the ordinary administration of the Poor Law by the parish officers, was too close for the one not to be influenced by the other. The success of the vagrancy laws depended on the treatment which the vagrant received once he or she was returned to the parish, and this unfortunately was the reverse of sympathetic. In one instance a certain Ann Peacock complained to the Justices that the overseers had deducted a shilling a week from her allowance, and had offered " that if the petitioner would by stealth and privately kreepe into the parish of All Saints Hartford, or into any other parish," they would give her £5. Therefore, while the parishes were as interested in inducing the chargeable poor to become vagrants as the magistrates were in preventing them, and while the contractors were employed in reconveying those whom the overseers bribed to wander, the whole process may be compared to that of pouring water out of a cask with a large meshed sieve, and in such circumstances it was hopeless to expect that the problem of vagrancy could be solved.

CHAPTER VII

CONCLUSION

Such were the results of leaving the responsibility for the Poor of the realm to the officers of the individual parishes. In this respect the Act of Settlement, though passed with the best intentions, proved in practice almost wholly bad. By 1660 it was clear to those interested in the problem that the provisions made for the relief and employment of the Poor by the 43 Eliz. c. 2 would no longer work without some measure of adjustment. But unfortunately, though perhaps almost inevitably, the new Act, passed in 1662, instead of organizing larger districts for the administration of the Poor Laws, retained the old parochial basis of the Elizabethan statute, and merely attempted to give its provisions fresh life by defining the responsibility of each parish more carefully. The result was to hamper the free movement of individuals from place to place and to restrict the ebb and flow of labour between the rapidly specializing industrial districts of the country.

The degree to which these new restrictions penalised both individuals and the development of the country as a whole, has been, and, to a certain extent, must continue to be, a matter of controversy. That it did inflict severe hardships on certain categories of individuals, such as single women, widows with dependent children, and, in the rural districts, married labourers, it is impossible to deny. In certain cases also the operation of the settlement laws tended to split up families, as when a widow with children married for her second husband a man whose settlement was in another parish, for then the mother was separated from such of her children by her former husband, as had attained the age of seven, and therefore could not be regarded as nurse children. But in the wider sphere of the development of the country as a whole, the consequences of the Act are more difficult to trace. Adam Smith clearly considered that its provisions hampered industry, but Howlett, on the other hand, produced evidence to show the contrary to be true. It would seem that the truth lay between the two points of view. For we have seen that the administration of the law was so weighted that few men who were capable of earning their living, were in practice hampered from moving. But the fact that a man could legally claim relief only from that parish where he was settled deprived all but the most capable and energetic of any incentive to go in search of work, when for some reason they could not obtain it within easy reach of their own parish. Speaking of the average labourer a witness stated before the Commissioners in 1833, " The present system makes them believe that, when their own supply of work is interrupted, the parish officers are bound to find work for them or give them relief ; and that no one is obliged, or ought to leave his parish in search of work." To such a pass the Poor Laws brought the English workman. This illustration is taken from a later date than the close of the eighteenth century, when poor relief was granted with a more lavish hand. Against this, however, should be balanced the fact that in 1833, unlike the period before 1795, no man could be removed until he was actually chargeable, so that a man had more freedom to move as he chose. In this way the enterprise and self-reliance of the labouring poor were subtly undermined. This attitude on the part of labour helps to explain the seemingly contradictory facts that, on the one hand, manufacturers were crying out for labour at a reasonable rate, while on the other, the expense of maintaining the Poor was rising steadily. It explains, too, the lack of initiative displayed by the agricultural labourers. They preferred to stay in a district where wages were low, rather than face the hazard of the road and go elsewhere.

For this attitude there was good reason ; the law declared that any person found wandering and begging should be whipped until his or her back was bloody. This penalty was as likely to fall on an honest but unlucky workman as on a professional beggar. Accordingly to go on the tramp to look for work, unless furnished with sufficient money for the journey, was a hazardous proceeding. Massie was firmly of the opinion that no one factor contributed so much to the encouragement of begging as the fact that honest persons in search of work could get no relief outside their own parish, if their store of money failed them. Perforce they turned to begging, and often to stealing ; and since both were punishable, there was the less need to discriminate. Then, once having become accustomed to this trade, they never cared to turn to laborious work again. Thus the settlement laws in this respect were double-edged. Firstly they terrified men from leaving their own parish by the spectre of the whipping post and constable if ill-luck should pursue them ; and secondly, men who did leave their parishes often fell into vagrancy and were lost to the effective industrial force of the country. In both these ways, indirectly, the settlement laws prevented the free circulation of labour. If the law had simply enacted that relief was only to be granted at a person's legal settlement, and had put no restriction on movement apart from that, a large number of people would still have clung to their place of settlement. But by providing maintenance on the one hand and the threat of physical violence on the other, the law ensured that the rural labourer, at least, should become not unlike the shell-fish, which cling to the rocks and let the drifting tide bring them their daily food.

This danger was intensified by the lack of adequate educational facilities, from which the labouring population suffered. Throughout the eighteenth century there were very few recreations which appealed to any but the most material and least elevated side of human nature. In all ranks of society, high and low alike, drinking and gambling abounded, while cock fighting was a favourite sport. Moreover, that part of the population which laboured for its daily bread was cut off from those more intellectual enjoyments which helped to gild life and provide mental refinements for their more fortunate fellows. Addison and Steele, Swift and Defoe, Reynolds and Gainsborough, Goldsmith and Johnson, the wits and the coffee houses, at least stimulated the mind of the eighteenth century gentleman, if they did little to check his habits of indulgence. But for the working man there was no such counterweight. Where overcrowding was the rule of life, where gin drinking was its relaxation, then was life indeed " mean, nasty, brutish and short," and there was little to encourage the virtues of sobriety and providence. In such conditions the administration of poor relief, as carried out by the parish officers, tended to encourage those very faults which were already most prominent in that age.

It was in its unexpected results that the Act of Settlement was so uniformly disastrous. Both the administration of the clauses dealing with parish apprentices and the enforcement of the bastardy regulations stain the law with a brutality, a callousness, and a lack of both decency and morality that are utterly repellant. But before we condemn this strange heartlessness too severely, some account should be taken of the eighteenth century in its more general aspect. It is not fair to the Poor Laws to study them apart from their environment, when a broad survey will show that the same brutality ruled in every sphere. It was an age when debtors as well as criminals were thrown into prison, and when the whole prison system was so wretchedly organized that in some gaols the very warders did not dare to go into the felons' cells for fear of contamination. If the workhouses shock every modern susceptibility, the prisons outrage it. Then, again, such punishments as public whippings and the pillory were common incidents in every town, while hangings ranked as a favourite exhibition with the mob, and often with their betters, too. In every way men were more used to pain and discomfort, because fewer methods of alleviation were known then than now. Even in their daily life their wants were fewer than are ours to-day, and what would now be looked upon as intolerable hardships were then regarded as the normal incidents of life. The eighteenth century seems so near to our own, that it is easy to forget the great differences, both in material conditions and in men's outlook, that divide it from the England of to-day.

The tragedy of the Poor Law lay in the fact that it failed so miserably to achieve those ends at which it aimed. This was not for lack of public interest, for no one can read contemporary writers on the question of poverty, without seeing that they were both tremendously keen and inordinately hopeful. Certainly the objects at which they aimed were worthy of all success. To relieve the old and impotent, to train children so that each one should have a trade to follow, and to provide work for the unemployed—what social platform to-day offers more ? Yet they aimed at no less. The distinguishing mark of the Poor Law administration, during these years, was the enormous gulf between theory and practice. As has been seen, the latter was a miserable travesty of the former. The apprenticing of poor children was a farce, and the workhouses soon ceased, if, indeed, they ever began, to afford real employment ; only the relief of the parish Poor was carried out. The granting of out-door relief without adequate safe-guards, and without any real efforts to reduce the amount of pauperism in the next generation, led to the general failure of the law, and finally to utter collapse. In theory men knew what was the right course to follow, but in practice administrative difficulties proved too great. The result was mirrored in the Commission of 1834.

Contemporary writers adduce many reasons for this failure of the Poor Laws to prevent, or even adequately to relieve, poverty ; but the real reason appears to have been the inadequacy of the administrative machinery with which they set out to solve a problem of the first magnitude. The great fault lay in their leaving so much to the parish. In the first place, the average type of officer was absolutely unfitted to cope with the responsibility. In the second, the parish was much too small and feeble a unit to take any effective action. This parish isolation was accentuated by the Act of 1662, after which it was increasingly difficult to organize any action on a larger scale, thanks to perpetual inter-parish jealousies and squabbles. Moreover, the parishes were not well equipped financially for the work they had in hand. Such power as there was to rate in aid was infrequently used, while the resources of each separate parish were too frail to do much more than relieve the absolutely necessitous. In addition to these very real handicaps the local administration was almost always slack, and more often than not corrupt. Consequently it was not an organization which ought to have been entrusted with the carrying out of any important business, unless at the same time a strict system of supervision had been provided.

If the problem had been, as it purported to be, merely one of relieving the Poor, the parish might have proved equal to its task. We have seen that of all the branches of the poor laws, that of out-door relief had been the most constantly and the best executed. But the real intention of the legislators had been to provide work, not maintenance, and this had introduced a situation far too complicated to be tackled by untrained administrators. Firstly, the difficulty of finding work that would employ all the poor, regardless of their previous history or training,was almost insurmountable. Secondly, such work, when found, was rarely remunerative enough to afford a bare subsistence for the Poor who were employed upon it. Consequently such work had to be either subsidised by the rates or abandoned. In many cases, where the parish Poor were few, it proved cheaper to pay an allowance than to take steps to find employment of such a character, and certainly less trouble was involved. Frequently the parish could not stand the financial strain of subsidising this work, and so it was quietly dropped, the workhouse being used both as a receptacle for the destitute and as a test of their need.

The results of this lopsided administration of relief were almost entirely unfortunate. The parish expenses were heavy, while its means were small. That the overseers were forced to judge everything from a financial standpoint was not altogether their fault, though the fact remains that the Poor Law had a degrading influence on almost everything with which it came into contact. We have seen how marriage was penalised, and how immorality thereby was indirectly encouraged. We have seen how family ties were slackened until men ran away, leaving their wives and children behind, secure in the knowledge that the parish was bound to provide for them. In the same way children had to be forced by law to keep the parents, and if they were not " persons of substance " they would seldom support them without some payment from the parish. The results of so insidious an influence could be hardly anything else than a lowered moral tone. The eighteenth century was a fit seed-time for the harvest of pauperism which distinguished its close. Men had neither respect for, nor gratitude towards the parish, and when the rigour of the administration was slackened, under the influence of the new humanitarian movement, no barrier remained against a wholesale dependance on the parish for relief.

The legacy which the old Poor Law left behind was an increased consciousness of class differences. The " poorer sort " took relief as their right, while the

ratepayers despised them for their indolence and inso-
lence, and even for their very misery. The persistence
of such an atmosphere for several generations cannot
have been without its psychological effect. It is one of
fate's ironies that a law which was designed to stabilize
the existing order, and to make for political security,
should have had the unfortunate results of the old Poor
Law.

Yet though from the vantage point of to-day it is
impossible not to condemn its inefficiency, stupidity and
brutality, we must not forget that England, in her earnest
attempt to discharge her responsibility for her poorest
citizens, was in the van of social history. It is to her
efforts in the past that the modern world owes the
greater part of what knowledge it possesses of the
practical difficulties of dealing with the problem of
poverty. Even so the lessons of the past are not easy to
interpret. The difficulties which faced the men of the
seventeenth and eighteenth centuries still exist. The
problem of finding suitable work, the expense of subsidising it, the fear of injuring the industrious to find
occupations for the idle, the hardships which under-
payment brings to the *bona fide* unemployed workman,
and the danger of bringing a whole class to rely on an
outside authority and not on themselves, are all as
prominent to-day as they were then. But from this
chaos of unsolved problem one fact stands out in clear
relief. Since poverty is a malady which attacks an
entire nation, it must be dealt with by the central
government acting for the nation as a whole, and not
by the separate localities which compose the nation.
Any attempted solution which does not regard the
problem in its integrity is foredoomed to failure. Even
then, so long as destitution remains to be relieved, the
administration of the Poor Law must be at the best a
thankless task. The only true solution for the Poor Law
reformer must be sought in drastic reforms of our social
system whereby undeserved poverty can be eliminated.

That such changes will take place with any rapidity is unlikely, and until that time the difficulties which obstruct even a reform of the Poor Law must continue to be very great. But unlike their predecessors the reformers of to-day are no longer sailing an uncharted sea. For awash, above the waves, lie the wrecked hulls of past experiments, proclaiming their mute warning, " Here danger lurks. Beware ! "

NOTES

CHAPTER I

THE CONTEMPORARY ATTITUDE TOWARDS THE PROBLEM OF POVERTY

[1] *A Method of Government for such Working Alms Houses*, etc. R. Hains. 1679. p. 7.
[2] *A Treatise on the Utility of Workhouses.* Wm. Bailey. 1758. p. 1.
[3] *Essay on the East India Trade.* C. Davenant. 1698. p. 28.
[4] *Prevention of Poverty.* R. Hains. 1674. p. 1.
[5] *Provision for the Poor.* Sir M. Hale. 1683. p. 12.
[6] *A New Discourse on Trade.* Sir J. Child. 1594. p. 4.
[7] *The True and Only Cause of a want of Money in these Kingdoms.* T. Hodges. 1673. (A single sheet.)
[8] *Discourse on the Trade of England.* Sir J. Child. 1698. p. 29.
[9] *The Trade of Great Britain in its Imports and Exports.* C. Whiteworth. 1776. pp. 1, 3, 63. E.
[10] *An Essay on Charity Schools.* G. Mandeville. 1723. p. 329.
[11] *An Account of Several Workhouses*, etc. 1732. pp. 94-5.
[12] *A New Discourse on Trade.* Sir J. Child. 1694. p. 81.
[13] *Proposals for Raising a College of Industry.* J. Bellars. 1695. p. 11.
[14] *Provision for the Poor.* Sir M. Hale. 1683. p. 3.
[15] *Report to the Board of Trade.* J. Locke. 1697. p. 102.
[16] *Proposals for promoting the Woollen Manufactury.* R. Hains. 1679. p. 3.
[17] *Report to the Board of Trade.* J. Locke. 1697. p. 110.
[18] *A Proposal for Relieving, Reforming, and Employing all the Poor of Great Britain.* L. Braddon. 1721. p. 65.
[19] *Essays about the Poor.* J. Bellars. 1699. p. 5.
[20] *Some Proposals for the Employment of the Poor for the Prevention of Idleness.* T. Firmin. 1681. pp. 38, 18.
[21] *An Account of the Proceedings of the Corporation of Bristol.* J. Cary. 1700. p. 13.
[22] *Provision for the Poor.* Sir M. Hale. 1683. p. 6.
[23] *Essay upon the Probable Means of Making a People*, etc. C. Davenant. 1699. p. 57.
[24] *A View of the Present State of the Cloathing Trade.* J. Haynes. 1706. p. 5.
[25] *A Plain and Easie Method*, etc. R. Dunning. 1686. p. 22.
[26] *Provision for the Poor.* Sir M. Hale. 1683. p. 18.
[27] *Tracts on Trade.* (Brit. Mus. 1887. 6, 60 [15].)
[28] *The Case of the Woollen Manufacturers of Great Britain.* (Brit. Mus. 1887. 6, 60 [32].)
[29] *The Trade of England Revived.* 1681. p. 8.
[30] *A Plain and Easie Method*, etc. R. Dunning. 1686. p. 1.
[31] *Report to the Board of Trade.* J. Locke. 1697. p. 102.
[32] *The Miseries of the Poor*, etc. L. Braddon. 1722. p. 18.

[33] *The Behaviour of Servants.* D. Defoe. 1724. p. 84.
[34] *The Gentleman's Magazine.* March, 1734. p. 15.
[35] *The Trade and Navigation of Great Britain Considered.* J. Gee. 1729. p. 38.
[36] *The Trade of Great Britain in its Imports and Exports.* C. Whiteworth. 1776. pp. 5, 22, 23, 27, 42, 43, 48
[37] *Considerations relating to the Poor* J. Massie. 1757. p. 58.
[38] *An Essay on Charity Schools.* G. Mandeville. 1723. p. 326.
[39] *Bread for the Poor.* R. Dunning. 1696. p. 1.
[40] *Charge of Sir John Gonson to the Grand Jury of Middlesex, etc.* 1728. p. 33.
[41] *Considerations relating to the Poor.* J. Massie. 1757. p. 69.
[42] *A New Discourse on Trade.* J. Child. 1694. p. 87.
[43] *Essay upon the Probable Means, etc.* C. Davenant. 1699. p. 55.
[44] *The Miseries of the Poor, etc.* L. Braddon. 1722. p. 62.
[45] *England's Weal and Prosperity Proposed.* R. Hains. 1680. p. 5.
[46] *The Prevention of Poverty.* R. Hains. 1674. pp. 2–4.
[47] *The Interests of England Considered.* E.J. 1720. p. 6.
[48] *England's Improvement by Land and Sea.* A. Yarranton. 1677. p. 52.
[49] *The Trade of England Revived.* 1681. p. 58.
[50] *Some Proposals for the Imployment, etc.* T. Firmin. 1681. p. 14.
[51] *Proposals for a Working Hospital, etc.* R. Hains. 1678. p. 4.
[52] *Plain and Easie Method.* R. Dunning. 1686. pp. 8–15.
[53] *A New Discourse on Trade.* J. Child. 1694. pp. 91–101.
[54] *The State of the Poor.* Sir F. Eden. 1797. Vol. 1, p. 188.
[55] *An Essay upon the Probable Means, etc.* C. Davenant. 1699. p. 59.
[56] *Proposals for Raising a College of Industry.* J. Bellars. 1695. p. 1.
[56] *Ibid.*, p. 11.
[57] *Essays about the Poor.* J. Bellars. 1699. p. 6.
[58] *A Proposal for Relieving, Reforming, and Employing, etc.* L. Braddon. 1721. p. 19.
[58] *Ibid.*, p. 55.
[59] *A Plain and Easie Method, etc.* R. Dunning. 1686. pp. 8–15.
[60] *Giving Alms no Charity.* D. Defoe. 1704. p. 13.
[61] *An Account of the Proceedings of the Corporation of Bristol.* J. Cary. 1700. p.
[62] *An Essay on the East India Trade.* C. Davenant. 1690. p. 28.
[63] *Reasons for Erecting in Every County, etc.* R. Hains. 1778. p. 4.
[64] *A Proposal for Making an Effectual Provision for the Poor.* H. Fielding. 1752. p. 35.
[65] *Argument proving that the Poor of England cannot be employed in the Wool Trade, but to the National Loss and Ruine of the Clothing Trade.* Philanglus. 1701. p. 2.
[66] *Parochial Tyranny.* A. Moreton. 1727. p. 34.
[67] *A Proposal for Making an Effectual Provision, etc.* H. Fielding. 1752.
[86] *The Manifold Causes of the Increase of the Poor.* J. Tucker. 1760. p. 9.
[68] *Considerations on Several Proposals, etc.* C. Grey. 1751. p. 5.
[69] *An Inquiry into the Management of the Poor.* 1767. p. 68.
[70] *Consideration of the Bills, etc.* T. Gilbert. 1787. p. 10.
[71] *Observations of the State of the Parochial and Vagrant Poor.* J. Scott. 1773. p. 97.
[72] *A Plea for the Poor.* R. W. Applegarth. 1790. p. 23.

CHAPTER II

THE ADMINISTRATIVE AND FINANCIAL EQUIPMENT OF THE PARISH

[1] " that the overseers shall within four days after the End of their Year, and after the other overseers nominated, as aforesaid, make and yield up to Two such Justices of Peace, as aforesaid, a true and perfect Account of all Sums of Money by them received, or rated and sessed, and not received, and also of such Stocks as shall be in their Hands or in the Hands of the Poor to work and of all things concerning their Office." (43 Eliz. c. 2, f. 2.)

[2] " If overseers have all this sway in the raising and disposal of the parish money, it seems highly reasonable that there should be an account and controul somewhere ; and this is placed in a justice of the peace, the other officer, upon whom the execution of the Poor laws is to depend. But this passes, in general, as a matter of mere form. It is true, the overseer, as directed by law, submits his accounts to the inspection of the parishioners, in vestry ; this, however, being left to the whole parish, is rarely undertaken by any. Afterwards the overseer swears to his accounts ; and the justice passes and signs it, as a thing of course, without any examination of the items. It is also requisite, that the justice should allow the rate made by the overseers ; but this is only a ceremony, and consists merely in fixing his name to it ; which, indeed, is the utmost the law requires of him, as it has been held he only acts ministerially." (*Considerations on the Bills*, etc. T. Gilbert. 1787. pp.14-15.)

[3] *Retford Churchwardens Accounts* in *Northampton Notes and Queries.* p.18.

[4] " That though a large book is provided to enter the Churchwarden's Accounts, yet there is a deficiency of about twenty four or twenty five Years Accounts, from 1690–1714." (Report on the Parish of St. Botolph. Feb. 22, 1733. p.22.)

[5] *The State of the Poor.* Sir F. Eden. 1797. Vol. III, p. 74.

[6] *The House of Commons Journals.* Vol. 18, p. 392.

[6] *Ibid.* Vol. 18, pp. 393-4.

[7] *Historical Account of the Vestry of St. Dunstan's in the West.* 1714. pp. 17-19.

[8] (Brit. Mus. 816, m. 9 ; single sheet.)

[9] *Historical Account of the Constitution of the Vestry of St Dunstan's in the West.* 1714. p. 129.

[10] *Ibid.* pp. 21, 28.

[10] *House of Commons Journals.* Vol. 18, p. 393.

[11] *Records of Batley.* M. Sheard. 1894. p. 217.

[12] *Records of Harrogate.* W. J. Kaye. 1922. p. 139.

[13] *History of the Parish of Leyton.* J. Kennedy. 1894. p. 38.

[14] *House of Commons Journals.* Vol. 18, p. 392.

[15] *Parochial Tyranny.* A. Moreton. 1727. p. 7.

[16] *House of Commons Journals.* Vol. 18, p. 394.

[17] *History of the Parish of Leyton.* J. Kennedy. 1894. p. 381.

[18] *Peep into an old Monkwearmouth Rate Book.* J. T. Middlemas. p. 6.

[19] *Parochial Tyranny.* A Moreton. 1727. p. 7.

[20] *Ancient Account Book of Cowden.* (Sussex Arch. Soc. Vol. XX,

[21] p. 115.)
Hawkshead, the Northernmost parish in Lancashire. H. S. Cooper. 1899. p. 428.

[22] *History of King's Lynn.* H. J. Hillen. 1907. Vol. 1, p. 389.

[23] *House of Commons Journal.* Vol. 21, p. 644.

[24] *Liverpool Vestry Book.* H. Peet. 1912. pp. 91–129.

[25] *Burton on Trent.* Wm. Molyneaux. 1869. p. 102.

[26] " What might have been the amount of the assessments for the poor during the seventeenth and eighteenth centuries, the Committee have no means of ascertaining ; for although the Preamble of 13 & 14 Charles II. states ' necessity, number and continual increase of the poor, to be very great and exceeding burthensome ; ' and in the year 1699 King William thus expressed himself in a speech from the throne : ' that the increase of the poor has become a burden to the kingdom ; and their loose and idle life does in some measure contribute to that depravation of manners which is complained of, I fear with too much reason ; whether the ground of this evil be in defects in the laws already made, or in the execution of them, deserves your consideration ; ' and although complaints appear to have been continually since made of the increasing number of the poor, yet it was not until the present reign in the year 1776, that authentic accounts of this expenditure were required under the authority of the legislature." (*Report from the Select Committee on the Poor Laws.* 1817. p. 5.)

[27] " The money, yearly paid by the subjects for the relief of the Poor is nigh as much as an assessment of seventy thousand pounds a month to the king." (*The Grand Concern of England Explained,* printed in *The Harleian Miscellany.* Vol. 8. p. 581.)

[28] " Every Man ", he wrote, " who hath any Property, must feel the weight of that Tax which is levied for the Use of the Poor ; and every Man who hath any Understanding, must see how absurdly it is applied. So very useless indeed is this heavy Tax, and so wretched its Disposition, that it is a Question whether the Poor or the Rich are actually more dissatisfied, or have indeed greater Reason to be dissatisfied ; since the Plunder of the one serves so little to the real Advantage of the other : for while a million yearly is raised among the former, many of the latter are starved ; many more languish in Want and Misery ; of the rest, Numbers are found begging and pilfering in the Streets to-day, and to-morrow are locked up in Gaols and Bridewells." (*A Proposal for Making an effectual Provision, etc.* H. Fielding. 1753. pp. 8–9.)

[28] In the Hundred of Blything in Suffolk the accounts were produced " of the Poor's Rates for the several Parishes, which appear to be increased about one Half in the last Ten Years." (*House of Commons Journals.* Vol. 24, p. 771.)

[28] In the Hundreds of Bosmere and Claydon it was asserted " that the Expence of supporting them for the last Eight Years is, in many places double to what it was in the Eight preceeding years." (*House of Commons Journals.* Vol. 29, p. 770.)

[28] The parish of St. Phillip and St. Jacob, in Gloucester, stated, " That the Poor's Rates are very much increased : That in the year 1723 they amounted to £446 and in the years 1728 and 1729 they amounted to £812 each Year ; and apprehends, that this Year the said Rates will amount to £900 or upwards, occasioned by the

Weaving Trade being lessesned, and the Manufactures wanting Employment." *House of Commons Journals.* Vol. 21, p. 684.)

[29] *Proposals for Building in every County a Working Alms House.* R. Hains. 1678. p. 1.

[30] *Bread for the Poor.* R. Dunning. 1686. p. 1.

[31] *House of Commons Journals.* Vol. 28, p. 772.

[32] *House of Commons Reports.* Vol. 9, p. 241.

[33] *An Essay upon Ways and Means.* C. Davenant. 1695. p. 79.

[34] *Political Conclusions.* G. King. 1696. p. 48.

[35] *The Poor Book of Westbury on Trym.* H. J. Wilkins. 1910. pp. 70, 87, 156.

[36] *A Warwickshire Parish.* R. Hudson. 1904. p. 204.

[37] *A History of Kettering.* F. W. Bull. 1891. p. 59.

[38] *The State of the Poor.* Sir F. Eden. Vol. 11, pp. 20, 144–5, 208, 291, 587. Vol. 111, p. 742.

[39] *The Liverpool Vestry Book.* H. Peet 1912 pp 48, 86

[40] *The State of the Poor.* Sir F. Eden. 1797. Vol. ii, pp. 5, 41, 221, 387

[41] *The History of Local Rates in England* E Cannan 1896. pp. 78–101.

[42] *House of Commons Journals.* Vol. 22, p. 270.

[43] *Ibid.* Vol. 24, p. 163.

[44] *Ibid.* Vol. 28, p. 41.

[45] *Ibid.* Vol. 36, p. 265.

[46] *A Peep into an old Monkwearmouth Rate Book.* J. T. Middlemass. 1901. p. 5.

[47] " It is the opinion of this vestry that all persons within this town who are assessed to pay for their stock in trade are liable to pay for what they are assessed unless they appeal and show cause to the contrary. Also it is ordered by this vestry that Mr Fazakerley's opinion be immediately taken whether a person's Stock in Trade is liable to pay towards the Poor's Rate." (*The Liverpool Vestry Book.* H. Peet. 1902. p. 502.)

[48] *Provision for the Poor.* Sir M. Hale. 1683. p. 7.

[49] " Upon hearing the appeal of Francis Hill against a rate for the relief of the Poor of the parish of Bradford in this county, complaining that he was assessed and rated for and in respect of his stock in trade in the said parish, whereas he was advised he was not by law liable to be so assessed and rated in respect of such stock in trade, it appeared in evidence, that the said appellant was a clothier, and that he was and for some years past had been, an inhabitant of the said parish of Bradford, where many other tradesmen, particularly clothiers and manufacturers of woollen goods, likewise lived ; and that he there carried on the business of a clothier, and that he was, and at the time of making the rate in question was actually possessed of a considerable stock in such his trade within the said parish of Bradford. And that the churchwardens and overseers of the poor of the said parish, at Easter 1775, made the rate in question, which was properly allowed by two justices of the peace, for the relief of the poor of the said parish ; and therein charged the appellant a penny as his share or contribution towards the relief of the poor of the said parish for the said year 1775, in respect of his stock in the said clothing trade, which he then had in the said parish ; and which said charge of a penny a rate was proved to be no more than his just proportion and share towards the said rate, if, in respect of his said stock in trade, he was legally bound to contribute anything towards the

relief of the said poor of the said parish.   Whereupon, and upon due consideration of the premises, this Court doth order and adjudge, that the said rate be, and the same is, hereby confirmed." (*Decisions of the Court of King's Bench*, etc., ed. F. Bott.   1793. Vol. 1, pp. 137–9.)

[50] *A History of Brighthelmstone.*   J. A. Erredge.   1862.   p. 53.

[51] " Oct. 7, 1679.   Whereas it appears to this Court by the petition of the Inhabts of Anderly Steeple that they are overburdened and charged towards the maintenance of the poor within the said town and that the town of Wallaby within the said parish hath few or none within it :   Ordered that the Inhabts of Wallaby do contribute towards the maintenance of the poor of Anderly Steeple according to the statute of the 43rd of Elizabeth."   *Quarter Session Records of the North Riding*, ed. A. C. Atkinson.   1884.   Vol. 6, p. 26.

[52] *Hertford County Records*, ed. W. T. Hardy.   1905–8.   Vol. 1, p. 368.

[53] " in the Year 1698, there was a Surplus of £300 in the Overseer's Hands, for that Year, above what maintained the Poor ;   and which, as the Law directs, ought to have been paid into the Hands of the Subsequent Overseers ;   but was, by a majority of St. Martin's Vestry, voted to be paid into their Hands :   And that, in the Year 1699 the said Hill being One of the Overseers, there did likewise remain, in his and his Partner's Hands, an overplus of about £220, which he the said Hill would have paid over to the succeeding Overseers ;   but his partner opposing the same, and the vestry, taking cognizance of their Dispute, did, not withstanding all the Opposition he could make to so illegal a Practice, by Majority of Voices, oblige him to pay the said £220 to them, and not to the succeeding Overseers as he has since been informed he might by Law have done, without their Consent or Approbation.   And the said Hill further said, That he being afterwards in the Year 1705, required to pay his Proportion of the Arrears of an Additional Assessment, made in the said parish for the maintenance of the Poor for four or five Years before, and refusing to pay the same because the Additional Charge was unnecessarily laid ;   he knowing of the aforesaid great surplusages, which would have saved the said additional Assessment, if those sums had been applied as the Law directs ;   Mr Price and Mr Vincent and Mr Ithell, the church-wardens and vestrymen of St. Martin's Parish, with a Constable, Two Collectors and a Beadle, of a distant ward, did distrain a Silver Pepper Box out of his House, and detain the same, till he had paid his Proportion of the said additional Assessment ;   Also, that several of his Neighbours were frightened into Payment of the said Assessment, under the Apprehension of the like distraint, being summoned to the Vestry ;   and there threatened to have their Goods seized, if they did not pay ;   by which means, great Sums were raised out of the Deficiencies of the Poor's Rates for several Years after the Books were delivered up, wherein they returned such as insolvent."   (*House of Commons Journals.*   Vol. 18, p. 394.)

CHAPTER III

THE PARTIAL SUCCESS OF THE PARISH IN THE SPHERE OF POOR RELIEF

[1] *Lancashire Quarter Sessions.* July. 1686.

[2] *Cambridgeshire Order Books.* 16th Jan. 1717–18.

[2] " Whereas complaint was made to this Court by Alice Chapman of Swaffam Prior in this county, spinster, for a weekly allowance to be made to her the said Alice Chapman, she being poor and indigent and not able to maintain herself and being neglected by the inhabitants of the said Parish of Swaffham Prior. This Court . . . do order the overseers of the poor of Swaffham Prior do pay the said Alice Chapman six pence per week in the summer season and a shilling in the winter till further order." (*Cambridgeshire Order Book.* 1718.)

[3] *Quarter Session Records of the North Riding of Yorkshire,* ed. A. C. Atkinson. 1884. Vol. 6, p. 111.

[4] *Cambridgeshire Order Book.* 10th Oct. 1700.

[5] For example at Leyton a certain Jane Sneed had obtained an order for relief but, " At a vestry the order of the Justice was read by George Hockerhull to the Vestry after which he desired Wm. Wood, one of the overseers to take itt and perform the order butt he refused itt and told the vestry he would not trouble his head about itt, and scornfully went out of the church. The other overseer Dirvall at last was persuaded to take itt, but nothing was done with Jane att that time thro' the vestry was very willing to allow a weekly relief according to the order, had the overseers demanded itt of them." (*History of the Parish of Leyton.* J. Kennedy. 1894. p. 375.)

[6] *The Poor Book of Westbury on Trym.* H. J. Wilkins. 1910. p. 44.

[6] *Ibid.,* pp. 50, 67, 114, 130.

[6] List of Poor receiving weekly pensions at Westbury in 1664.

Imp payd to	Joane Wade 12 moneths at 4.0. a.m.	02–08–00
,,	,,	,,	Jane Lane 12 moneths at 2.6. a.m.	01–10–00
,,	,,	,,	John Hunt 12 moneths at 2.6. a.m.	01–10–00
,,	,,	,,	William Coats 12 moneths at 3.0. a moneth	01–16–00
,,	,,	,,	Robert Smith 12 moneths at 2.6. a moneth	01–10–00
,,	,,	,,	Richard Dean 12 moneths at 2.6. a moneth	01–10–00
,,	,,	,,	Agnes Smith 12 moneths at 1.0. a moneth	00–12–00
,,	,,	,,	Edward Lansdown 12 moneths at 4.0. a moneth	02–08–00
,,	,,	,,	Widow Wood 12 moneths at 4.0. a moneth	02–08–00
,,	,,	,,	Widow Wickham 12 moneths at 3.0. a moneth	01–16–00
,,	,,	,,	Widd. Thomas 12 moneths at 3.0. a moneth	01–16–00
,,	,,	,,	Katherine Drinkwater 12 moneths at 1.6. a moneth	00–18–00

(*The Poor Book of Westbury on Trym.* ed. H. J. Wilkins. 1910. p. 43–5.)

[8] List of Poor receiving weekly pensions at Tysoe. 1728, January.

```
To Edward Plestoe .........................2–0
   Juda Brewer .............................5–0
   Widow Wells ............................1–6
   Widow Lively ...........................1–6
   Widow Capp .............................1–6
   Widow Wilkins .........................1–6
   Francis Howell .........................1–0
   Eliz. Elliot .............................1–0
   Joe Ball .................................2–0
   Henry Wilkins .........................2–0
   Given to David Plestoe .................1–0
```

(*One Hundred Years of Poor Law Administration in a Warwickshire Village*, by A. W. Ashby, in *Oxford Studies in Social and Legal History*, Vol. III, p. 117.)

[8] *A Warwickshire Parish*. R. Hudson. 1904. p. 208.

[9] Ad. MSS. (Brit. Mus.). Eg. 2437.

[10] *Olde Leeke*. M. H. Miller. 1891. p. 30.

[11] *The Vestry Minutes of St Margeret Lothbury*, ed. Edwin Freshfield. 1887. pp. 143–4.

[12] List of the Poor receiving weekly pensions at Tooting Graveney.

```
Wido Wilson Pension from ye 17th of April 1702 till Decem-
  ber 14th, 36 weeks at 3 Shillings pr Weeke ..............£5– 8–0
  and 15 weeks at 2s. Weeke.............................£1–10–0
Wido Bespitch 51 Weeks at 1/6 Pr Weeke..................£3–16–0
Tho. Day from April ye 13th 3 weeks at 1/- Pr Weeke ......   3–0
  and 8 weeks at 1/6 pr Weeke .........................  12–0
  and 29 weeks at 2 Shill pr Weeke .....................£2–18–0
Wm Ely from October ye 12th till March ye 29th 1703 being
  25 weeks att 1/6 pr week .............................£1–17–6
```

(*History of the Parish of Tooting Graveney*, by W. E. Morden. 1897. pp. 118–19.)

[13] *A History of the Parish of Ribchester*. T. C. Smith. 1890. p. 67.

[14] *Quarter Sessions Records for the North Riding of Yorkshire*. A. C. Atkinson. 1884. Vol. 6, pp. 118, 191.

[15] *The Account Book of St Bartholomew Exchange*, ed. E. Freshfield. 1895. p. 193.

[16] " Att a vestry lawfully called and met the 29th of Juley 1662 it was put to the vott and Carried by al handes that Care should be tacken for a malle Child that was laidd in the Parish of St Margeret Lothbury the 28th of Juley at night and that the Collecter should pay the Charges ther of from tim to tim as it shall groe Due." (*The Vestry Minutes of St Margeret Lothbury*, ed. E. Freshfield. 1887. p. 117.)

[17] *The Poor Book of Westbury on Trym*. H. J. Wilkins. 1910. pp. 232, 270, 233, 260.

[18] *The Poor Booke of Poole*. Add. Mss. Eg. 2437 (Brit. Mus.)

[19] *The Poor Book of Westbury on Trym*. H. J. Wilkins. 1910. pp. 160, 168, 207, 174, 175.

[20] Expences incurred on behalf of Ned Hatter.

```
" Edward Hatter 13mon. at 6s p. mo end ye 13th of aprill  ..04–01–00
" payd for a Coat and breeches and making it for Edward
                                    Hatter .......00–11–00
" payd for two Shirts and two payre of stocking and shooes
                          for Hatter (1687) ..
" Edward Hatter 5 mo ½ at 6s p.m.  ...................01–13–00
```

NOTES TO CHAPTER III 263

" payd for two suits of clothes for Ned Hatter & Sarah P
Pullins boy 01–02–00
" for 4 shirts and hatts for these boys..................... 00–16–00
" payd for two payre of shooes and 2 payre of Stockins for
these boyes ...00–07–08
(*The Poor Books of Westbury on Trym*, ed. H. J. Wilkins. 1910.
p. 200.)

[21] *The Natural and Political Observations upon the Bills of Mortality.*
Jasper Gaunt. 1676. p. 27.
[22] *Middlesex County Records*, ed W. J. Hardy. 1909. p. 110.
[23] *House of Commons Journals.* Vol. 18. 8th March. 1715. p. 396.
[24] *An Earnest Appeal for Mercy to the Children of the Poor.* J. Hanway.
1766. p. 39.
[25] *House of Commons Journals.* Vol. 31. 24th March. 1767. p. 248.
[26] *A Discourse of the Poor.* R. North. (pub.) 1753. p. 33.
[27] *Some Details of the Parish of Tonbridge.* B. Wadmore. 1906. p. 78.
[28] *Middlesex County Records*, ed. W. J. Hardy. 1905. p. 124.
[29] *History of Brighthelmstone.* J. H. Erredge. 1862. p. 54.
[30] *Ancient Account Book of Cowden.* (Sussex Arch. Soc. Vol. 20, p. 115)
[31] *Middlesex County Records*, ed. W. J. Hardy. 1905. p. 291.
[32] *Hertford County Records*, ed. W. J. Hardy. 1905–8. Vol. 2. p. 70.
[33] *Some Proposals for the Imployment of the Poor.* T. Firmin. 1681.
p. 2.
[34] *Report to the Board of Trade.* J. Locke. 1697. p. 111.
[35] " 1766 Gave to John Benson's wife on account of the largeness of her
family..o–2–6." (*A History of the Church of St Giles, Northampton.*
R. M. Serjeantson. 1911. p. 238.)
[36] *A Discourse of the Poor.* R. North. 1753. p. 43.
[37] *Journals of the House of Commons.* Vol. 28, 30th May.
[38] *Victoria County History: Hampshire.* Vol. 5, p. 431.
[39] *A Plan of Police.* T. Gilbert. 1786. p. 15.
[40] *History of Leytonstone.* W. G. Hammock. 1904. p. 42.
[41] *Hertford County Records*, ed. W. J. Hardy. 1905–8. Vol. 1, p. 347.
[42] " Upon the complaint of Robt Baines of Sutton that he wanteth a
place of habitation for himself his wife and children to live in and
that he hath obtained the consent of the lord and freeholders in
Sutton to erect a cottage there it is . . . ordered by this Court that
it shall and may be lawful to and for the said Robt Baines to erect
a cottage in Sutton in such place as the lord and freeholders of the
saud towne have sett forth for him." (*Lancashire Order Book.*
19th April. 1686.)
[43] *Lancashire Order Book.* 1666. July.
[44] *Ibid.*, Oct. 1666.
[45] " itt is A Greed that the parish shall sett her house in repaire and take
it to the parishes owne handes." (*The Vestry Minutes of the
Churchwardens of the Church of St Mary's*, ed. J. R. Abney. 1912.
p. 65.)
[46] *Records of Batley.* M. Sheard. 1894. p. 217–18.
[47] *Lancashire Order Books.* Oct. 1666.
[48] *Ibid.* 1700.
[48] *An Account of Several Workhouses*, 1732. p. 133.
[49] *The Liverpool Vestry Book*, ed. H. Peet. 1912. p. 89.
[50] *The Vestry Book and Churchwardens Accounts of St. Mary Leicester*,
ed. J. E. Abney. 1912. p. 132.
[51] " paid John Reynolds rent 06–08
" pd for house rent for Abigal Parker 20s this yeare and halfe
a yeare that was behind for last yeare 01–12–00

" Payd for ye Widd: Wild one whole yeare rent 02–00–00
" for Goody Hughes rent 00–15–06
(*Poor Book of Westbury on Trym.* H. J. Wilkins. 1910. pp. 194, 233, 237.)

52 *The Vestry Minutes of St Margaret's Lothbury,* ed. E. Freshfield. 1887. p. 114.

53 *Records of Batley.* M. Sheard. 1894. p. 237.

54 *Sussex Arch. Coll.* Vol. 20, p. 114.

55 *Ibid.* Vol. 23, p. 98.

56 *A Cornish Parish.* Jos. Hammond. 1897. pp. 88, 89.

57 *The Poor Book of Westbury on Trym.* H. J. Wilkins. 1910. pp. 259, 282, 280, 192.

58 *Hawkshead, the Northmost Parish in Lancashire.* E. S. Cooper. 1899. p. 422.

59 *The Poor Book of Westbury on Trym.* H. J. Wilkins. 1910. p. 282.

60 *East Anglia.* Vol. 9, p. 274.

61 *The History of Leytonstone.* W. G. Hammock. 1904. p. 45.

32 *Hawkshead, the Northmost Parish in Lancashire.* H. S. Cooper. 1899. p. 422.

63 *Cambridgeshire Quarter Sessions*: Miscellaneous Papers.

64 *Memorials of a Warwickshire Parish.* W. Hudson. 1904. p. 206.

65 *Memorials of Herne, Kent.* J. Buchanan. 1887. p. 55.

66 *The Poor Book of Westbury on Trym.* H. J. Wilkins. 1910. p. 262.

67 Westbury.
   In 1668 " paid for coals for William Coats 00–03–04
            " paid for 2 horse load of coals for John Reynold 00–02–00
   In 1686 " Given Goody Evans her husband being in
              prison & she and her children being in Great
              Want at several tymes in money and cole .00–14– 0
            " Given to Goody Haskins towards cole for firing 00–01– 0
   1689   " Paid for 3 Horse loade of Cole for William
              Smith 00–03– 0
(*The Poor Book of Westbury on Trym,* ed. Wilkins. pp. 68, 168, 193, 213.) See also *A Hundred Years of Poor Law Administration in a Warwickshire Village,* by A. W. Ashby in *Oxford Social and Legal Studies.* Vol. 3, p. 128–9.

68 *The Poor Book of Westbury on Trym.* H. J. Wilkins. 1910. p. 169, 199, 123–155, 161, 130, 118.

69 *The Ancient Account Book of Cowden.* Sussex Arch. Soc. Vol. 20, p. 112 & 118.

70 *A Parochial History of St Mary's of Bourne.* J. Stevens. 1888. p. 239 & 240.

71 *A Cornish Parish.* J. Hammond. 1897. p. 90.

72 *Memorials of a Warwickshire Parish.* R. Hudson. 1904. p. 206.

73 *The Poor Book of Westbury on Trym.* H. J. Wilkins. 1910. p. 148

74 Small Pox.
   " To John Dogget when Grace Loynes had the small Pocks ...£1– 1–0
   " For nursing Wickam's boy with small pocks £00–12–0
(*Ancient Acct. Book of Cowden,* p. 117.)
   " For the small pox to Isace Munday £5–7–6
   " To four men for carrying the small pox people £1–4–6
(*A Parochial History of the Church of St Mary of Bourne.* J. Stevens. 1888. p. 240.)

75 *Ancient Account Book of Cowden* (Sussex Arch. Soc. Vol. 20, p. 117.)

75 *A Parochial History of the Church of St Mary of Bourne.* J. Stevens. 1888. p. 240.

NOTES TO CHAPTER III 265

[76] *A History of the Parish of Tooting Graveney.* W. E. Morden. 1897. p. 191.

[77] *A History of the Parish of Leyton.* J. Kennedy. 1894. pp. 146, 149, 150.

[78] *History of the Parish of Ribchester.* T. C. Smith. 1890. p. 67.

[79] *Quarter Session Records for the North Riding of Yorkshire.* A. C. Atkinson. 1884. Vol. 7.

[80] *Histories of Manningham, Heaton, and Alterton.* Wm. Cudworth. 1896. p. 23.

[81] *The Poor Book of Westbury on Trym.* H. J. Wilkins. 1910. p. 193.

[82] *A Parochial History of St Mary of Bourne.* J. Stevens. 1888. p. 240.

[83] *Ye Parish of Camberwell.* H. C. Blanch. 1875. p. 123.

[84] *The Quarter Session Records of the North Ridnig of Yorkshire,* ed. A. C. Atkinson. 1884. Vol. 6, p. 127.

[85] *The Account Book of the Parish of St Bartholomew Exchange,* ed. E. Freshfield. 1895. pp. 166–7.

[86] *Fenland Notes and Queries.* Vol. 11, p. 167.

[87] *A Cornish Parish.* J. Hammond. 1897. p. 90.

[88] *Ye Parish of Camberwell.* H. C. Blanch. 1875. p. 123.

[89] *Burton on Trent.* Wm. Molyneaux. 1869. p. 201.

[90] "1709, By cash returned by Mrs. Burden for not curing Creppers head..1–1–0." (*A Cornish Parish.* J. Hammond. 1897. p. 91.)

[91] *The Poor Book of Westbury on Trym.* H. J. Wilkins. 1910. p. 260.

[92] *East Anglian.* Vol. 4, p. 13.

CHAPTER IV

THE FAILURE OF THE PARISH TO EMPLOY THE POOR

[1] *The Quarter Sessions Records for the North Riding of Yorkshire*, sd. A. C. Aitkinson. 1884. Vol. 6, p. 112.

[2] *East Anglian.* Vol. 13, p. 70.

[3] *Records of Batley.* M. Sheard. 1894. p. 214.

[4] *History of the Parish of St. Giles, Northampton.* J. C. Cox. 1911. p. 238.

[5] *Burton on Trent.* Wm. Molyneaux. 1869. p. 96.

[6] *A History of the Parish of Leyton.* J. Kennedy. 1894. p. 147.

[7] *St John Baptist, Church and Parish, Chester.* S. Cooper Scott. p. 130.

[8] " Agreed That Twentie poundes p' cell of the monies given by Mr Packer to be ymployed to sett the poore on worke, be delivered to Mr John Mayatt woollen Draper, upon his owne bond, to be ymployed to sett the poore to worke." *(Records of the Borough of Abbingdon,* ed. B. Challoner. 1896. p. 144.)

[9] " That to imploy and sett most at worke It is conceived that ye woollen trade is most useful and that wooll bee wrought into yarn or worsted fitt both to make into cloth stuffs and into stockings. That there be a Workhouse fitt to work in and storehouse wherein to receive all ye stocks, And thereout to deliver such quantities of wooll and other commodities as from time to time there shall be occacion, And for ye place to work in do pprose one barne now in ye possession of Mr. Thomas Jepson and ye barnes called ye old school house. That wheels, spindles, wharles, combs, cards and other instruments and utensils bee made ready and fitt to worke withall. That there be a master workman to teach and instruct those who are to learne and to direct and appoint those who can work. That ye churchwardens and overseers of the Poor doe deliver unto ye Mayor and Councell ye names of all ye poore people in ye town and there out may bee choyse made whom of them shall be sett on work. That one or more fitt and solvent ppson or ppsons be appoynted to buy in wooll, and deliver out ye comodyties and to bee Master or Masters of ye store house and keep acompts of all receipts and payments and from time to time to deliver upp their accounts to ye said Mayor and Councell. That ye Mayor and Councell shall sett ye rates of ye wages of any who are workers and also of all other servants according to ye statutes of this Realm. Ye wages of such as shall be imployed in ye house bee weekly paid unto every pson working or unto their parents upon every Friday night at such time as they leave of working."

Five years later new regulations were made to the effect that :—
" The saide children and other persons who are imployed and sett to work at the saide Workhouse shall every yr between the 1st day of March and the 1st of October dayly go and repair unto the Workhouse by 6 of the clock in the morneing and there continue working till 12 of the clock at noon, and shall in the afternoons return again at one o'clock and there continue working until

7 at night ; and between the 1st of October and the 1st of March
shall dayly go to ye worke at 7 in the morning and continue till
12 at noone, and then return at one and continue till six in the
evening, and shall respectively receive such wages and rates . . .
as the said master workman shall think fitt and shall be allowed
and approved of by the sd Mayor and Councell or the mayor part
of them." (*A History of Preston*. A. Hewitson. 1883. pp. 398
& 400.)

10 *The State of the Poor*. Sir F. Eden. 1797. Vol. 11, pp. 35, 53, 76.
11 *An Account of Several Workhouses*. 1732. p. 130.
12 " There are 12 Governors chosen annually for the management of
it of which the two churchwardens and the two Overseers of the
Poor, are always of the Number ; two Governors, in their Turns,
take Care Weekly to visit the Workhouse every Day, to see good
Orders and to inspect into the Affairs of the House : And the first
Sunday of every Month, as many of the Governors as can meet
at the House to give Directions, if there be occasion, for cloathing,
etc." (*Rochester Workhouse : an Account of Several Workhouses,
etc*. 1732. p. 135.)
13 " 1 That the Master and Misstress be sober and orderly Persons,
and not given to swear, and that they see the Orders strictly performed. 2 That they rise by seven a Clock in the Morning from
Michaelmas to Lady Day and by six from Lady Day to Michaelmas.
3 That they see the Family a Bed eight a Clock, and their candles
out, during the Winter half Year ; but in the Summer half Year,
that they be in Bed by nine. 4 That they have their Breakfast
in the Winter half Year at eight in the Morning, and in the Summer
half Year by seven. 5 That they have their Dinner by one
o' Clock all the Year. 6 That they have their Supper at six in
the Evening during the Winter half year, and in the Summer at
seven. 7 That the Beer be drawn by one Person for a whole Day
in his Turn. 8 That the Cloth be laid by Turns for Breakfast,
Dinner and Supper. 9 That they sit at the Table to eat their
meals in a decent manner. 10 That the Master say Grace before
and after their Meals. 11 That they have the House swept from
top to bottom every Morning, and washed once a Week. 12
That they are called to work in Summer by seven and in the
Winter by eight in the morning. 13 That they leave work at
seven o' Clock at Night in the Summer, and six in the Winter.
14 That no Person go out of the Gate without the Master's Leave.
15 That if any Person steals, or is heard to swear or curse, for such
Crimes the first time to stand on a stool at one Corner of the
Working Room, the whole Day, with the Crime pinned to their
Breast. 16 That for the Second Offence he or she shall stand in the
like Posture, and have half a Pound of Bread, and a Quart of Water
for that Day. 17 That for a third Offence, he or she be ordered
by a Justice of the Peace to be publicly whippt. 18 That the
Master read, or cause to be read, Prayers every Morning before
Breakfast, and every Evening before Supper, and call together as
many as can conveniently be there. 19 That these Prayers shall
be out of ' The Whole Duty of Man,' or some other good Book as
the Minister shall appoint. 20 That the Master and Misstress shall
every Lord's day attend at the Public Worship, with as many of
the House as are not hindered by a just Reason. 21 That on the
Lord's Day either before Church, or after Dinner, he do read, or
cause to be read, the Psalms and lessons appointed for the Morning
Service : and after Evening Prayer, the Psalms and Lessons for

the Evening Service ; and also a section or chapter out of the
' Whole Duty of Man.' That the Master and Misstress do receive
the Holy Sacrament four Times every Year at least. 22 That
the Master do give an Account every Monthly Meeting of all such
as are negligent and disorderly." *(An Account of Several Workhouses*, etc. 1732. pp. 107–8.

WORKHOUSES

[13] *Bedford :—*

Sunday	Bread & Cheese.	Boil'd Beef & Suet Pudding.	Bread & Cheese.
Monday	Broth.	Cold meat left from Sunday.	,, ,, ,,
Tuesday	Bread & Cheese.	Boil'd Beef & a little mutton & Suet Pudding.	,, ,, ,,
Wednesday	Same as Monday.		
Thursday	Same as Tuesday.		
Friday	Same as Monday.		
Saturday	Bread & Cheese.	Hasty Pudding or Milk Porridge.	Broth or Bread & Cheese.

(An Account of Several Workhouses, etc. 1732. p. 81.)

Cartmel :—

Sunday	Bread & Cheese or Bread & Butter & Beer.	Meat with Broth & Herbs or Roots as in Season.	
Monday	Broth & Bread & Beer.	Pease Porridge or Pudding.	Bread & Cheese or Butter or cockles or Potatoes or Parsnips or meat left at Dinner at the discretion of the Master or Mistress for daily supper.
Tuesday	Milk Porridge.	Meat, etc.	
Wednesday	Same as Monday.	Rice Milk.	
Thursday	Water Porridge.	Meat, etc.	
Friday	Same as Monday.	Same as Monday.	
Saturday	Milk Porridge.	Rice Milk or Hasty Pudding.	

Beer was to be allowed " at the discretion of the Master and Mistress
not exceeding a pint at one meal to each person. (*Annals of
Cartmel*. By J. Stockdale. 1872. p. 172.) (*An Account of
Several Workhouses.* 1732. pp. 91, 104, 144, 146.)

[13] At Onley, " the poor People, if of healthful Bodies, and able, shall in
Summer rise at five, or before that time, and go to bed at nine."

[13] At Kingston upon Hull, " the healthful and strong " were to rise at
six in the summer and eight in the winter, and to be in bed at nine
in the first case and eight in the second. (*Account of Several
Workhouses.* 1732. pp. 95, 175.)

[14] *Ibid.* pp. 146, 91, 104, 144.

[15] " Itm Agreed with the Parish of Hendley to allow Jno. Bloss to take
all such persons as shall become chargeable to the sd Parish as
followeth for Mary Kettle 2s. per week for Eliz. Ward 1/6 for Rose
Ward 1s. & for Sarah Lord 1s. 6d. & to allow him two Loads of
Wood & a chaldcon of coals & for all the other Persons herein

after mentioned as the said Parishtioners shall hereafter agree to allow for them & the sd Jno. Bloss in consideration of the sd Agreement doth prommise to provide, keep & maintain all the persons before mentioned with good & sufficient meat, Drink, Washing & Lodging during the Terme they are so put out to him fr Easter 1763 to Easter 1764." (*East Anglian*, N.S. Vol. 4, p. 95.)

[16] *History of the Parish of Tooting Graveney.* W. E. Morden. 1897. pp. 282, 64, 67, 68.

[17] *Report on the Relief and Settlement of the Poor* (*House of Commons Reports.* Vol. 9. pp. 272–83.)

[18] Sums paid for farming out the City Poor.

At Hoxton.

St Helen	4–3	per head per week.
St John Zachary	4–3	,, ,, ,, ,,
St Orga	4–3	,, ,, ,, ,,

At Mile End.

St Faith under St Paul's	3–6	including clothes.
All Hallows	3–6	for grown persons.
, ,,	3–0	for children with allowance of £1–7–0 for clothes if necessary.
S Margaret, Lothbury		ditto.
St Margaret Moses (since 1761)		ditto.
St Martin Vintry		ditto.

At Black Fryers.

St Olave, Silver Street	3–9	for grown persons.
	3–3	for children.
St. Katherine, Colman St.	4–0	for grown persons.
	3–6	for children (exclusive of clothes.)
St Lawrence, Pountney		ditto.

(*Reports* (1715–1802) *from Committees of the House of Commons printed by order of the House and not inserted in the Journals.* Vol. 9. 21st Feb. 1776. pp. 272–83.)

[19] *An Account of Several Workhouses.* 1732. pp. 72, 86, 117, 110.

[20] *Some Details of the Parish of Tonbridge.* B. Wadmore. 1906. p. 84.

[21] *A Letter to the Author of Several Considerations*, etc., 1752. pp. 26 & 44.

[22] *Observations on the Present State of the Parochial and Vagrant Poor.* J. Scott. 1773. pp. 39–40.

[23] *The State of the Poor.* Sir F. Eden. 1797. Vol. 3, p. 90.

[24] *Observations on the Present State of the Parochial and Vagrant Poor.* J. Scott. 1773. p. 36.

[25] *Observations on the Poor Laws*, etc. Dr Trotter. 1775. p. 52.

[26] *A Letter to the Author*, etc. 1752. p. 43.

[27] *Observations*, etc. J. Scott. 1773. p. 41.

[28] *A History of the Poor Poor.* T. Ruggles. 1793. p. 285.

[29] *House of Commons Journals.* Vol. 35. p. 154.

[30] *Bedfordshire County Records*, ed. W. J. Hardy and Page. 1907. p. 14.

[31] *A Brief Statement of the Facts*, etc. 1796. p. 20.

[32] *House of Commons Journals.* Vol. 34. p. 617.

[33] *Ibid.* Vol. 22, p. 270.

[34] *An Account of Several Workhouses*, etc. 1732. p. 38.

[35] *House of Commons Journals.* Vol. 25. p. 135.

[36] *Ibid.* Vol. 32, p. 698.

[37] *Ibid.* p. 617.

[38] *An Earnest Appeal for Mercy to the Children of the Poor.* J. Hanway. 1766. pp. 8 & 43.

[39] *House of Commons Journals.* Vol. 31. p. 248.

[40] *An Account of Several Workhouses*, etc. 1732. p. 147.

[41] *The State of the Poor.* Sir F. Eden. 1797. Vol. 11, p. 143.

[42] *An Account of Several Workhouses*, etc. 1732. p. 164.

[43] St Albans, "Give me leave to warne you and your friends not to promise yourselfe too much from the labour of the people when they engage in such a management for the public good . . . so that if you keep them employed thro' the Produce be no more than will pay for the Articles of Firing and Candels it is something not to be despised." (*An Account of Several Workhouses.* 1732. p. 115.)

[44] Expenses of various workhouses for food, clothes and firing in 1772 contrasted with sums earned.

Place.	Expenses.	
Hundred of Blything	£1790– 7–2	£453– 9– 2
Norwich	£7224– 9–3	£398– 0– 7
Beverley	£176– 5–0	£6– 0– 0
King's Lynn	£796– 0–0	£77– 0–10
St George, Hanover Square	£4370–19–7	£208– 9– 9
St. James, Westminster	£3680–18–9	£112–12– 5

(*Reports from Committees of the House of Commons printed by order of the House and not inserted in the Journals.* Vol. 9. pp. 256–60.)

[45] *An Account of Several Workhouses.* 1732. p. 146.

[46] *Ibid.* 1732. pp. 61, 65, 255, 258–9.

[47] *Reports from the Committees of the House of Commons printed by order of the House.* Vol. 9, pp. 258–9.

[48] *An Account of Several Workhouses.* 1732. p. 164.

[49] "At the first opening of the House, there were Trustees or Governors chosen to inspect the management of it, who lived in the Town near the Workhouse, but these Gentlemen were rarely willing to take the Trouble upon them, by reason of the Small Share they paid towards the Support of it, in comparison to what the Farmers do ; and therefore the Management has been chiefly in the Hands of the Officers, who are generally the most substantial Farmers ; and they having had the Happiness to choose a good Master, they depend on his Conduct . . . there have been very few Complaints, the Shopkeepers and Butchers generally having their turns in serving the House."

"Hitherto we have suffered no inconvenience worth Notice by the Management of the Parish Officers, there having been a Succession of them that have had Regard to the Rules at first established for the Government of it and tho' there may seem some Partiality in serving the Workhouse themselves with Corn and Wood, yet as those Articles have been delivered at Market Price, they could not be censured. However, as we cannot be assured of the Integrity of their Successors, it is to be wished that the Trustees could be prevail'd on to make their visits more frequent to prevent any Possibility of future Irregularities."

(*An Account of Several Workhouses.* 1732. pp. 141–2.)

[50] *House of Commons Journal.* Vol. 22, p. 270.

[51] *A History of the Parish of Leyton.* J. Kennedy. 1894. p. 229.

[52] *House of Commons Journals.* Vol. 28, p. 667.

[53] *Ibid.* Vol. 25, p. 368.

[54] *A History of the Parish of Leyton.* J. Kennedy. 1894. p. 389.

[55] *A History of Leytonstone.* W. G. Hammock. 1904. p. 41.

[56] *An Account of Several Workhouses.* 1732. p. 114–15.

[57] *Ibid.* pp. 15, 121, 92, 101, 61.

[58] *The State of the Poor.* Sir F. Eden. 1797. Vol. 1, p. 270.

[59] *House of Commons Journals.* Vol. 34, p. 617.

[59] At Clerkenwell it was reported that " the Number of poor Persons had greatly increased of late Years, and is now so large that the Workhouse being too small to receive them, many are obliged to be relieved as Out Pensioners, which is attended with much inconvenience and additional expence." (*House of Commons Journals.* Vol. 35, p. 135.)

[60] *An Account of Several Workhouses,* etc. 1732. p. 128.

[61] *Reports from the Committees of the House of Commons printed by order of the House.* Vol. 9, pp. 256–62.

[62] *House of Commons Journals.* Vol. 35, p. 154.

[63] *Ibid.* Vol. 29.

[64] *Observations on the Poor Laws.* etc. Dr Trotter. 1775. pp. 37–38.

CHAPTER V

THE EFFECT OF PAROCHIAL ADMINISTRATION OF THE LAW ON THE STATE OF THE POOR

[1] e.g. " Whereas Richard Booker of the parish of St George the Martir within the cittie of Canterburye husbandman, is lately comed unto the parish of St. John's near Laughton, and there desireth to reside and continue, haveing had no legal setting or aboade there, but was last settled and remained at the cittye of Canterburye in the Said parish of St. George the Martir by the space of fowre moneths last past befire the 8th of Septemebt last past as appeareth by a certificate under the hands of William Whiting defunctic and Richard Tuxon common clerk, of the cittie, and for that it appeareth that the said Richard Booker is noe wandering beggar, ordered that the said Booker shall be remaunded and sent back unto the cittie of Canterburye unto the said parish of St. George the Martir there to be settled and remain." (*Records of the West Riding of Yorkshire*, p. 334, Doncaster 13th Oct., 1641.)

[2] " Order of Richard Goulsdon and Henry Chauncey, justice of the peace. Whereas upon the examination of John Bull, labourer, we find that he was lately a settled inhabitant in the parish of Aspeden, and he has since unduely removed himself into the parish of Layston, where he has obscured himself in a cottage about the space of three months last past, unknown to the inhabitants until exigency and necessity compelled him to crave their charity and relief, to the burdening of the parish of Layston ; it is therefore ordered that unless the parish of Aspeden show good cause at the next Quarter Session, why they should not receive the said John Bull and set him on work or otherwise relieve him, the constables of Layston shall forthwith convey him to Aspenden." (*Hertford County Records*, ed. W. J. Hardy. Vol. 1, p. 142.)

[3] " As it is not strange to see labourers have four or five children apiece, which they maintain by their labour, so it is common to see many maintain three children apiece in a decent manner : now admitting the wife maintains herself and one child, which is the most a woman can and what few will do ; what is needful to maintain himself and two children the husband must bear·; he must pay house rent which is yearly 20s., is upwards of .... 4d.
He must buy wood which cannot be less than .... 3d.
His own clothes, in 20s. yearly, cost above .... 4d.
His Sunday diet 2d. and his working tools weekly 1d. .... 3d.
There remains of his weekly wage to maintain 2 children in meat and drink, cloathes, attendance, washing etc. scarce above 1d. a day for each child .... 1s. 2d.
(*Bread for the Poor.* R. Dunning. 1698. p. 3.)

[4] " William Godfrey, an inhabitant of the town of Hitchin hired a house of Thomas Cowley, situate in the parish of Kingswalden, under the yearly rent of £2–5, for the term of one year, to commence from Lady Day, 1685, by virtue whereof Godfrey with his appren-

tice, did enter into the said house on the 25th March 1685, and laid goods there, but did abide there and some time at Hitchin, until the 24th of June following. Then Godfrey brought his wife and children who settled themselves there in the said house, by reason of their residence there the overseer of the poor for Kingswalden did charge him for the same house 6d. to their poor rate for the first year, and continuing there they charged him 2d. for the second year, and he paid that likewise, and the surveyors of the highways required the wife of Godfrey to gather stones for the repair of the highways in Kingswalden, by reason of her residence there, and she performed that duty in the year 1687, and Godfrey and his family continued in the said house until the time of his death which was almost five weeks before Michalmas 1687, but his wife and children continuing in the said house after the death of Godfrey, the overseers of the poor of the said parish of Kingswalden complained to the justices, at the next quarter sessions that Godfrey's wife and children endeavoured to settle themselves at Kingswalden in a cottage under the yearly value of £10, and were likely to become chargeable." (*Hertford County Records*, ed. W. J. Hardy. 1905–7. Vol. I, p. 376.)

[4] " A vast number of those who are employed in manufacturing towns are parishioners of different villages (particularly those in thei vicinity), and whenever infirmity, age, or check in trade happens, these men are not supported by those who have had the benefit of their labour, but are sent for subsistence to their respective parishes." (Wedge, writing in 1794 of Warwickshire, quoted A. W. Ashby, *One Hundred Years of Poor Law Administration in a Warwickshire Village.* p. 67. *Oxford Studies in Social and Legal History.* Vol. III, 1912.)

[5] *Middlesex County Records*, ed. W. J. Hardy. 1905. p. 10.

[6] *The Quarter Session Records of the North Riding of Yorkshire.* A. C. Atkinson. 1884. Vol. 6, p. 158.

[7] *Observations on the Defects of the Poor Laws.* T. Alcock. 1752. pp. 19–20.

[8] *Dunstable Parish Papers.*

[8] " Examination of Wm Fosses now Resident in the Parish of Dunstable tin plate worker :—This examinant (being duely sworn) sayeth that the last place of his legal settlement is in ye Parish of St Sephuleres in the County of Middlesex, which he gained by being apprentice to one Wm Miller of the said Parish Tinman and serving six years and seven months under indenture and that he hath not gained any other legal settlement." (*Dunstable MSS.*)

[9] " Paide for orders for carrying Betty Crowder to St Peter's parish and charge about finding out witnesses .. 00–13–06
Paide goeing to Gloucester on the Tryall of Elizabeth
and two witnesses and 4 horses and all charges about
the Bussiness against the Pish of St Peter's 06–17–06
(*The Poor Book of Westbury on Trym.* H. T. Wilkins. 1910, p. 280.)

[10] *The Poor Book of Westbury on Trym.* H. T. Wilkins. 1910. pp. 234, 193.

[11] *Hawkshead, the Northmost Parish in Lancashire.* H. S. Cooper. 1899, p. 422.

[12] *Dunstable MSS.*

[13] *Hertford County Records.* W. J. Hardy. 1905–7. Vol. I, pp. 271 & 210.

[14] " Forasmuch as it is duely proved to this Court," runs the entry, " that a man and his wife having lately come from his settlement

in Great Fencoate to inhabit in Danby Wiske in a tenement under the yearly value of £10 and having refused to give security for saving harmless the said town of Danby Wiske, were by a warrant from two Justices removed out of Danby Wiske unto Great Fencoate, the place of their last lawful settlement ; nevertheless the said man did not remain at Great Fencoate, but of his own accord returned to Danby Wiske : Ordered that the Constable of Danby Wiske do convey him to the Ho of Corr to be punished as a vagabond, until he be delivered etc. or settle himself at Great Fencoate according to the warrant above mentioned." (*Quarter Session Records for the North Riding of Yorkshire.* A. C. Aitkinson. 1884. Vol. 6, p. 241.)

14 " Forasmuch as two women were sent by warrant by two Justices from Thirske unto Walk, the place of their last lawful settlement, notwithstanding which they have returned unto Thirske aforesaid : Ordered that if they shall not, in obedience to the sd warrant, remain and abide at Warth, but contemptuously return to Thirske, that then they shall be conveyed to the Ho of Corr[n] there to remain." (*Ibid.* Vol. 6, p. 158.)

15 " That if any Person or Persons whatsoever, that from and after the first day of May, which shall be in the year of our Lord 1697, shall come into any Parish or other Place, thereunto inhabit and reside, shall at the same time produce, bring and deliver, to the Churchwardens and Overseers of the Poor, or to any or either of them, a Certificate, under the hands and seals of the Churchwardens and Overseers of the Poor of any other Parish, Township, or Place, or the major part of them, or under the hands and seals of the Overseers of the Poor of any other Place where there are no Churchwardens to be attested respectively by two or more credible Witnesses, thereby owning and acknowledging the Person or Persons mentioned in the said Certificate to be an Inhabitant or Inhabitants legally settled in that Parish, Township or Place, every such certificate having been allowed and subscribed by two or more of the Justices of the Peace of the County, City, Liberty, Borough or Town corporate, wherein the Parish or Place from which any such certificate shall come, doth lie, shall oblige the said Parish or Place to receive and provide for the Person mentioned in such certificate, together with his or her family, as Inhabitants of that Parish, whenever he, she, or they shall happen to become chargeable to or be forced to ask relief of the Parish, Township or Place to which the certificate was given, and then, and not till then shall it be lawful for any such Person, or his or her children, though born in that Parish, not having otherwise acquired a legal settlement there, to be removed, conveyed and settled in the Parish or Place from whence such certificate was brought." (*Decisions of the Court of King's Bench,* ed. F. Bott. Vol. 11, pp. 717–18, 882.)

16 " No person whatsoever who shall come into any parish by such certificate shall gain a settlement therein, unless he shall really and bona fide take a lease of a tenement of the value of ten pounds or shall execute any annual office being legally placed therein." (9 & 10 *W. & M.,* 3 *c.,* 11.)

16 " An apprentice or hired servant to a certificated person shall not, by virtue of any apprenticeship or hiring and service, gain any settlement in the parish, but every such apprentice and servant shall have his settlement in such parish, as if he had not been bound apprentice or served as a hired servant with such certificated person." (12 *Anne. c.* 18.)

[17] *Decisions of the Court of King's Bench*, ed. E. Bott. Vol. 11, pp. 717–18, 882.

[18] *History of the Parish of Tooting Graveney.* W. E. Morden. 1897. pp. 578, 65.

[19] *Burton on Trent.* Wm. Molyneaux. 1869. p. 98.

[20] *A History of the Church of the Holy Sepulchre, Northampton.* J. C. Cox. 1897. p. 217.

[21] " The difference in the several parishes it is said, arises in a great measure from the facility or difficulty of obtaining settlements, in several parishes a fine is imposed on a parishoner who settled a new comer, by hiring or otherwise, so that a servant is very seldom hired for the year. Those parishes have for a long time been in the habit of using such precautions, are now very lightly burdened with Poor. This is often the case where the farms are large and of course in few hands ; while other parishes, not politic enough to observe these rules, are generally burdened with an influx of poor neighbours." (*The State of the Poor.* Sir F. Eden. 1797. Vol. 3, p. 743.)

[22] *St Bartholomew Smithfield.* E. A. Webb. 1921. Vol. 1, p. 525.

[23] *History of the Parish of Tooting Graveney.* W. E. Morden. 1897. p. 78.

[24] *Voyage of Gonzales.* 1730 (*Pinkerton's Travels.* Vol. 2). pp. 33, 29.

[25] *A Plan of English Commerce.* D. Defoe. 1728. pp. 89–90.

[26] " The day abovesaid it was ordered that Tho. Scott a man that makes woman's pattown clogs in this city and he not being a brother of this gild or freman of this city be prosecuted if he will not move out of the liberty according to a discharge giuen him in this guild-hall." (*Municipal Records of Carlisle*, ed. R. S. Ferguson. 1887. p. 207.)

[27] *Hertford County Records*, ed. W. J. Hardy. 1905-7. Vol. 1, pp. 133, 166, 171. Vol. 11, pp. 141, 151, 206, 277.

[28] *History of the Company of Cutlers in Hallamshire.* R. E. Leader. 1905. p. 76n.

[29] *Report of the Commissioners of* 1833. Appendix A, Part 1. pp. 543 & 432,

[30] " Whereas by Indenture bearing date the first day of March instant and made by and between the said Overseer abovesaid of the one part and the abovebounded Henry Abraham of the other part, they the said James Bold and Richard Lancaster by and with the consent and allowance of Two of his Majesty's Justices of the peace (one of the quorum) of and for the County aforesaid Did put place and bind one John Brearley a poor Boy of the age of Eleven Years or thereabouts to be an apprentice to the above-bounded Henry Abrahams to serve from the day of the date thereof until he the said John Breadley should attain the age of Twenty One years and hath paid unto the said Henry Abraham the sum of one pound Fifteen shillings with the said John Brearley as and for his Apprentice ffee And Whereas the said Henry Abraham residing in the said Township of Latham by a License of a Certificate from the Township of Bisherstaffe in the County aforesaid it may happen that the said John Brearley by reason of such Apprenticeship may gain no settlement within the said Township of Latham ; but, it being agreed before the Execution of the said Indenture that the said Henry Abrahams should procure a Settlement for him the said John Brearley before the Expiration of the said Terme in some parish Township or place in that part of Great Britain called England otherwise than in the Township of Skelmersdale aforesaid.

The condition of this Obligation is such That if the abovebounded Henry Abraham his executors or administrators shall and do before the Expiration of the said Indenture of Apprenticeship obtain procure and get him the said John Brearley A Legall Settlement within some parish Township or place within that part of Great Britain Called England other than in the said Township of Skelmersdale. That then this Obligation to be void or else to be and remain in full force and value." (Brit. Mus. Add MSS. 36882 f.1.)

[31] *The Vestry Minutes of St Christopher le Stocks*, ed. E. Freshfield. 1886. p. 46.

[32] " That Abigail Short one of the Children at the charge of this parish shal be placed forth by and at the discretion of Mr. Nathaniell Booke and Mr. Thomas Hooten the present churchwardens whereby the parish may be freed from further charge about the said child And the Churchwardens shall given any Some for so placing forth the said child not exceeding Seaven pounds." (*The Vestry Minutes of St Christopher le Stock*, ed. E. Freshfield. 1886. p. 46.)

[32] " Att the aforesaid vestry it was oredred That Mr. Batt upper Churchwarden Should Bind out William Lucas Apprentice to what Person or Business he shall think Most Proper & to make as cheape a Bargaine For putting him out as he can." (*The Vestry Minutes of St Margaret's Lothbury*, ed. E. Freshfield. 1887. p. 8.)

[33] " At a meeting of the Parishioners of St. Peter's in Chester the 10th day of August 1686 it was then agreed and ordered by the said Parishioners that the churchwardens doe putt foth apprentice Thomas Brinion sonn of Richard Brinion (deceased) an Orphan of this Parish to any trade not exceeding £4 to give with him att his binding, and twenty shillings yearly to his master for seven years." (*St Peter's in Chester.* J. Simpson. 1909.)

[33] *History of the Parish of Tooting Graveney.* W. E. Morden. 1897. pp. 62, 53, 67, 51, 169, 51.

[34] *Dunstable MSS.*

[35] Brit. Mus. Add. MSS. 36882 f.1.

[36] *The Poor Book of Westbury on Trym.* H. J. Wilkins. 1910. p. 207.

[37] *London Life in the XVIIIth Century.* M. D. George. 1925. p. 234.

[38] *The Trade of England Revived.* 1681. p. 18.

[39] *A History of Machine-Wrought Hosiery.* Wm. Felkin. 1867. p. 227.

[40] In 1684, it was ordered " that the Present Churchwardens bind Samuell Christopher Apprentice to William Palmer Citizen and frameworke Knitter for Eight Yeares and that Six pounds bee given to his Mr upon that Consideration hee Giveing Security to the Parish to save the same harmelesse from the said Samuell." (*The Vestry Minutes of St Christopher le Stocks*, ed. E Freshfield. 1886. p. 63.)

[41] *Middlesex County Records*, ed. W. J. Hardy. 1905. p. 336.

[42] *Hertford County Records*, ed. W. J. Hardy. 1905–8. Vol. 1, p. 191.

[43] *Middlesex County Records*, ed. J. C. Jeafferson. 1887. Vol. 4, pp. 364, 229.

[44] *Middlesex County Records*, ed. W. J. Hardy. 1905. p. 140.

[45] *Calendar of State Papers Domestic.* Vol. 1689–90, p. 538.

[46] *Hertford County Records*, ed. W. J. Hardy. 1905–8. Vol. 1, p. 183.

[47] *The Parish Register.* G. Crabbe. Pub. 1807. p. 62.

[48] *The Utility of Workhouses.* Wm. Bailey. 1758. p. 5.

[49] *An Account of Several Workhouses.* 1732. p. 137.

[50] *A Discourse on the Poor.* R. North. Pub. 1753. p. 51.

[51] *Political Arithmetic.* A Young. 1774. pp. 93-4.

[52] " If they marry therefore," he wrote, " where are they to live ? No

cottage is empty—they must live with their fathers and mothers or lodge ; the poor abhor both as much as their betters, and certainly in many cases run into licentious amours merely for want of a cottage or a certificate. The whole system of our poor laws is so mischievous, that it must be attended with this effect. Suppose an unmarried labourer applies to the lord of the manor for leave to build a cottage on the waste—' No,' says the gentleman, ' the cottage when built will be a nest of beggars and we shall have them all on the parish.' Can you wonder at such language from a man who probably can let land worth 20s. an acre for no more than 14s. on account of high poor rates." (*Political Arithmetic.* A. Young. 1774. pp. 93–4.)

[53] Eden. Vol. I.

[54] " Whereas upon application made unto Christopher Jefferson and Theodore Smith Two of His Majesty's Justices of the Peace for the said Count of Cambridge (whereof one is of the Quorum) by the Churchwardens and Overseers of Soham within this County it appeareth to them that Richard Horsely the putative father of a bastard child borne in the parish of Soham within this County had lately run away out of the said parish of Soham and left the said bastard child upon the charges of the parish although he had sufficient estate to discharge the said parish. They the said justices of the Peace by warrant or order dated 22nd September did require the said Church wardens and Overseers of the said parish of Soham to seize and receive so much of the annual rents as amount unto £1–11–5 for the discharging of the said parish and £5 per annum for the bringing up and maintenance of the said child." (*Cambridge Quarter Sessions.* 8th Oct. 1724.)

[55] " That if any single woman shall be delivered of a bastard child, which shall be chargeable, or likely to become chargeable, to any parish or extra parochial place, or shall declare herself to be with child, and that such child is likely to be born a bastard, and to be chargeable to any parish or extra parochial place, and shall, in either of such cases, in an examination to be taken in writing, upon oath, before any one or more justices of the peace of any county, riding, division, city liberty or town corporate, wherein such parish or place shall lie, charge any person with having gotten her with child, it may and shall be lawful for such justice or justices, upon application made to him or them by the overseers of such parish, or by any other of them, or by any substantial householder of such extra parochial place, to issue out his or their warrant or warrants for the immediate apprehending such person, so charged as aforesaid, and for bringing him before such justice or justices, or before any other of his Majesty's Justices of the Peace of such County etc."

[56] " To the Constables of Dunstable and all other Constables of the sd County, Whereas Allice Briggett Came this day Voluntarily before me and Made Oath that she was Delivered of a Female Bastard Child in the said Parish of Dunstable on or about the 13th of July Last wch said Bastard Child is now Living & Chargeable to the sd Parish of Dunstable & on her Oath Charges one John Midgley Late of the Parish of Dunstable Breeches Maker wth being the father of the said Bastard Child. These Therefore in his Mays Name to Require you apprehend the sd John Midgley if he can be found in ye said County to answer the Premises to be dealt with according to Law." (*Dunstable MSS.*)

[57] " Whereas May Church of the Parish of Dunstable in the County of

Bedford Spinster having this Day made Oath that she is now
pregnant and bigg with Child and that Thomas Cripps of the aforesaid Parish Carpenter is the Father of such Child And wherefore
it is agreed by and between the said Thomas Cripps and May
Church that a Marriage shall be shortly had & Solemnised between
them the said Thomas Cripps and May Church and which by reason
of the absence of the Minister of the aforesaid Parish cannot at
present be performed.   Now Edward Ashley of the Parish of
Dunstable in the said County Waggoner do hereby agree to and
promise with the present Churchwardens and Overseers of the said
Parish of Dunstable and their Successors for the time being to save
harmless & keep Indemnifyed the said Parish of Dunstable from
all Costs and Charges Damages & Expences which the said Parish
may be outt to or sustain on Account of the said May Church being
with Child as aforesaid untill such times as the Said Marriage shall
be had and solemnised between the said Thomas Cripps & May
Church as aforesaid.   As witness my hand this 30th Day of Dec^r
in the Year of our Lord 1761.   Edward Asply."   (*Dunstable MSS.*)

[58] *Middlesex County Records*, ed. J. C. Jeafferson.   1887.   Vol. 4,
p. 77.
[59] *Report of the Commissioners of* 1833.   Appendix A.   p. 77.
[60] *Quarter Sessions Records of the North Riding of Yorkshire*, ed. A. C.
Atkinson.   1884.   Vol. 7, p. 81.
[61] *Hertford County Records*, ed. W. J. Hardy.   1905–7.   Vol. I, p. 173.
[62] *Ibid.*   Vol. II, p. 24.
[63] *St Bartholomew, Smithfield.*   E. A. Webb.   1921.   Vol. II, pp.
527–8.
[64] *Memorials of Herne, Kent.*   J. Buchanan.   1887.   p. 55.
[65] *The Poor Book of Westbury on Trym.*   H. J. Wilkins.   1910.   p. 53.
[66] *The Account Book of St Bartholomew Exchange* ed. E. Freshfield.
1895.   pp. 177 & 197.
[67] *History of Leyton.*   J. Kennedy.   1894.   pp. 148, 152, 159.
[68] *Hertford County Records*, ed. W. J. Hardy.   1905–7.   Vol. I, pp. 319,
409, 412.
[69] *St Bartholomew, Smithfield.*   E. A. Webb.   1921.   Vol. II, p. 526.
[70] " 1750 8th October.   The order made by William Hall Esq. and
Thomas Plumbe Clerk two of His Majesty's Justices of the Peace
(one being of the quorum) in and for the said county under their
Handes and Seals bearing date the 18th Day of September last
wherein and where by James Peep of UpHolland in the said county
mason is adjudged and declared putative Father of Thomas
a male bastard child born of the Body of Esther Knowles late of
Upholland aforesaid, single-woman, in Upholland aforesaid and he
ordered to pay to the Churchwardens and Overseers of the Poor
of Upholland aforesaid the Sum of ten shillings expended in her the
said Esther Knowles lying in Childbed and also the yearly sum of
thirty shillings to commence from the Birth of the said bastard
child and continue payment whereof Quarterly so long as the said
child shall be chargeable to Upholland aforesaid and with which
payments from the said Churchwarden and Overseer of the Poor
the said Esther Knowles is to provide for the further maintainance
of the said Bastard Child.   And Lastly both Parties ordered to
give Sufficient security to indempnifie the inhabitants thereof.
The same is by this Court ratified and confirmed no appeal being
made and due service of the said order proved upon the oath of
James Hilton."   (*Lancashire Quarter Sessions MSS.*)
[71] *Cambridgeshire Order Book.*   1st Oct.   1713.   16th Jan.   1723.

[72] *Lancashire Order Book.* 3rd May. 1750.

[73] *Report of* 1833. Appendix A. Part 1. p. 890.

[74] *Reports of Committees of the House of Commons,* etc. Vol. 6, pp. 274–279.

[75] *History of the Parish of Tooting Graveney.* W. E. Morden. 1897. p. 76.

[76] *Reports of Committees of the House of Commons,* etc. Vol. 9, pp. 283–287.

[77] *Lancashire Order Book.* 6th Oct. 1726.

[78] *Cambridgeshire Order Book.* 9th April, 1730. 17th Jan., 1727.

[79] *Lancashire Order Book.* July, 1686.

[80] *Cambridgeshire Order Book.* 25th Jan., 1709.

[81] *Lancashire Order Book.* 22nd Jan., 1700.

[82] *The Vestry Minutes of St Bartholomew Exchange,* ed. E. Freshfield. 1890. p. 90.

[83] *The History of the Parish of Tooting Graveney.* W. E. Morden. 1897. p. 195.

[84] *East Anglian.* Vol. 11, p. 329.

[85] *Cambridgeshire Order Book.* 16th Jan., 1747.

CHAPTER VI

THE FAILURE OF THE ACT OF SETTLEMENTS

[1] *Hertford County Records*, ed. W. J. Hardy. 1905-8. Vol. 1, p. 272.
[2] *Quarter Sessions from Queen Elizabeth to Queen Anne.* A. H. A. Homilton. 1878. p. 248.
[3] *Hertford County Records*, ed. W. J. Hardy. 1905-7. Vol. 11, p. 29.
[4] *Ibid.* Vol. 11, p. 23. Vol. 1, p. 414.
[5] *The State of the Prisons in England.* J. Howard. 1777. pp. 13-19.
[6] *Hertford County Records*, ed. W. J. Hardy. 1905-7. Vol. 1, p. 279.
[7] *Northamptonshire Notes and Queries.* Vol. 111, p. 26.
[8] *Memorials of Herne, Kent.* J. Buchanan. 1887. p. 55.
[9] *Calendar of State Papers Domestic*, ed. F. H. B. Daniels. pp. 233, 285, 509.
[10] *Hertford Quarter Sessions*, ed. W. J. Hardy. 1905-7. Vol. 1, p. 375.
[11] *Ibid.* Vol. 1, p. 255.
[12] *State Papers Domestic.* 6 May 1689. p. 92.
[13] " I desire that it may be considered that where there is one person come to this city to find work, there is two come to beg or worse . . . and until this easie and gainful, though Wicked Trade of Begging shall be supressed, I do not expect to see fewer, but more Beggars every day. It is well known that of late years many persons have come from the furtherest parts of the nation to set up this trade here, and if speedy care be not taken to prevent it this City and Suberbs will drain all the Poor people of England unto them, Begging being here a better Trade than anywhere else, and greater Encouragement given to it." (*Proposals for the Imployment of the Poor*, etc. By. T. Firman. 1681. pp. 25–6.)
[14] *Middlesex County Records.* J. C. Jeafferson. 1887. pp. 285, 319, 237.
[15] *An Inquiry into the Cause of the Great Increase in Robbers*, etc. H. Fielding. 1751. p. 92.
[16] *Giving Alms no Charity.* D. Defoe. 1704. pp. 11–12.
[17] *The Trade and Navigation of Great Britain Considered.* J. Gee. 1729. p. 38.
[18] *Some Proposals for the Imployment of the Poor*, etc. T. Firmin. 1681. p. 25–6.
[19] *A Plain and Easie Method.* R. Dunning. 1686. p. 23.
[20] *Surrey Arch. Coll.* Vol. 17, p. 114.
[21] *The Trade and Navigation of Great Britain Considered.* J. Gee. 1729. p. 41.
[22] " Deal in the County of Kent, to wit. These are to desire you to permit and suffer the bearers thereof, John Mason and Th. Jones belonging to the John and Thomas, a merchant ship of London, upon their homewards bound passage from Jamacia, was taken by a spanish privateer and taken to the Island of Queba, and by good fortune they made their escape and these poor creatures were landed in a poor sickly condition, peaceably and quietly to pass unto Yarmouth in the county of Norfolk, we desiring and requiring all proper officers, and all well desposed Christians to relieve them

on their way home to Yarmouth." In this case the impostiture was detected and the imposters whipped and sent back to their own parish. (*Hertford County Records*, ed. W. J. Hardy. Vol. 11, p. 80.)

[23] *Cambridge Order Book.* Jan., 1749.

[24] *Bedfordshire County Records*, ed. W. J. Hardy and Page. 1907. Vol. 1, p. 10.

[24] Another deposition among the Bedfordshire records is that of Tobias Burke,

" a vagrant aged forty years.   That his father who was in the service of King William III. and Queen Anne, told deponent that he was born in Flanders.   On the death of his father deponent was brought to London.   That his father was a legal inhabitant of St. Cairns, within three miles of Burr, in King's County Ireland.   Deponent was left with his mother with his uncle in St. James Clerkenwell, in the county of Middlesex, where he learnt to drive hackney carriages and ride postilion.   He afterwards lived with his present wife in a cellar, where he sold a spiritous liquor called gin, but an information being laid against him he went to his wife's friends in Lancashire.   On hearing from his wife about three weeks ago that all matters were made up he started to return to London, but his money giving out he was forced to beg in the parish of Clop-hill, and was relieved by several of the parishioners.   He was arrested in Campton.   Deponent says he was never a hired servant by the year or bound apprentice to anyone." (*Bedfordshire County Records*, ed. W. J. Hardy. 1907. Vol. 1, p. 25.)

[25] *Hertford County Records*, ed. W. J. Hardy. 1905-7. Vol. 1, p. 307.

[26] " Upon the petition of Andrew Ward, late Constable of Finchley Parish showing that he served the said office last year and ex-pended in passing cripples and vagabonds through the said parish, together with other incidental charges, £13-14-7, and praying that a rate may be assessed for the reimbursement of the same, it is ordered that two justices named do examine the accounts of the said petitioner, and do levy a rate for the settlement of the same." (*Middlesex County Records*, ed. W. J. Hardy. 1909. p. 69.)

[27] " Whatever they at first were, the Fact is, they are at present in general, no other than Schools of Vice, Seminaries of Idleness, and Common stores of Nastiness and Disease . . . And with regard to work, the Intent of the Law is, I apprehend, as totally frustrated.   Insomuch that they must be very lazy Persons indeed who can esteem the Labour imposed in any of these Houses as a Punishment.   In some, I am told, there is not any provision made for Work.   In that of Middlesex in particular, the Governor hath confessed to me that he hath no work to employ his Prisoners, and hath urged as a Reason that having generally great numbers of the most desperate felons under his charge, who, notwithstanding his utmost Care, will sometimes get access to the other Prisoners, he dares not trust those committed to hard Labour with any heavy or sharp Instrumnets of work, lest they should be converted into weapons by the Felons."

" What good consequences then can arrive from sending idle and dis-orderly Persons to a Place where they are neither to be corrected or employed, and where the Conversation of many as bad or worse than themselves, they are sure to be improved in the Knowledge and confirmed in the Practice of iniquity ? Can it be conceived that such People will not come out of those Houses, much more Idle and Disorderly than they went in ? The Truth of this I have often experienced in the Behaviour of the Wretches brought before me ; the most impudent and flagitious of whom, have always been such as have been before acquainted with the Discipline of Bride-well ; A Commitment to which Place, tho' it often causes great Horror and Lamentation in a Novice, is usually treated with Ridicule and Contempt by those who have already been there." (*An Inquiry into the Cause of the Late Increase in Robbers*. H. Fielding 1751. p. 63.)

[27] *Middlesex County Records*. W. J. Hardy. 1905–7. p. 302.

[28] *Ye Parish of Camerwell*. H. C. Blanch. 1875. p. 119.

[29] " And whereas several great sums of money since the making of the said act have been levied and expended for the conveying of vagrants and that some Justices of the Peace give greater Allow-ances to Constables for conveying vagrants than may seem to be necessary and that the Owners of Waggons, Horses, Carts are often more Extravagant in their Rates and Demands, for Remedy thereof and for better regulating and ascertaining such Allowances be it enacted by the Authority aforesaid that the Justices of the Peace in their first Quarter Sessions that shall be held for the several Counties, Ridings, Divisions and Liberties after the Commence-ment of this act and so yearly at every Easter Quarter Sessions During the continuation of this act are hereby empowered to ascertain and set down the several Rates that shall be for the Year Ensueing to be allowed for maintaining, conveying and carry-ing of such vagrants as shall be passed or carried through their respective Counties, Ridings, Divisions and Liberties." (1 An, st. 2, c. 13.)

[30] " Pursuant therefore to the said act and to the end that the rates hereafter mentioned and the other rates in the said act may be strictly observed in this County. It is ordered by this Court that where there shall bee Occasion for the passing and conveying vagrants by Cart and Horse 9d bee allowed every mile and no more to the constable or his deputy and that where there shall be occasion only for a Horse and Man 3d for every mile and no more and for every mile that a person is conveyed on foot 1d a mile and no more and that every vagrant that is to be conveyed aforesaid that is healthy to bee allowed only 1½ per day, And every Vagrant that is Sickly and ill 3d per day and no more . . . And further ordered that every petty constable do bring all and every vagrant and vagrants to bee passed and conveyed before the next Justice of the Peace of the county which justice is desired so to regulate the allowances and to Tax them on the back of the Certificate by them to bee given to the severall petty constables : And that no high constable do pay the rated tax upon such certificate brought to them by their petty constables unless the said petty constable shall produce to the high Constable a receipt from the constable of the Adjacent County to which such petty constable was Ordered to deliver the said vagrant or vagrants of such constables having received the said vagrant or vagrants which constables of every adjacent county are by the said act required to doe." (*Three Centuries of Derbyshire Annals*. J. C. Cox. 1890. p. 155.)

[31] *Middlesex County Records*, ed. W. J. Hardy. 1905. p. 258.

[32] *Hertford County Records*, ed. W. J. Hardy. 1905–7. Vol. 2, p. 52.

[33] *Report of Committees of the House of Commons, printed by order of the House*, etc. Vol. 9, pp. 289–90.

[34] Warwickshire Quarter Sessions 1709, Michaelmas.
" That whereas W. Bright, constable . . . hath this day in open

court declared that he is willing to undertake the conveyance of vagrants through this county for £150 per year, it is therefore thought fit and so ordered that the said W. Bright shall have the said £150 paid him for the year ensuing for the conveyance of vagrants. Which sum shall be paid to him for the cause aforesaid by the treasurer of the stock of this county." (*A Hundred Years Poor Law Administration in a Warwickshire Village*, by A. W. Ashby, in *Oxford Studies in Social and Legal History*, Vol. III, p. 72.)

[35] *Quarter Sessions from Queen Elizabeth to Queen Ann.* A. H. A. Hamilton. 1878. p. 268.

[36] *Victoria County History : Buckingham.* Vol. II, pp. 81–2.

[37] *Quarter Session Records of the North Riding of Yorkshire.* A. C. Atkinson. 1884. Vol. 6.

[38] *Report on Mendicity in the Metropolis.* 1815. p.p 125, 125.

BIBLIOGRAPHY

MANUSCRIPT SOURCES.

Cambridgeshire Quarter Session Minute and Order Books. (County Hall, Cambridge.)

Cambridgeshire Quarter Sessions Recognisance Book. (County Hall, Cambridge.)

Justices Warrants, Vagrants Passes, etc. (County Hall, Cambridge.)

Lancashire Quarter Sessions Order Books. (County Hall, Preston.)

Dunstable Parish Papers, Orders of Removal, Certificates, Vagrants Passes, Apprentices Indentures, Bills of Parish Expences, etc. (In the Chest in the Priory Church, Dunstable.)

Churchwardens' Accounts, Sidbury. (Brit. Mus. Add. MSS. 34696.)

The Poor Book of Poole, co. Dorset. 1697–98. (Bri. Mus. Eg. papers, 2437.)

Parish Apprentice Indentures, Worcester. (Brit. Mus. Add. MSS. 32465. f. 28.)

Parish Papers, Skelmersdale, Ormskirk. (Brit. Mus. Add. MSS. 36882. f. 1. and 36876.)

PRINTED CONTEMPORARY WORKS

Resolutions of the Judges of Assize. 1633. (Brit. Mus. 1027. L. 16.)

An Appeal to Parliament that there may not be one Beggar in England. T.L. 1660.

The True and Only Cause of a Want of Money in these Kingdoms. J. Hodges. Single Sheet. 1673.

The Prevention of Poverty. R. Hains. 1674.

Natural and Political Observations upon the Bills of Mortality. Jasper Gaunt. 1676.

England's Improvement by Land and Sea. A. Yarranton. 1677.

Reasons for Erecting in every County a Working Alms House. R. Hains. 1678.

A Method of Government for such Working Alms Houses, etc. R. Hains. 1679.

Proposals for Promoting the Woollen Manufacture. R. Hains. 1679.

England's Weal and Prosperity Proposed. R. Hains. 1680.

Some Proposals for the Imployment of the Poor for the Prevention of Idleness. T. Firmin. 1681.

A Provision for the Poor. M. Hale. 1683.

A Plain and Easie Method. R. Dunning. 1686.

A New Discource on Trade. J. Child. 1694.

Essays upon Ways and Means of Supplying the War. C. Davenant. 1695.

Proposals for raising a College of Industry. J. Bellars. 1695.

Political Conclusions. G. King. 1696.

Bread for the Poor. R. Dunning. 1696.

Report of the Board of Trade. J. Locke. 1697.

The Grand Concern of England Explained.   Harleian Miscellany.
Discourse on the Trade of England.   J. Child.   1698.
Essay on the East India Trade.   C. Davenant.   1698.
Essay upon the Probable Means of Making a People Gainers in the Balance of Trade.   C. Davenant.   1699.
Essays about the Poor.   J. Bellars.   1699.
An Account of the Proceedings of the Corporation of Bristol.   J. Cary.   1700.
Arguments proving that the Poor cannot be employed in the Wool Trade, etc.   Philanglus.   1701.
Giving Alms no Charity.   D. Defoe.   1704.
A View of the Present State of the Cloathing Trade.   J. Haynes.   1706.
Case of the Middling and Poorer Sort of Master Shoemakers.
Case of the Woollen Manufacturers of Great Britain.   1887. 6. 60.   (32).
An Historical Account of the Constitution of the Vestry of the Parish of St Dunstan's in the West.   1714.
Great Britain's Glory.   J. Haynes.   1715.
The Interests of England Considered.   1720.
A Proposal for Relieving, Reforming, and Employing all the Poor of Great Britain.   L. Braddon.   1721.
The Miseries of the Poor are a National Sin, Shame, and Charge.   L. Braddon.   1722.
Essay on Charity Schools.   G. Mandeville.   1723.
The Behaviour of Servants in England.   D. Defoe.   1724.
Everybody's Business is Nobody's Business.   D. Defoe.   1725.
The Complete English Tradesman.   D. Defoe.   1727.
A New System of Agriculture.   J. Lawrence.   1727.
Parochial Tyranny.   A. Moreton.   1727.
A Plan of English Commerce.   D. Defoe.   1728.
The Charge of Sir John Gonson to the Grand Jury, etc.   1728,
A Humble Proposal to the People of England.   D. Defoe.   1729.
The Voyage of Gonzales (Pinkerton's Travels, Vol. 2).   1730.
The Trade and Navigation of Great Britain Considered.   J. Gee.   1729.
The Enclosure of Commons and Common Fields is contrary to the Interests of the Nation.   J. Cowper.   1732.
An Account of several Workhouses, etc.   2nd edition.   1732.
Gentleman's Magazine.   March, 1734.
A New Scheme for Reducing the Laws relating to the Poor into one Act of Parliament.   1737.
Essay on the Decline of our Foreign Trade.   M. Decker.   1739.
The London Tradesman.   R. Campbell.   1747.
Kalin's Account of his visit to England, translated by Joseph Lucas, pub. 1892.
Considerations on Several Proposals.   C. Grey.   1751.
An Inquiry into the Cause of the late Increase in Robbers.   H. Fielding.   1751.
Letter to the Author of Several Considerations.   1752.
Observations on the Defects of the Poor Laws.   T. Alcock.   1752.
A Proposal for Making an Effectual Provision for the Poor.   H. Fielding.   1753.
Discourse on the Poor.   R. North.   Pub. 1753.
Considerations relating to the Poor.   J. Massie.   1757.
A Treatise on the Utility of Workhouses.   Wm. Bailey.   1758.
The Comfortable Provision of the Poor in Workhouses.   Wm. Bailey.   1758.
The Manifold Causes of the Increase of the Poor.   J. Tucker.   1760.

An Earnest Appeal for Mercy to the Children of the Poor.   J. Hanway.
1766.
An Inquiry into the Management of the Poor.   1767.
A Farmer's Letters to the People of England.   A. Young.   1767.
A Six Weeks Tour through the Southern Counties.   A. Young.   1768.
Tour through the Northern Counties.   A. Young.   1770.
Tour through the Eastern Counties.   A. Young.   1771.
Observations on the State of the Parochial and Vagrant Poor.   J. Scott.
1773.
Political Arithmetic.   A. Young.   1774.
Observations on the Poor Laws.   Dr. Trotter.   1775.
Report on the Laws which concern the Relief and Settlement of the Poor.
1776.   General Reports.   Vol. 11.
*Abstract of Returns from the Governors. Directors, Assistants, Guardians,
Treasurers, etc., of the several Houses of Industry and Workhouses.*
1776.   General Reports.   Vol. 9.
*Abstracts of Returns made from the Clerks of the Peace and other Officers
concerning Vagrants and the Houses of Correction.*   1776.   General
Reports.   Vol. 11.
The Trade of Great Britain in its Imports and Exports.   C. Whiteworth.
1776.
The State of the Prisons in England.   J. Howard.   1777.
An Essay on Modern Luxury.   1777.
Reasons for the late Increase in the Poor Rates.   1777.
A Plan for the Better Relief and Employment of the Poor.   T. Gilbert
1781.
A Sentimental History of Chimney Sweeps.   J. Hanway.   1785.
A Plan of Police.   T. Gilbert.   1786.
Considerations of the Bills, etc.   T. Gilbert.   1787.
A Plea for the Poor.   R. W. Applegarth.   1790.
History of the Poor.   T. Ruggles.   1793.
Decisions of the Court of King's Bench upon the Laws relating to the Poor.
E. Bott (revised F. Const).   1793.
Annals of Agriculture.   A.   1792.
Case of the Labourers in Husbandry.   D. Davies.   1795.
A Brief Statement of Facts.   1796.
Report on Mendicity in the Metropolis.   1815.
Report from the Select Committee on the Poor Laws.   1817.
Report of the Commissioners of 1833.   Appendix A, Part I.

COLLECTIONS OF RECORDS

Calendar of the State Papers Domestic.
Journals of the House of Commons.
Abingdon : Records of the Borough of, ed. B. Challoner.   1898.   Abingdon.
Batley : Records of, ed. M. Sheard.   1894.   Worksop.
Bishop Stortford : Records of St Micheal's Church of, ed. J. L. Glasscock.
1882.
Carlisle : Municipal Records of, ed. R. S. Ferguson.   1887.   Carlisle.
Hertford County Records, ed. W. J. Hardy.   1905–8.
*Leicester : The Vestry Minutes of the Churchwardens of the Church of
St Mary's of,* ed. J. E. Abney.   1912.   Leicester.
Liverpool : Vestry Book of, ed. H. Peet.   1912.
Middlesex County Records, ed. J. C. Jeafferson.   1887.
Middlesex County Records, ed. W. J. Hardy.   1905.

Reading, Records of, ed. W. Guilding. 1892.
St Albans : The Corporation Records of, ed. A. E. Gibbs. 1890. St Albans.
St Bartholomew Exchange (London) : The Vestry Minutes of, ed E. Freshfield. 1890.
St Bartholomew Exchange : The Account Book of the Parish of, ed. E. Freshfield. 1895.
St Christopher le Stocks : The Vestry Minutes of, ed E. Frishfield. 1886.
St Margaret Lothbury : The Vestry Minutes of, ed. E. Freshfield. 1887.
Swarthmoor Hall : The Household Account Book of Sarah Fell, ed. N. Penny. 1920. Cambridge.
Westbury on Trym : the Poor Book of, ed. H. J. Wilkins. 1910. Bristol.
Yorkshire Quarter Sessions Records, for the North Riding of, ed. A. C. Atkinson. 1884.
Yorkshire West Riding Session Rolls, ed. J. Lister. (Yorkshire Archæological and Topographical Association.)
County, Municipal, and Parish Histories. (Containing Records similar to those in previous section.)
Bilson : A History of the Parish of. G. T. Lawley. 1893. Bilson.
Bourne : A Parochial History of St Mary of. J. Stevens. 1888.
Brampton : A History of. J. A. Giles. 1847. Brampton.
Brighthelmstone : A History of. J. A. Erredge. 1862. Brighton.
Bristol : The Annals of in the Eighteenth Century. J. Latimer. 1893. Bristol.
Burton on Trent. Wm. Molyneaux. 1869.
Camberwell : Ye Parish of. H. C. Blanch. 1875.
Cartmel : The Annals of. J. Stockdale. 1872. Ulverston.
Chew Magna : Collections for a Parochial History of. F. A. Wood. 1903. Bristol.
Chester : St Peter's in. F. Simpson. 1909. Chester.
Cuckfield : History of the Parish of. W. Cooper. 1912. (Haywards Heath.)
Derbyshire : Three Centuries of Derbyshire Annals. J. C. Cox. 1890.
East Anglian, N.S. Ipswich.
Fenland Notes and Queries. Peterborough.
Gloucestershire Notes and Queries.
Hawkshead : the Northernmost Parish in Lancashire. H. S. Cooper. 1899.
Herne : Memorials of. J. Buchanan. 1887.
Hoddesdon : A History of. J. A. Fregalles. 1908. Hertford.
Hungerford : An Historical Sketch of the Town of. W. Money. 1894. Newbury.
Kettering : A History of. F. W. Bull. 1891. Northampton.
King's Lynn : A History of the Borough of. H. J. Hillen. 1907 Norwich.
Lapworth : Memorials of a Warwickshire Parish. R. Hudson. 1904.
Leeke : Olde. M. H. Miller. 1891. Leeke.
Leyton : A History of the Parish of. J. Kennedy. 1894. Leyton.
Leystonstone : A History of. W. G. Hammock. 1904.
Manningham, Heaton, and Alterton : Histories of. W. Cudworth. 1896. Bradford.
Monkwearmouth : Peep into a Monkwearmouth Rate Book. J. T. Middlemass. 1901. Sunderland.
Northampton : A History of the Church of the Holy Sepulchre. J. C. Cox. 1897. Northampton.
Northampton Notes and Queries. Northampton.
Preston : A History of the Parish of. A. Hewitson. 1883. Preston.

288 ENGLISH POOR IN THE 18TH CENTURY

Quarter Sessions from Queen Elizabeth to Queen Anne. A. H. A. Hamilton. 1878.
Ribchester : A History of the Parish of. T. C. Smith. 1890.
St Austell : a Cornish Parish. J. Hammond. 1897.
St Olave (London) : The Annals of the Parish of. A. Povah. 1894.
Smithfield : St Bartholomew.
Stroud : A History of. Smetham. Chatham.
Sussex Archæological Collections.
Tonbridge : Some Details of the Parish of. B. Wadmore. 1906 Tonbridge.
Tooting Graveney : A History of the Parish of. B. Wadmore. W. E. Mordem.
Victoria County Histories.

GENERAL WORKS.

Cannan, E. *The History of Local Rates in England.* 1896.
Clarke, A. *Working Life of Women in the Seventeenth Century.* 1919.
Dunlop, O. *English Apprenticeship and Child Labour.* 1912:
Felkin, W. *A History of Machine Wrought Hosiery.* 1867.
George, D. *London Life in the Eighteenth Century.* 1925.
Gras, N. S. B. *The Evolution of the English Corn Market.* (Cambridge, Mass. Harvard University Press.) 1915.
Leader, R. E. *The History of the Company of Cutlers in Hallamshire.* 1905. Sheffield.
Rogers, T. E. *History of Agriculture and Prices.* 1887–1902. (Oxford).
Trotter, E. *Life in a Seventeenth-Century Parish.* (Cambridge.)
Turner, C. J. *History of Vagrancy.* 1887.
Webb, S. & B. *English Local Government. The Parish and the County* 1906. *Statutary Authorities.* 1922.

INDEX